Mosaic of Thought

Teaching Comprehension in a Reader's Workshop

Ellin Oliver Keene & Susan Zimmermann

HEINEMANN
Portsmouth, NH

Heinemann
A division of Reed Elsevier Inc.
361 Hanover Street
Portsmouth, NH 03801-3912

Offices and agents throughout the world

The authors and publisher thank those who gave permission to reprint borrowed material:

"First Reader" from *Questions About Angels* by Billy Collins. Copyright © 1991 by Billy Collins. By permission of William Morrow and Company, Inc.

Excerpt from *Woman Hollering Creek*. Copyright © 1991 by Sandra Cisneros. Published by Vintage Books, a division of Random House, Inc., New York and originally in hardcover by Random House, Inc. Reprinted by permission of Susan Bergholz Literary Services, New York. All rights reserved.

Excerpt from *A Leak in the Heart* by Faye Moskowitz. Reprinted by permission of David R. Godine, Publisher, Inc. Copyright © 1985 by Faye Moskowitz.

Excerpt from *A Chorus of Stones* by Susan Griffin. Copyright © 1992 by Susan Griffin. Used by permission of Doubleday, a division of Bantam Doubleday Dell Publishing Group, Inc.

Excerpt from *An Unspoken Hunger: Stories from the Field* by Terry Tempest Williams. Copyright © 1994 by Terry Tempest Williams. Reprinted by permission of Pantheon Books, a division of Random House, Inc.

Excerpt from *Knots on a Counting Rope* by Bill Martin Jr. and John Archambault. Copyright © 1966, 1987 by Bill Martin Jr. and John Archambault. Reprinted by permission of Henry Holt and Co., Inc.

"Three Small Oranges" copyright 1993 by Jane Kenyon. Reprinted from *Constance* with the permission of Graywolf Press, Saint Paul, Minnesota.

"Lost in the Stars" by David Remnick. From *The New Yorker*, January 29, 1996. Reprinted by permission of the author.

Excerpt from "Comrade Past & Mister Present" is from *Comrade Past & Mister Present* by Andrei Codrescu, Coffee House Press, 1986. Used by permission of the publisher. Copyright © 1986 by Andrei Codrescu.

Library of Congress Cataloging-in-Publication Data

Keene, Ellin Oliver.
   Mosaic of thought : teaching comprehension in a reader's workshop
/ Ellin Oliver Keene, Susan Zimmermann.
      p.   cm.
   Includes bibliographical references.
   ISBN 0-435-07237-4
   1. Reading comprehension.   2. Literature—Study and teaching.
I. Zimmermann, Susan, 1951– . II. Title.
LB1050.45.K435 1997
      372.47—dc21   96-53181
                                                                  CIP
                                                                  AC

Consulting Editor: Thomas R. Newkirk
Production: Melissa L. Inglis
Cover design: Linda Knowles
Manufacturing: Elizabeth Valway
Back cover photo of Susan Zimmermann by Lee Hovey-King

Printed in the United States of America on acid-free paper
02 01   EB   15

for our children

Contents

Foreword

I've been looking for some time for a book that would take me inside the reading process and show me what reading comprehension is all about. We've seen the *anatomy* of reading comprehension in one taxonomy after another. What we've needed is the *physiology*, the actual working of the parts as a reader interacts with lively text. We've needed to see the full, rich circulation of solid thought as readers explore text on the page. Finally that book is here, a jargon-free look at how teachers can help their students think as good readers need to think.

Educators and the public are in a frenzy over how to boost reading comprehension scores. In some school systems children fill out comprehension skill sheets, again and again. In others they struggle diligently through thick workbooks in an effort to improve their SAT scores. Neither approach teaches students to use strategies that will, in fact, help them understand texts better. Worse, neither approach develops the love of reading, the very engine that invites the student into a lifetime of reading. Keene and Zimmermann's work does both. It is a very practical book, and it evinces a passion for reading that engenders the same in us. We are taken into classrooms where that passion exists. However, this is a passion with a difference: the children and teachers know what they are doing.

For too long, children have been reading extensively without becoming better readers. The shift from basals to trade books has been a good one—children read more books than before. But they don't necessarily read them well. This book shows teachers how to get children to read trade books better, as well as how to integrate literature into their lives so they will, in fact, live better.

There are any number of publications that show how children write and craft their texts. Since the early seventies I and many others have been working at trying to show the writing process in action. When written text is changed on the page, we are able to surmise the kinds of thinking the child entertains. Reading is another matter. When the reader engages with print, we have no idea where he or she is or what types of thinking are in process. This book shows how both teachers and children think as they read.

We are taken inside classrooms where reading comprehension is taught in the context of real engagement between teachers and children, children and children. We witness just how social the act of comprehension needs to be. Keene and Zimmermann talk with each other, and children offer wide ranges of interpretation as they build meaning together in small discussion groups.

Keene and Zimmermann take the lid off the reading process and show the operation of the various skills that people need in order to read well. What they show isn't from a distance. They invite us inside their own minds, they bring their lives to the page, read, back off, and show specific strategies for taking in meaning. Most reading texts *talk about* prior knowledge. Here, the authors bring their own lives to the text and walk away with new meanings.

This book is a series of invitations. Each chapter begins with texts—poetry, essays, personal memoirs, fiction. The authors apply various reading skills, from schema to synthesis, to enrich their own reading and quest for learning. The authors then take the same skill inside the classroom, where superior teachers show how they teach the skill with their children. We meet teachers and children in the process of learning to read and, above all, comprehend.

The authors wisely advise, "If you wish to understand these skills, observe them in operation as you do your own reading." This is not a book for nonreading teachers. After reading this book, I am convinced that if we are to take children into the upper reaches of comprehension we have to have been there ourselves. How can we teach children how to synthesize ideas if we don't do this with our own reading? This book, then, is an invitation to the reading dance: you will find yourself in bookstores asking for the very books the authors are reading. I jotted down quite a list of book titles that evoked pictures I wanted to encounter directly.

Teachers will enjoy this friendly, personal book that takes the best of reading comprehension research and shows us how to actively apply it to our own reading and how to help children do the same. Join Keene and Zimmermann on the page as they read and in the classroom where they redefine the purpose of comprehension: new thinking and worthwhile living.

Donald H. Graves
Professor Emeritus
University of New Hampshire

Prologue

*. . . The Great Debate over reading methods has raged
for centuries. Educator Horace Mann warned in the 19th
century that letters of the alphabet were "bloodless, ghostly
apparitions." California passed the "ABC" bill last year,
requiring, among other things, that textbooks include
lessons on spelling and alphabet sounds. Another bill
would require new teachers to take phonics courses to get
certified. North Carolina is urging schools to teach
alphabet sounds. . . . Even GOP presidential candidate
Bob Dole cast his ballot for phonics, saying recently that
California's whole language "fad" has produced disastrous
results.*

"If You Can Read This . . . You Learned Phonics. Or so its Supporters Say,"
Newsweek Magazine, May 13, 1996.

I sit in a teachers' lounge late in the spring, waiting for an after-
school study group to convene. There is a tension present, almost
like another face in the room. Two teachers sink into chairs, exhausted less by their day with children than by the inevitable after-
school conversation about the new principal who will be hired,
colleagues who are transferring to other schools, and what will become of the children with whom they've worked so hard this year.

"Is she *whole language* or *basal?*" one asks about a teacher who wants to transfer to the school.

"I can't remember, but I think she taught in a basal school," the other replies.

I remain silent, feeling too weary for the debate myself. As they talk, I flash back with a chuckle to the final stages of labor and delivery when Elizabeth was about to be born. The nurse anesthetist asked me what I did professionally. My response was followed immediately by his anxious questions about his first-grader who, he believed, was receiving inadequate phonics instruction. I recall my husband David's face, somewhere between a laugh and incredulity. "Don't get into it!" he warned, "not now!"

The whole language versus phonics debate has resulted in two competitive rather than collaborative factions in the field of reading research and education. The Public Education Coalition's Reading Project and the work described in this book were created in an attempt to bridge this widening chasm. We believed at the project's inception—and still do now—that learning to read depends on two critical factors: the teacher's thorough understanding of the reading process itself, and his or her determination to understand and respond to each child's needs as a reader. When both conditions are present, the debate becomes a mirage.

The purpose of the Coalition's Reading Project, described throughout this book, was to help teachers infuse in-depth, explicit, meaningful instruction in reading into literature-rich classrooms where teachers and children explore, learn from, and react to a wide variety of books. We wanted children to develop a command of the cognitive strategies known to be used by proficient readers to create memorable interpretations of books and to read with passion and purpose. We wanted children to read critically, ask questions, develop the habits of mind of avid readers, succeed in comprehending ever more challenging texts, and use a wide variety of problem solving strategies to remedy comprehension problems independently.

In this book we piece together a mosaic of reading experiences for the adult reader and portraits of classrooms in which explicit comprehension instruction has been successful: classrooms that provide intimate places for children to read; places where books line the walls, where teachers continue to learn about reading for themselves and their children, and where children are learning to be skillful and thoughtful readers.

We consciously avoid the great debate, believing that it divides professionals unnecessarily. Children need to learn letters, sounds, words, sentences, books, and they need to learn to comprehend literally and inferentially. Our hope is that this book gives teachers new ways to think about their own reading, and effective ways to inspire children to read deeply and carefully. Ultimately, we will be most gratified if teachers move beyond this book—expanding and deepening the concepts, sharing their insights with other teachers and parents, working through obstacles together, creating new mosaics of thought.

Acknowledgments

Writing this book has caused us to read differently. We remember the children who interrupted precious writing time, the friends and family members who usually accommodated but sometimes chafed at the evenings and weekends spent writing and rewriting, the background voices of colleagues asking questions, making demands, lending support. Having written this book, we know how vital those voices are, and how interwoven they are in a writer's work. Now, when we pick up books, we wonder about the writers' families and friends, about the spaces where they live and work, about the offices or cafes where they sip coffee and talk with their editors.

Colleagues, friends, and family are a part of each page of this book. But it was born principally of a collaboration and friendship between an educator and a lawyer who dreamed of schools where children become proficient and passionate readers. This decade-long relationship shaped a body of work in schools throughout the Denver area and then spurred a new adventure: coauthoring this book. As we planned each chapter, we asked questions, lobbed thoughts back and forth, and scrutinized what we were really trying to say. In a small converted garage in the mountains west of Denver, Ellin wrote the drafts, then Susan sculpted the work to final form. Throughout this back-and-forth process, the questions continued, the molding went on, until we were satisfied that each chapter captured the clarity and simplicity of what we wanted to say. From this partnership and sharing, we are both immeasurably changed and enriched.

We are forever grateful to Tom Newkirk, professor at the University of New Hampshire, celebrated author, and our editor for this volume. As Tom and Ellin sat poolside at a San Diego conference hotel reviewing a draft of Chapter 6, he looked at her and said he didn't believe it was saying exactly what we needed it to say. Shortly after that comment—and Ellin's acknowledgment that he was absolutely right—a gust of wind blew most of the chapter into the pool. We're both sure Tom somehow planned that gust, his powers as an editor being nothing short of divine.

The Public Education and Business Coalition (known as the Public Education Coalition [PEC] prior to July 1995), particularly Stephanie Maddox and Barbara Volpe, were generous in their support. The PEBC's quaint and cozy offices—in a converted apartment building across the street from the Colorado Capitol—have been home to innumerable conversations among the Coalition's staff developers, whose work continues to be the backbone of the Coalition's work. It was through those discussions that the model for reading described in this book was invented. It is difficult to imagine a more rewarding collaboration or friendship than the one we've shared. To describe each staff developer's unique creativity and passion for learning and children would take pages. Our thanks go to all for their contribution to the thinking behind this book and, more importantly, for their work in hundreds of classrooms where the concepts were developed and refined.

Special thanks go to Chryse Hutchins for her boundless trust in children and relentless need to understand how best to teach and learn with and from them; to Anne Goudvis' piercing intellect and persistent drive to ensure our actions actually benefit teachers and children; to Stephanie Harvey for her humor and knack for continually raising the standard for our work; to Cris Tovani, who had the foresight to return to the high school classroom and develop these ideas in a secondary school; to Liz Stedem, whose wisdom and love for children shaped the Coalition's earliest work in schools; to Marjory Ulm, whose savvy grounded our ideas in the real world of an inner-city school system; to Colleen Buddy who extended these ideas in the classroom further than any of us imagined possible. Because of the acumen and insight of this team of staff developers, which now has grown to nearly fifty, we were able to use reading comprehension research as a foundation and undertake the most intoxicating of intellectual exercises—generating new knowledge together.

To the teachers with whom we worked and tested the ideas in this book, our gratitude is profound and permanent. Bruce Morgan, an extraordinary teacher and friend, read the manuscript with a critical but gentle eye, reminding us of the real audience for this book: those who teach thoughtfully and live full lives outside the classroom.

Debbie Miller's classroom embodies the vision in this book. Debbie is an artist, able to give shape and substance to theory. Through her work, she has enhanced the lives of hundreds of children at Knapp, University Park, and Slavins Elementary schools in Denver. Her experiments with the comprehension research have proved unimaginably effective, and continue to inspire other teachers, children, and their parents.

The teachers whose stories are told in this book are also artists: Sharon Sherman-Messinger, Pat Benyshek, Kristin Venable (now a Coalition staff developer), Todd McLain, Enid Goldman, Mimi DeRose (now a principal), Charline Mize, Paige Inman, Jody Cohn, and, once again, Cris Tovani created the kind of classroom environments where learning is inevitable. It is not just the quality of their teaching that makes this happen, but how they have chosen to live their lives.

Our colleagues around the country have shaped and deepened the PEBC's work over the years. In 1985, Mary Ellen Giacobbe joined us for our first conference. What a mentor she became and what a kick-off she provided! The Teachers College Writing Project at Columbia University founded by Lucy Calkins provided a model for our early work. Lucy's gift as a writer and speaker continues to inspire us. During hot, crowded summer institutes in Colorado, Don Graves made hundreds of teachers believe they were capable of absolutely anything as both writers and teachers. He ignited that passion for learning—in teachers and children—that lasts a lifetime. Shelley Harwayne and Joanne Hindley have crafted a new standard for teaching and learning at the Manhattan New School and through their excellent books. They have been generous in sharing their experiences and their friendships with us.

Georgia Heard has illuminated our work and our lives with rare insight and poetry. Janice Dole at the University of Utah opened her mind and heart to Ellin for nearly twenty years. Their conversations provided the real genesis of the Coalition's work in reading.

Finally, this book would not have happened without the support of the Helen K. and Arthur E. Johnson Foundation in Denver. Its executive director, Stan Kamprath, listened intently, asked questions, and believed in our ideas. We are forever grateful to the Foundation for its grants supporting the development of our work in schools, and its commitment to the development of this book.

Ellin Oliver Keene and Susan Zimmermann

ONE

The Mosaic Takes Shape

First Reader

I can see them standing politely on the wide pages
that I was still learning to turn,
Jane in a blue jumper, Dick with his crayon-brown hair,
playing with a ball or exploring the cosmos
of the backyard, unaware they are the first characters,
the boy and girl who begin fiction.

Beyond the simple illustration of their neighborhood
the other protagonists were waiting in a huddle:
frightening Heathcliff, frightened Pip, Nick Adams
carrying a fishing rod. Emma Bovary riding into Rouen.

But I would read about the perfect boy and his sister
even before I would read about Adam and Eve, garden and gate,
and before I heard the name Gutenberg, the type
of their simple talk was moving into my focusing eyes.

It was always Saturday and he and she
were always pointing at something and shouting, "Look!"
pointing at the dog, the bicycle, or at their father
as he pushed a hand mower over the lawn,
waving at aproned mother framed in the kitchen doorway,
pointing toward the sky, pointing at each other.

They wanted us to look but we had looked already
and seen the shaded lawn, the wagon, the postman.

We had seen the dog, walked, watered and fed the animal,
and now it was time to discover the infinite, clicking
permutations of the alphabet's small and capital letters.
Alphabetical ourselves in the rows of classroom desks,
we were forgetting how to look, learning how to read.

BILLY COLLINS,
from *Questions About Angels: Poems*

It is late, the house quiet. My five-year-old sleeps with sixteen dolls
and stuffed animals. I hear my husband let the dogs out and back in
for the last time this evening. I read through the poem "First Reader"
and find my eyes drawn back to the line, "They wanted us to look but
we had looked already." I skip up a stanza to "It was always Saturday. . . ."

The poem brings an image to my mind. It is Tanika, a first-grader
from an inner-city Denver school, a child with whom I had a writing
conference earlier that day. She wrote about what it was like when
her dad packed his bags and left the night before. "He took my mom's
last seven dollars. It says right here," she says, pointing to her notebook where a string of letters is punctuated with a dollar sign. No
shaded lawn, wagon, or postman in her life, I suspect.

My thoughts leap to my sleeping daughter and circle around to
the Billy Collins poem. The first word in the last stanza, "They" becomes me—a parent, a teacher, a teacher of teachers. I become the
one wanting the children "to look," but hearing now, in the quiet of
my bedroom, their cumulative cry, "but we had looked already."
Please, we have looked already.

I flash through a brisk chronology of my own learning-to-read
days. Miss Gregg looks down fondly from her desk. My six-year-old
fingers prop my book at an angle on the desk, just like all the other
children in the classroom who hold the same reader, in the same position. I see Dick and Jane standing politely on those wide pages. I
must have liked Dick and Jane. They, no doubt, affirmed my small
place in the world. My family looked a lot like theirs: mom, dad, one
brother. The apron and wave are a stretch. My spirited mother would

2

have stood at the door, not calling us for dinner, but more likely enticing us to enter a make-believe world or play a game with her. For me, Dick and Jane were familiar and comforting. They preserved the status quo. They didn't invite me to look beyond the pages into their lives. They didn't encourage me to think.

Now I'm back to the first stanza in the poem. Who were the first characters for me after Dick and Jane? Why is it so difficult for me to remember them? Mrs. Schoonmaker was my fourth-grade teacher. She played bridge with my grandmother on Wednesday nights and was always a little grumpy on Thursday morning. She introduced me to *Black Beauty* and *National Velvet*, but she also put me in the middle math group with Miss Schakelford. I was very clear about what that meant.

My eyes refocus on the poem. Billy Collins' last line "we were forgetting how to look, learning how to read" characterizes the next few years of my life as a reader and writer. I had already learned how to read, but I rarely bothered to look. We learned that words on the page held a literal, finite truth that wasn't challenged by the reader. We learned to identify main ideas and write short book reports. We answered comprehension questions at the end of abridged stories in basal readers. We worked diligently through the rainbow of colors (why was green better than red?) on our SRA (Scholastic Research Associates individually programmed reading program) cards.

Looking at layers of meaning in text was never considered possible for us. Examining text was abandoned in favor of three reading groups a day and free reading on Friday afternoons. There were no questions about why Cathy wouldn't marry Heathcliff, or what drove Emma Bovary to suicide. Rereading, understanding symbolic meanings, or talking with others about books—the activities that define my reading as an adult—were not part of my life as a reader in those years.

I remember almost nothing of my junior high school years and very little of high school, until senior year Honors English. Jan Call was the teacher and she suggested, I believe for the first time, that I look beyond the text, consider multiple meanings, propose an interpretation different from the rest of the class, or ponder the symbolism.

Willy Loman, the protagonist in *The Death of a Salesman*, became the subject of several weeks of discussion. It would never have occurred to me that his name could symbolize his plight. Jan Call suggested we embrace many ways of knowing a book and that we—this was really radical—reread it in its entirety or in small pieces.

As I lie in bed eighteen years later, I clearly see the inside of that classroom at Greeley West High School. I recall how the anxiety lodged in my spine as I tried to formulate some kind of contribution to the discussion. My pulse raced as I raised my hand, ready to make and defend a point. Mostly, I remember feeling utterly ill-prepared for this level of discussion, concluding I wasn't intellectually capable of participating. And, given that school hadn't provided an opportunity for this kind of discussion before the twelfth grade, I *was* unprepared. Everyone joked that the notoriously talkative Ellin Oliver was mysteriously quiet in Honors English.

This thought causes me to reread the poem. I believe now that interesting and varied interpretations of text are rarely possible without rereading small sections or the whole text. I reread and find that I have not been aware of comprehending anything after the line, "But I would read about the perfect boy and his sister. . . ." I continue to read the words that follow, but in my mind's eye, I see my brother, a chubby little five-or-six-year-old with cavernous brown eyes. He is reading the encyclopedia and my mother is incredulous. She doesn't know whether to worry because he doesn't play outside like his older sister, or to indulge her pride in his remarkable early abilities by telling everyone she knows. In characteristic style, she opts for the former, but occasionally indulges the latter.

I realize I haven't paid attention to the rest of my rereading of the poem, so engrossed am I in this vivid picture from my childhood. I can see my brother with absolute clarity on the floor in front of the floor-to-ceiling bookshelves with the set of encyclopedias, recently moved to the lowest shelf. In the background I hear my mother on the phone, talking, I am sure, about my brother. My visual recollection is remarkably detailed, but I'm amazed at how the poem evoked auditory recollections as well.

My husband David enters the room and I share the picture

sparked by reading the poem. I am fascinated that this clear, twenty-five-year-old image came back to me because I reread the line about the perfect boy and his sister. I notice, and can't help commenting, that the adjective *perfect* preceded the word boy and not "his sister." I am tempted to launch into a diatribe about sexism, "perfect boy and his sister" implied in the line, but think better of it.

David listens to my ramblings peripherally. He has heard it before. He calls it an obsession. It has been over ten years since I began an immersion in professional literature and practical applications related to reading comprehension. Among many other effects, perhaps the most remarkable outcome of my exploration has been on my own reading.

I read differently now than I did fifteen years ago. I have moved from a passive to an active stance. I am acutely aware of my own reading process, the questions and challenges I have for the authors I read, the awareness I have of moments of confusion and disorientation in the text, and the tools I use to confront that confusion.

Guilty as charged, I am obsessed. I know now that my reading is not some finite, predetermined ability, pace, or style that was programmed in Miss Gregg's first-grade class. My thinking as a reader can be manipulated. I can help myself delve deeper, reflect more, remember more, make more conscious decisions about how I read and what I understand.

I realize David does not intend to engage in a discussion about reading comprehension with me at 11:00 on a Tuesday night. I mean to put the book down, roll over and turn the light off, but I can't resist one last foray into the Billy Collins poem. "Forgetting how to look, learning how to read" is the line that stays alive in my mind.

I read again and remember a song, popular when I was a little girl, " . . . little houses made of ticky tacky and they all looked just the same. . . ." That song, tune and all, springs to mind and leads me to think of the factory model that, in large part, still governs schools in this country. Little children made of ticky tacky and we teach them all just the same.

Our schools may, in many ways, look just the same, but the scene outside the schoolyard has changed and, I fear, our schools haven't responded. First-grader Tanika and thousands of others like her live lives quite distant from the scenes depicted in today's incarnation of Dick and Jane readers. A knot forms in my stomach as I consider the discrepancy between how we teach and what children need. I ask myself if Billy Collins is pointing an accusatory finger at predictable schools and homes where, "It was always Saturday and he and she were always pointing at something and shouting, Look!" Is he asking us to reexamine a system where the potential for children to grow up literate and intellectually curious is seriously limited when they must be more concerned with "the infinite, clicking permutations of the alphabet's small and capital letters"?

Maybe he intended nothing as conspiratorial as the conclusions I am drawing. I think again of Tanika, whose father left for points unknown the night before. I reread the poem thinking Billy Collins intended it to be a wake up call for families and schools and decide that I have arrived at my favorite interpretation so far. A little bit of the Honors English anxiety about forming my own interpretation creeps in. Am I taking too much liberty in interpreting this poem? Am I being too gloomy? Maybe the author had nothing like this in mind. This poem was just his way of remembering those days of beginning reading. But the more I think about it, the more I conclude that Emma Bovary and Heathcliff are in the distant background for a reason. The complex, dynamic characters prone to unpredictable actions are increasingly kept in the background of American classrooms. Eager to share my thinking, I turn to David and find him asleep.

I picked up Billy Collins' book *Questions About Angels* after Shelley Harwayne, Director of New York's Manhattan New School and author of *Lasting Impressions* (Heinemann, 1993) recommended it. She first read it on a plane returning from a speaking engagement and found it powerful. Shelley had done a great deal of work with Colorado teachers and had become a friend to many of the staff developers in one of the projects I direct at the Public Education Coalition (PEC), a business and education partnership active in five school districts in the Denver area. The books she recommended over the years—for children and adults—consistently appealed to me, so I purchased the book for myself and the staff developers at the PEC.

During Shelley's visit for a PEC summer institute, we read the poems and discussed them in small groups with teachers from throughout the region. Questions about certain poems, speculation about Billy Collins, and an occasional quote began to seep into the conversation among the PEC staff developers. They shared the poems with more teachers. The local bookstores had a run on the book and the poems, now read by dozens of summer institute participants, took on layers and layers of interpretation, each infused with the light of the reader's experience.

Months after the summer institute when this book of poems had made the rounds, months after the meanings expanded in concentric circles to dozens of teachers, I lay discussing one of the poems with a sleeping spouse. I was reminded of graduate school discussions about how meaning from text is constructed socially—how conversing about text deepens our understanding of virtually everything we read. I wondered if the social construction of meaning is dependent on a response from someone who is actually conscious.

My eye flashes again to the poem. Dick and Jane are gone. Now I think of the teachers with whom I've worked in the last twelve years. Teachers who, with great intelligence and not a little moxie, transformed their classrooms into workshops in which students are immersed in the real world of reading and writing every day. I recall how I read, reread, and ultimately relied upon the seminal work of Don Graves, Mary Ellen Giacobbe, Jane Hansen, Georgia Heard, and Lucy Calkins to help teachers create learning environments that rested on four key elements: time, ownership, response, and community (Hansen, 1987). I am struck now by the timelessness of those four elements, how relevant they are for teachers who are working to create meaningful environments, and how critical they are if children are to become passionately engaged in learning.

I also think about the work of the Public Education Coalition. In every life, there are a few defining moments—brief times that end up directing us, leading us, perhaps, to important work. One of those defining moments for me took place in the summer of 1984. A small group of educators from four school districts met on a hot summer evening at the Burnsley Hotel in downtown Denver with two attorneys and a corporate executive. An elegant dinner was brought into a dark paneled conference room. Wine was served. The talk was hushed at first. Most of those gathered had never met and weren't altogether sure why they had been invited to this meeting.

One of the attorneys spoke first. She thanked us for joining them and, with urgency in her voice, spoke of her perceptions of public education in our region and around the country. She talked of her four children, her wish they could be well educated in public schools, her fear they could not. She spoke of her interpretations of the recently issued report, *A Nation At Risk: The Imperative for Educational Reform*, that spoke of a "rising tide of mediocrity" in America's public schools. She told us that she shared the viewpoint of many in the business community: Public education was in trouble and the community was increasingly impatient with solutions proposed by teachers and administrators.

The educators gathered around the table listened intently. Perhaps some felt defensive. I remember wincing at the candor with which she spoke. I remember thinking not all schools are like that, but admitting to myself that even in my small suburban/rural school district, many were.

Then the conversation turned. One of the women, Susan Zimmermann, who would lead the PEC through its first ten years, posed a question. Often the most provocative questions are simple and hers may have been the most simple, provocative question I have ever heard. She asked the small group of educators what would happen if they were asked to design a small network of pilot schools in the four school districts represented at the table. What would it take, she wanted to know, to set up five to ten public schools that would serve as models for the community—places where the children and adults were deeply engaged and passionate about their own learning? What would it take?

I left the meeting with no specific answers, but knowing I wanted to be a part of this effort. The attorneys had proposed the formation of a local education fund designed to identify and support innovative practices in public schools while provoking systemic change from outside the system. They were going to move quickly. They intended to make a big difference and they were asking us for help.

Within six months, the PEC launched its Literacy League pilot school project in five schools—two in inner-city Denver, three in outlying suburban districts—initially with a focus on improving students' writing skills. Liz Stedem, an elementary teacher with broad experience in reading and writing, and I began by stepping cautiously into a few classrooms to work side-by-side with teachers. We wanted to serve as coaches, not experts. We wanted to learn alongside the teachers. We were eager to help them analyze their strengths and weaknesses, but also to examine their classrooms in light of what we were coming to understand from the groundbreaking writing process work of teachers and researchers in New Hampshire, New York, and around the country. Teachers and scholars Don Graves, Lucy Calkins, Shelley Harwayne, Mary Ellen Giacobbe, and dozens of others had scouted new territory in teaching writing. Language Arts classes were being converted into workshops in which children wrote every day, wrote from their own experiences, learned to make their own decisions about revising their work, and shared their writing with classmates. With those types of changes in the way children learned to write, we knew changes in reading instruction couldn't be far behind.

I remember walking up the stairway of a turn-of-the-century Denver school early in the project. I had books crammed in a bag slung on my shoulder, my own writing notebook under my arm, and adrenaline pumping through my veins. I wasn't completely sure how to help another teacher create a writing workshop in her classroom. But Maria Romero, a teacher with twenty-four years experience waited for me, one floor above. Humble doesn't begin to describe how I felt. Stupid gets closer, but fortunately, Maria loved kids, was eager to work with a colleague, and had an annoying itch—a feeling that all was not well for her fourth-grade writers. We dug in together, launching a journey that would bring hundreds of teachers and staff developers together over the next ten years.

As we went into those first classrooms, we hoped to be able to ask the kinds of provocative questions we had been asked at that dinner at the Burnsley. If we were able to do that, we were confident teachers would undertake their own transformations in personal and sustainable ways. We asked teachers to set goals for themselves as teachers of reading and writing, then we worked with them in their classrooms to realize those goals.

Instead of conducting endless workshops and talking about the research in reading and writing, Liz and I worked collaboratively with the classroom teachers solving problems, observing, conducting writing conferences with children, and puzzling over children's work. We also conducted demonstration lessons on widely varying aspects of the writing process: how to create strong, believable characters; how to draft a powerful lead or a gripping ending; or how to read literature with the eye of a writer. The conversations that followed the demonstrations were intense. "Why did you focus on character development instead of commas or quotation marks?" a teacher would probe. As staff developers, we were forced to become more aware of what led to our decisions in the course of a lesson. And, after the lessons, we always saved time to debrief with the teachers over coffee in the lounge.

Today, nearly fifty PEC staff developers work with teachers in six Denver-area school districts. Over one hundred schools have been involved in the PEC teaching and learning projects known as the Literacy League, Reading, and Math Projects. Much has changed and, of course, much remains the same. Teachers and staff developers still puzzle over the reluctance of a child to write from the heart, still agonize over the child who reads fluently but comprehends little, still long for the day when a child can move seamlessly through elementary, middle, and high school, working with teachers who value classrooms built upon the foundations of time, ownership, response, and community; they still wonder when all the pieces of the teaching and learning mosaic will come together for children in every school.

Listening to my sleeping house, I alternate between worry that no matter what we do it will never be enough, and deep satisfaction in the work we've done. I marvel at the extraordinary accomplishment and potential of teachers and staff developers—heads bent over a child's writing folder or reading response log, mulling over the complexities of children's thought captured on paper.

As I lay comfortably ensconced in my bed, reading Billy Collins' poetry, my mind took a journey. In the space of three to five minutes, I considered what I already knew that related to the poem; I wove past experiences into the fabric of the poem, posed questions, drew conclusions, visualized, inferred, synthesized, and considered what I didn't know, at least as much as what I did know. I longed to talk about what I had discovered through rereading. I created more interpretations because I had already talked to others and my meaning was layered on top of theirs.

My thinking led me on a journey many of us take. The journey itself, however, is rarely discussed. This book is about having that conversation with ourselves and with children. It is about revisiting the myriad ways in which we construct meaning as we read. It is about lively talk in classrooms and what happens when children develop an awareness of their thought processes as they read. It is about explicit comprehension instruction that is rich and deep and invites children to contribute significantly to the conversation about the mental journey we take when we read. It is about a different kind of first reader from the one described in Billy Collins' poem.

This is a book about the mosaic each of us creates as we read—a mosaic constructed of diverse pieces, each integral to the whole, each essential to the texture of learning.

TWO

Mind Journeys

You can smell the classroom from down the hall. Not a late-spring-temp-in-the-low-eighties-we've-just-been-out-to-recess smell, but the light floral scent of a slowly burning potpourri that draws you right to room 203. A first-grader's sign on the door asks visitors to "Sn n plz." I cross the threshold into the classroom and trip on the curling corner of an imitation oriental rug.

As I recover from the near fall, Joaquin comes to my rescue with an outstretched hand. "You okay?" he asks. I nod.

"This is our foyer," he tells me, making a sweeping gesture with his arm. "You want to see the den?" He leads me to a four-by-four-foot area bordered on three sides by three-foot-high bookcases. The den is set off by another throw rug that fits neatly into the space created by the bookshelves.

"That's Casandra. She likes hardcover fiction." Joaquin points to a prone body, lying on her tummy. Casandra doesn't budge. One pudgy finger holds *Sky Dogs* by Jane Yolen open. The other hand moves over the illustrations as if they're braille.

"Want to see the art studio?" Joaquin asks; but his teacher, Debbie Miller, approaches and suggests that he continue his tour later.

Joaquin collapses next to Casandra and picks up his own book. Debbie and I smile and begin to look around the classroom she has moved into after transferring from another school. I immediately notice the abundant natural light. No overhead neon needed in this room. The darker corners are illuminated by standing floor lamps—vintage Wal Mart and garage sale—and half a dozen table lamps sit in the center of the groups of desks around the room.

Debbie's infectious laugh precedes her description of spending more on extension cords and electrical tape than on the lamps themselves. "I got the twelve-foot ladder from the custodian's closet." Her voice takes on a mock conspiratorial tone. "I climbed up there and took down all the old blinds that hung there for thirty years and the light is amazing, don't you think?" I do.

University Park Elementary is a circa 1940s Denver Public School building. The sixteen-foot ceilings, pale green walls, and tile floors in most rooms create an acoustic and visual nightmare. Not here. An odd assortment of throw rugs and lamp shades, vividly decorated by children's markers, define the work areas, minimize the noise, and soften the light. Long stretches of Stewart plaid fabric cover bulletin boards and the recesses of closets whose doors Debbie has removed, no doubt having snatched the appropriate tools from the custodian's closet. Joaquin's description of the foyer and den is becoming absolutely believable.

The *living room* is the central gathering place for this group of twenty-five six-year-olds. Again defined by a throw rug (anchored by more electrical tape), the room contains a rocking chair with an old rattan circular table next to it. A floor lamp throws light from behind. The turtle and gerbil have been moved to the veterinary office, a distant corner. Apparently, the smell was a bit strong for the living room.

Debbie invites the children to bring the books they have been working on to the living room for sharing time. As the children gather, I recall a conversation Debbie and I had several years ago as we watched another group of first-graders thumb through books.

"Reading has always been a mystery to me. I mean, what is it, really? How can we ever know what goes on in their minds when they're reading?" she'd asked.

I'd struggled with the same question beginning in my undergraduate teacher training courses. "How can I actually teach kids to read?"

The boxes of "reading activities" I developed for my reading methods classes certainly didn't answer my question.

Debbie pushed her point. "I remember Tip and Mitten. I remember SRA. I remember 'read the chapter and answer the comprehension questions' and, you know what?" she challenged, "I learned to read just fine with all those methods we now consider obsolete. I don't really know what to say when parents or my principal ask me why I'm doing things differently now. I have a hard time answering their questions. I can't very well tell them I'm having much more fun teaching a new way, though that is very true!"

With that question Debbie voiced the sentiment of many of her colleagues: What we call teaching reading has come to mean something dramatically different than it did when many of today's teachers learned to read.

We have made great strides. Debbie and teachers around the country have redefined the time children spend each day learning to read. They have created readers' and writers' workshops where every day children are given extended opportunities to read, have ownership for the selection of many of their own books, and spend time responding to what they've read by talking to others and writing about their reactions.

But Debbie, who by then had several years of teaching in a workshop format under her belt, was still uncomfortable. "You know, Ellin, these classrooms look and feel different from a year or two ago. Children choose to read. They read for long periods of time. They are totally excited to share books. They recommend books to each other. They meet in book clubs and ask to go to the library. It's an incredible difference. They're more engaged for longer periods than I've ever seen them; and, it's so much more fun to teach this way. . . ." Her voice lowered and her eyes narrowed. "But something isn't right. I don't want to teach out of the basal again." Her voice trailed off. "But I'm not teaching." She emphasized the word teaching. "I'm not teaching these kids how to read."

It wasn't the first time I had heard this. As I listened to

Debbie's searching questions, I recalled numerous conversations (including one memorable poolside talk) with a friend and colleague, Janice Dole, a leading researcher in the field of reading comprehension. Jan reminded me that, historically, teachers and researchers have believed that the ability to comprehend text is "caught rather than taught" (Pearson, Roehler, Dole, and Duffy, 1992). If reading meant *catching* a meaning known only to the author, teaching reading had to mean finding out whether or not students *got it*.

Instruction in America's elementary reading classes has been based on this theory: a series of comprehension questions—coming from the basal reader or the teacher—were posed, and the goal was to see if children could answer them (caught them) in the way the teacher believed they should. Many teachers taught what the basals told them to teach: *skills* such as homonyms, suffixes, main ideas, as well as scores of other fragments of reading. Reading classes were typically structured and predictable: three reading groups a day and plenty of *seat work* time to complete skill sheets. Rarely were students taught how to comprehend and analyze whole sections of text.

For decades many educators believed that teaching reading meant dealing with the visible or audible, rather than cognitive, manifestations of reading. If children completed drill sheets and workbook pages, and sat in their ability groups to discuss the story, the spiral curriculum built into the basal series would ensure that students could comprehend complex text. But we never really considered what they might have been thinking about while they were reading. In fact many children were not (and are not) learning to comprehend using this approach, and they certainly weren't becoming proficient, independent, confident, critical readers. The belief system that formed the foundation for reading instruction in most American schools appeared to rest on quicksand.

As a first-year teacher, I asked a fifth-grader in my class to decorate two legal-sized folders which I stapled to the bulletin board. One said "completed assignments," the other read "corrected assignments." The fifth-graders dutifully (usually!) put their completed worksheets into the first folder. My job was to read them and return them in the second folder. The first folder bulged and eventually tore the staples out of the wall. The second folder remained embarrassingly light. I realized quickly I didn't want to spend my time grading worksheets students completed and forgot. I felt guilty every time I looked at that empty folder, but no one ever asked for a worksheet back.

Meanwhile, as a class, we started to talk about books. I read J. R. R. Tolkien's *The Hobbit* aloud while the students sketched illustrations. The museum table, a place where the class treasures were exhibited, became a place to display, share, and recommend favorite books, as well as other artifacts. At parent conferences, we talked about new books parents might check out: books I knew their children would enjoy, based on what they'd read and shared in a reading class that was quickly veering off its expected course as I ignored conventional wisdom and mandated practices.

All the fifth-graders with whom I worked that year were readers, technically. They had no problems with word identification. They could usually decipher unknown words. They could recite a basic summary of a story. I changed course for one reason. They were disengaged. They were sick and tired of worksheets and repetitive assignments. And so was I.

There were six first-year teachers in my school that year. We were all young, mostly single, and just out of college. We loved teaching, but we had full lives. Our routine Friday afternoon clubs were sprinkled with conversations about our new profession, kids who worried us, and our lives. We crowded chairs around tables sticky with spilled beer and talked, our conversations crisscrossing around our students, our loves, our disappointments, and our dreams. We talked about books we read and passed paperbacks around until they were tattered. One teacher was writing a novel; several of us kept journals; one wrote poetry. During those freewheeling discussions, it dawned on me and the others that the classes we called reading didn't make sense. They were inadequate imitations of real life.

I was lucky. My colleagues and I supported each other as we moved away from traditional, textbook-bound instruction. We discussed the awakenings we saw in our students and shared our enthusiasm. For many other teachers, the process of change was lonelier.

In the 1980s teachers around the country began to abandon basal-driven reading instruction for several reasons. Like my fifth-graders, their students were disengaged and bored. As teachers, they were uncomfortable with an instructional model based on rote learning that left little room for serious analysis and exploration. But, most alarming, they were moving away from this type of instruction because too many of their students were not learning how to comprehend what they read.

For six years I directed the Chapter One (now Title I) Program in the Douglas County, Colorado, school district. During that time the Chapter One teachers and I spent many hours observing and scrutinizing the work of elementary students identified for Chapter One services. The profiles of many of these children—thirty percent or more—troubled us. These were children who successfully read words from word lists on comprehension inventories. They were able to decode words accurately with acceptable pronunciation. Some even read passages fluently. Yet after they read, many were unable to tell us what the passages meant. These children didn't know when they were comprehending. They didn't know when they were not comprehending. Many didn't know what they were supposed to comprehend when they read. Others didn't seem to know that text is supposed to mean something.

Often when these children listened to stories read aloud, their behaviors suggested they weren't aware they should be thinking about the story during the read-aloud time or that they should be prepared to talk about it afterward. They paid little attention to the illustrations and showed only slight interest as their classes undertook activities related to the content of the books. Increasingly, we became aware of a growing group of students who could decode words, but couldn't really understand what they'd read.

Debbie Miller, my own teaching colleagues, the Douglas County Chapter One teachers, and thousands of others rejected traditional reading instruction because their students weren't engaged and too many of them weren't comprehending what they read. These teachers knew there had to be a better way. They knew that teaching reading implies much more than hoping that all the worksheets and comprehension questions add up to the real thing.

Nonetheless, when they'd made significant changes in their reading classrooms, the questions they posed about really teaching reading raised a collective voice: "We have moved on. We have left controlled, teacher-proof reading programs where we read 'Say this' in bold print. We have created readers' workshops instead of reading classes and they are inviting places for children to learn to love to read. We have filled our shelves with wonderful children's literature. We read to our students for hours every week. Children in our classrooms love books and spend time with them every day. As teachers we are happier and more creative than ever before, but if we don't want to return to programmed reading instruction, we're going to have to know what to teach instead."

It became clear that many of these important questions focused on what should be taught. Teachers felt increasingly confident about their progress in how the classroom environment and management should be handled. They were absorbed and enthused about the process they had undergone in transforming their classrooms into readers' workshops, and they felt an enhanced sense of engagement for their students, as well as for themselves. These teachers were beginning to understand the need to teach reading by articulating and focusing instruction on the mental processes that underlie reading.

The teachers who posed important questions believed the compendium of skills lifted from the basal scope and sequence was irrelevant, uninteresting, and inadequate in terms of teaching children how to comprehend, but they didn't know what skills or strategies with which to replace that scope and sequence.

"If we don't return to programmed reading instruction, what do we teach instead?" If a handful of teachers or only one or two staff developers had pressed us with the question, it might have gone the way of many provocative questions in our profession. But the record remained stuck on the same groove: "I'm not teaching these children how to read, how to read, how to read."

A sense of urgency arose and the staff developers at the PEC began an exploration that would lead to some important early answers to these questions. The teachers and staff developers started with conversations about their own reading. When Liz Stedem read Wallace Stegner's *Crossing to Safety*, she told us to put down anything else we might be reading in order to read it immediately. We read Nadine Gordimer's *My Son's Story* and Lawrence Thornton's *Imagining Argentina* and talked about parts we loved, sections that surprised us, events we didn't understand fully, and mutual friends who might enjoy them. We started a PEC Book Club. By the time we talked about *Love in the Time of Cholera* by Gabriel Garcia Marquez and *Beloved* by Toni Morrison, a year or so later, our lives as readers had changed permanently.

We discovered new lives as adult readers, but the conversation around the PEC conference room table consistently circled back to children. We began to feel an urgency about children's reading, and reading instruction in the workshop setting. Were we making it possible for children to first understand and then analyze and write about books in the same probing way we were discussing them? We didn't think so.

By that time, the staff developers at the PEC had begun to read and consider the implications of reading comprehension studies undertaken in the 1980s. Frequently referred to as the proficient reader research, this body of work examined the cognitive processes (strategies) used most commonly by proficient readers, whether they were adults glued to a gripping novel or advanced placement seniors making their way through a physics text (see Table 2.1).

Surprisingly, many of the studies that examined the thinking of proficient readers pointed to only seven or eight thinking strategies used consistently by proficient readers. Even more surprisingly, the researchers described the same seven or eight strategies in their findings. Some researchers concluded that if teachers taught these thinking strategies, instead of much of the traditional isolated skills expected to lead inexorably to proficient reading, students who used the strategies would be better equipped to comprehend and analyze text independently. Since it is known which strategies are used most routinely by proficient readers, researchers suggested that teachers focus instructional time and creative energy on helping students gradually learn to use these strategies as they read a variety of texts in all grade levels.

The researchers recommended that each strategy be taught with singular focus, over a long period of time, to students from kindergarten through twelfth grade and beyond, and that teachers model and students practice the strategies with a variety of texts. If teachers focused their attention on a strategy, beginning with a great deal of modeling and gradually releasing responsibility (Gallagher and Pearson, 1983) to the children to practice it independently, the researchers believed students could actually be taught to think differently as they read. They would comprehend more deeply, critically, and analytically.

In reading groups and at PEC staff developers' meetings, we tested the strategies on our reading. We became more conscious of our own thinking processes as readers. We realized we could concentrate simultaneously on the text and our ways of thinking about it. What seemed most extraordinary, however, was that by thinking about our own thinking—by being metacognitive (literally, to think about one's own thinking)—we could actually deepen and enhance our comprehension of the text. We reminded ourselves that during the time we had worked together at the PEC, everything we felt was worth doing in classrooms we had first tested on ourselves, through our own reading and writing. These strategies were no exception.

"The only time I recall anyone teaching me directly how to

Researchers have confirmed what teachers of reading may have observed in themselves and in their students, namely, that thoughtful, active, proficient readers are metacognitive; they think about their own thinking during reading.

Proficient readers know what and when they are comprehending and when they are not comprehending; they can identify their purposes for reading and identify the demands placed on them by a particular text. They can identify when and why the meaning of the text is unclear to them, and can use a variety of strategies to solve comprehension problems or deepen their understanding of a text (Duffy et al. 1987; Paris, Cross, and Lipson, 1984).

As a reader is metacognitive, he or she frequently uses the following cognitive strategies:

· Activating relevant, prior knowledge (schema) before, during, and after reading text. Proficient readers "use prior knowledge to evaluate the adequacy of the model of meaning they have developed" and to store newly learned information with other related memories (Pearson et al. 1992; Gordon and Pearson, 1983; Hansen, 1981).
· Determining the most important ideas and themes in a text (Afflerbach and Johnston, 1986; Baumann, 1986; Tierney and Cunningham, 1984; Winograd and Bridge, 1986). Proficient readers use their conclusions about important ideas to focus their reading and to exclude peripheral or unimportant details from memory.
Asking questions of themselves, the authors, and the texts they read (Andre and Anderson, 1979; Brown and Palincsar, 1985). Proficient readers use their questions to clarify and to focus their reading.
· Creating visual and other sensory images from text during and after reading. These images may include visual, auditory and other sensory connections to the text. Proficient

TABLE 2.1 *Reading Comprehension Strategies*

readers use these images to deepen their understanding of the text.

· Drawing inferences from text. Proficient readers use their prior knowledge (schema) and textual information to draw conclusions, make critical judgments, and form unique interpretations from text. Inferences may occur in the form of conclusions, predictions, or new ideas (Anderson and Pearson, 1984).

· Retelling or synthesizing what they have read. Proficient readers attend to the most important information and to the clarity of the synthesis itself. Readers synthesize in order to better understand what they have read (Brown and Day, 1983).

· Utilizing a variety of *fix-up strategies* to repair comprehension when it breaks down. Proficient readers select appropriate fix-up strategies from one of the six language systems (pragmatic, schematic, semantic, syntactic, lexical, or grapho-phonic) to best solve a given problem in a given reading situation (i.e., skip ahead or reread, use the context and syntax, or sound it out). (Garner, 1987)

Pearson, Roehler, Dole, and Duffy propose that the strategies listed above become the kindergarten through twelfth-grade reading comprehension curriculum. They contend that a lengthy list of discrete reading skills does not add up to proficient reading as was once believed.

A new interactive definition of reading comprehension suggests that reading teachers understand the cognitive processes used most frequently by proficient readers and that they provide explicit and in-depth instruction focused over a long period of time on these strategies. Teachers need to use authentic and challenging texts (high quality children's literature and well-written nonfiction) to help their students move along the continuum from novice to proficient reader.

TABLE 2.1 *Continued*

improve my reading was a speed reading course my mother forced me to take the summer before I went to college," Chryse Hutchins, one of the PEC staff developers, said, shaking her head, "This stuff is incredible. I mean, I read and I'm thinking at two different levels now. I'm taking in the content, the events in the story, the editorial, the gardening hints, whatever, but I'm also posing and answering questions, pondering, really living in my visual images as I read. I'm thinking about experiences I've had and books I've read that relate to this text and I'm making decisions about what I think is most important. I'm talking about metacognition at cocktail parties," she laughed. After telling her to "get a life," the others nodded in agreement.

I remember asking, "Then, what does this mean for kids? Is it too simplistic to think that if proficient readers use the same strategies to construct meaning when they read in virtually any kind of text, that it might be possible to help kids become more aware of their own reading processes and then to teach them to improve their comprehension? Might we be able to help teachers focus their instruction on these strategies in order to help kids learn to comprehend in the first place, and deepen their comprehension once they're reading fairly independently?" I paused, hoping they wouldn't laugh at what I'd proposed. "Is it too simplistic?" I asked.

Another staff developer scanned the faces in the conference room and responded slowly. "My mother always told me that elegance and power are found in simplicity." Smiles spread around the table.

By then the connection to the classroom had become obvious. We were convinced that reading comprehension could be taught by showing children what proficient readers thought about as they read, and teaching children to use those same strategies themselves. We were further convinced that this explicit instruction could take place in the literature-rich learning communities many teachers had worked hard to create. The strategies became pieces in a mosaic, vital components of a strikingly beautiful design we had experienced and longed to share with other teachers and children.

As we worked with the strategies, it became clear that metacognition—thinking about one's own thinking—was an umbrella under which the other strategies fell. Each strategy was a variation of metacognition.

A search began. Through journals and visits to reading projects in school districts and universities around the country, we looked for settings in which children studied in workshop environments surrounded by high quality fiction and nonfiction; where they were given ample opportunity to read every day, and to talk and write about their interpretations of books; *and* where the teacher explicitly taught the comprehension strategies identified in the proficient reader research. We wanted to see if teachers anywhere in the country were implementing the proficient reader research by using the strategies and helping children gradually assume responsibility to use them independently. We wanted to know if they were doing so in the context of a reader's workshop.

Instead, we found classrooms where teachers had created readers' workshops that focused instructional attention primarily on selecting books and sharing in book clubs. Mini lessons centered on ways children, working alone or in groups, could create vivid representations of what they read.

We found classrooms where children developed elaborate projects to extend concepts from the books they read, and others where children created time lines of characters' lives and became those characters in dramatic representations of the books.

We found examples of instructional tools that had been developed to help children describe their comprehension. In many classrooms, teachers taught webbing and mapping processes that children used to remember significant actions taken by the characters in a book, or important details about the setting or conflict. The tools were primarily enrichment activities. They helped teachers to know what children remembered from their reading, but did little to actually change children's thinking while they were reading. The teachers who used the tools assumed that asking students to complete projects related to the books they read would teach them to read.

And, of course, we found many classrooms where there was a great deal of direct instruction, but it was focused on a random string of isolated and unrelated skills. The skills instruction and comprehension tools did not, however, teach children how to comprehend. In increasing numbers, the teachers we met were dissatisfied and asking the same questions we had.

Something was missing: It was, we came to believe, the juxtaposition of the study of literature in a workshop setting and deep, focused comprehension instruction—instruction that targeted the thinking that occurs during reading, thinking that determines how deeply the text is understood.

I watch Debbie Miller teach a mini lesson to her new first-graders. She sits in the rocker, reading *Amazing Grace* by Mary Hoffman, stopping every three or four pages to look up and think aloud. The first-graders are clustered at her feet.

"You know," she begins, "reading this reminds me of a time when I wasn't allowed to play basketball on the Springfield High School team because I was a girl. See, right here when Raj tells Grace that she can't be Peter Pan because she is a girl and when Natalie tells Grace she can't be Peter Pan because she's black?" Debbie points to the text. "Those words made me hear exactly what the coach said to me a long time ago. He said, 'Debbie, no girls have ever played on the Springfield High School basketball team and I can't see as how they ever will.' "

I sit, cross-legged in the midst of the children huddled around Debbie. As I listen, I see Debbie is teaching reading comprehension directly by helping the children use their relevant, prior knowledge to make sense of a story they are hearing for the first time—a cognitive strategy the research suggests is vitally important to comprehension.

Before Debbie had struggled with the question of teaching reading comprehension, mini lessons weren't this deliberate. The differences between only talking about books and talking about the thinking processes a proficient reader uses to understand them are subtle but key and Debbie had made the transition.

Debbie reads a few more pages and stops on the page where the character Grace and her grandmother, on their way to the ballet, stop to gaze at a marquee proclaiming "Stunning new Juliet."

"This book also reminds me of a book I'm reading right now. Let me show you." She reaches down and pulls Faye Moskovitz' *A Leak in the Heart* from her bag. "In this book," Debbie says, "the author is writing about when she was little and how hard and even embarrassing it was for her when her grandmother spoke Yiddish around her friends. It made her feel so different from the other kids."

A hand shoots up and Kent says "You know what book that reminds me of?" The heads rotate toward him. "*My Grandfather's Face*," he says triumphantly. "Remember how the girl's grandfather is an actor and he's acting in front of a mirror and she thinks he's really mad at her? Debbie, your book is like that." Debbie nods, "Yeah, Yeah! It is similar to *My Grandfather's Face*. Remember, you guys, how we have said that there are text-to-self connections, text-to-world connections, and text-to-text connections. What kind of a connection did Kevin just make?"

It's unanimous. "Text to text!" the class replies.

A few weeks later, I'm back in Debbie's classroom. It's quiet. The stream of a trumpet solo seeps into the lighted corners of Debbie's room from a small boom box. Golden leaves dart at the windows as a chilly fall wind picks up. Elan stretches and, book under his arm, moves from the den to his table. In his area, a well-loved bear and a picture of his dog in a frame define his space. Debbie and I pull first-grade sized chairs next to him for a reading conference. He is reading *Mrs. Wishy Washy* by Joy Cowley.

"Well, Mr. Elan, what do you think? When you were reading *Mrs. Wishy Washy*, what were you reminded of? Any text-to-text, text-to-self, text-to-world connections?" Debbie leans forward, elbows on her knees.

"Hmmmm . . . Well . . . Not . . . I don't think so Debbie." Elan's eyes stray to another book stacked in a plastic basket in the middle of his table. "Nope, but this one does." He leans to the center of the table and pulls out *Oliver Button Is a Sissy* by Tomie dePaola.

"This is a great book, Debbie," he says. "Do you remember when we read this in the living room? Josh and I have been reading it together and now I'm reading it alone. Well, it reminds me of stuff that always happens in day care after school. Kids, like even sometimes me, get really teased about some stuff and in this book, that's what happens to Oliver Button. Remember the part when," he flips immediately to the page he is looking for, "these older boys are throwing his tap shoes up in the air. They say he's a sissy because he likes to dance. That reminds me of when the kids in day care will only play Power Rangers and I don't want to and then they don't like me."

Debbie and I exchange a quick glance before she continues the conversation about the similarities between Oliver Button's conflict and the gang in day care.

Debbie leans back again and says, "Elan, I always like to tell readers after a conference something that is important to know about being a reader. I'd like for you to know that some books, like *Oliver Button Is a Sissy*, are great because they remind us of so many things: other books, other things we've learned about the world, and things that happen in our own lives. Books like *Mrs. Wishy Washy* are great, too, but for a different reason."

Elan agreed. "Yeah, I can read it easy!"

"Exactly!" Debbie says. "The words are predictable and you can read them, but the story doesn't really make you go on a journey in your mind, does it?"

"Nope, it doesn't have any poetic language and it isn't something that would really happen. If the story isn't about something that would really happen, you don't go on mind journeys."

As I leave the sweet sounds and smells of room 203 behind me, Elan's words live on in my mind. If reading is about mind journeys, teaching reading is about outfitting the travelers, modeling how to use the map, demonstrating the key and the legend, supporting the travelers as they lose their way and take circuitous routes, until, ultimately, it's the child and the map together and they are off on their own.

THREE

What Lies Beneath

Salvador, Late or Early

Salvador with eyes the color of caterpillar, Salvador of the crooked hair and crooked teeth, Salvador whose name the teacher cannot remember, is a boy who is no one's friend, runs along somewhere in that vague direction where homes are the color of bad weather, lives behind a raw wood doorway, shakes the sleepy brothers awake, ties their shoes, combs their hair with water, feeds them milk and corn flakes from a tin cup in the dim dark of the morning.

Salvador, late or early, sooner or later arrives with the string of younger brothers ready. Helps his mama, who is busy with the business of the baby. Tugs the arms of Cecilio, Arturito, makes them hurry, because today, like yesterday, Arturito has dropped the cigar box of crayons, has let go the hundred little fingers of red, green, yellow, blue, and nub of black sticks that tumble and spill over and beyond the asphalt puddles until the crossing-guard lady holds back the blur of traffic for Salvador to collect them again.

Salvador inside that wrinkled shirt, inside the throat that must clear itself and apologize each time it speaks, inside that forty-pound body of boy with its geography of scars, its history of hurt, limbs stuffed with feathers and rags, in what part of the eyes, in what part of the heart, in that cage of the chest where something throbs with both fists and knows only what Salvador knows, inside that body too small to contain the hundred balloons of happiness, the single guitar of grief, is a boy like any other disappearing out the door, beside the schoolyard gate, where he has told his brothers they must wait. Collects the hands of Cecilio and Arturito, scuttles off dodging the many schoolyard colors, the elbows and wrists criss-crossing, the several shoes running. Grows small and smaller to the eye, dissolves into the bright horizon, flutters in the air before disappearing like a memory of kites.

SANDRA CISNEROS,
from *Woman Hollering Creek and Other Stories*

The flight attendants hadn't yet risen. The seat belt sign was still illuminated. I was perfectly content, headed for New York by myself. I'd been eager for the trip, for some time alone, a short hiatus from phones ringing and calls for mom. Completely relaxed, I pulled *Woman Hollering Creek* from my well-worn Metropolitan Opera book bag—deliberately purchased years before to be a reminder of my favorite city.

It was 1993. I was traveling to New York to teach a session on reading comprehension at the Teachers College Writing Project at Columbia University. I was looking forward to seeing friends. I was looking forward to being alone in the city. I was looking forward to conversations with the sophisticated and curious teachers who frequent the workshops at Teachers College and to sharing our staff development team's growing enthusiasm about teaching reading comprehension in a workshop environment.

I wanted to open the session with a piece that would be challenging to comprehend on the first reading. As I had prepared at home, David had walked through my basement study. "Any thoughts on a good piece that will entice, but baffle a little?" I'd asked.

David, who is—and thinks like—an amateur cartoonist, suggested I take one of his legal texts and project a couple pages on the screen for the workshop participants to read. "I want to temporarily confuse, not permanently alienate," I'd laughed, as he slipped out the door.

I wanted the participants to experience what their students experience: to struggle as their students sometimes struggle; to be on the edge of understanding, but not quite there—at least initially. I knew I learned the most about reading comprehension when I was slightly off balance myself. Then I was forced to think more critically and carefully about my own thinking. I wanted to share that experience with the teachers in New York. I wanted them to relive the anxiety and effort children experience when they grapple with text just outside their understanding.

The white noise of jet engines forms a backdrop that sends me deep inside what I'm reading or thinking about. "Salvador with eyes the color of caterpillar, Salvador of the crooked hair and crooked teeth, Salvador whose name the teacher cannot remember, is a boy who is no one's friend. . . ." I leaned my head against the fuselage and let the vibration of the engines mingle with the words of the piece.

I turned and stretched my legs the full length of the row. Apparently few others were interested in leaving the west to travel to the city that day. The solitude brought me freedom to stare for awhile, reread, and try to determine whether I was truly able to understand this little piece of writing.

In Cisneros' poetic words, an impression, not really a clear picture, of a little boy emerged. My mental image was nothing more than a sprinkling of words, an elusive impression, sprayed with color and movement. Perhaps an impression was all I needed to understand this piece—a small dent in my memory where Salvador, Cecilio, and Arturito ran toward "homes . . . the color of bad weather." It was mine to decide.

As the plane leveled at cruising altitude, I reread the last paragraph, trying to keep all the elements straight in my mind. Was it "the hundred balloons of happiness, the single guitar of grief" that confused me? My eyes scanned back over the paragraph looking for a break in the barrage of images. There was none. I looked for a period and found it two thirds of the way into the long paragraph. I noticed the first paragraph never stopped for a breath. It was one long sentence. Though I understood each of the words, I had only blurry images of Salvador and his surroundings. I was reminded that understanding the words in a piece is a small fragment of what we call comprehension.

The next day, surrounded by educators from five boroughs and New Jersey, I scratched notes in the margin as I reread "Salvador, Late or Early." I asked the teachers to read the piece and do the same. Silence filled the room.

I underlined the words "let go the hundred little fingers of red, green, yellow, blue, and nub of black" and jotted the question, "Why is it the black that is a nub?" in the margin. I could feel his frustration as Salvador "collects them again." I wrote the word *whirring* next to the last paragraph, but I'm unsure why. I felt teachers' eyes on me and the heat of embarrassment rising up the back of my neck and into my face. I began to wonder how I was going to lead a discussion about this piece with the unsettling feeling that I didn't quite get it myself.

The woman who spoke first wore a brilliantly colored turban and had dark exotic eyes. Every head turned toward her voice, a voice gentle and magnetic with an undertow of pain. "When I read this piece," she paused as her head rolled upward and her eyes fixed on the water-stained ceiling tiles, "I see my mama. She is surrounded by ten of us, all sizes. Some are eating, some are sleeping. Some are choring. None are playing." Silence.

The voice of a young teacher came next. "It just makes me think of the kids in my school. They're all Salvadors. It makes me feel so inadequate. I wonder if I," her eyes returned to the sheet in front of her and her smooth brown hand ran over the lines, "somehow, I am like the teacher who can't remember the names?" Her voice trailed off and again the discomfort of silence forced everyone's eyes to their copies of the piece.

Another teacher stretched a long leg in black stirrup pants on to the table and leaned back in an old wooden chair. She looked briefly out the window, as if to collect her thoughts, and said, "You know, I'm sort of embarrassed. I had only a vague idea what the piece was about until I began to hear other people talk about it. Then it was like my memory kicked in. When she," the woman gestured across the room, "said something about the author's use of color as symbolic, I remembered that the colors were vivid in my mind when I read, too, but I didn't think about that until I heard her say it. By discussing this, it's like we decided what it meant together."

"I agree," another teacher jumped in, "I didn't understand this well enough in the time you gave us to read it to really understand the symbolism. Whatever I would say about it right now would be so literal."

"I was worse than that," another confessed. "When the first few lines seemed so strange to me, I just skimmed over the rest and I don't think I could say what it was about at all. What's more, I don't think I want to know."

"I don't think it was strange at all," came the voice from someone sitting on the floor who'd come into the session after the chairs had filled. "I found it disturbing and hopeful at the same time. I think it paints a picture of kids—like a couple I could name in my class right now. When I read this, I saw this really earnest little kid who has so much responsibility." She paused and glanced at me. "I don't know if this is what we were supposed to be thinking about and responding to as we read this, but I was thinking about a piece in the *Times Sunday Magazine* a few weeks ago. Listen to this: 'sooner or later arrives with the string of younger brothers ready. Helps his mama, who is busy with the business of the baby.' Doesn't that remind you of so many of your kids, or the piece in the *Times*, the agonizing detail about what these kids do when they go home to empty houses with a bunch of other kids. It's terrifying." Others nodded. "Powerful." More nods.

The conversation continued, following a winding path. Some in the room viewed Cisneros' writing as poetry and loved the impressions she drew; others seemed almost angry at Cisneros' nontraditional style. "Why does she purposely make it harder to comprehend? What's the point?"

"The point," I pulled them back together, "is engagement. The point is that you knew whether or not you understood. You knew what mental images you held during and after you read the piece. You knew what you needed to know in order to contribute to the conversation we've just had. You also knew, at some level, that it would be fine if you didn't fully understand or like this piece. You knew it would be perfectly acceptable to say so, and you knew that reading the piece only once, and not having an opportunity to talk about it in small groups or write about it more extensively before we had the large group discussion, made comprehending it more difficult."

"My concern," I told them, "is that many children are not so engaged as they read. They don't know when they're comprehending. They don't know when they're not. They don't know whether it's critical for them to comprehend a given piece. And if they don't comprehend, they don't know what to do about it." I saw nodding heads around the room, then told them about a classroom I'd visited the previous fall.

As I entered the room, children were throwing their backpacks into a 1950s era cloak room. The windows were wide open. A late summer breeze blew. The chatter rose to the fifteen-foot ceilings and filled the corners of the room. The children were the definition of first-grade exuberance and energy. "Who's she?" they asked, pointing at me as they gathered at their teacher's feet.

Sharon Sherman-Messinger, a highly respected teacher whose practices have influenced many of her colleagues around the Denver area, works with kids who have anything but a literate start to their lives. Each day her students come from gang territory to the oasis of her classroom.

That day Sharon started by reading to her students. I observed, knowing I'd learn a lot from Sharon, especially about launching a school year. Sitting in an old bentwood rocker, she opened *Tiki Tiki Tembo* retold by Arlene Mosel and began. She leaned forward, her voice playfully running the cadences, her face magnetic.

I was so enticed by her oral reading that we were halfway through the book before I became aware that I was more absorbed than just about anyone else in the room. Some of the children were looking out the window; others played with little pieces of paper or pencils; others stared vacantly as if they didn't know how to listen. A few appeared to be captured by the book, but many looked as if the reading had no purpose at all for them.

I thought about my daughter Elizabeth. The first time I read *Tiki* she was delighted; and, as a two-year-old, tried to say the words alongside me, "Tiki, Tiki, Tembo no sa rembo chari bari ruchi, pip peri, pembo." What was it about those words that made it almost impossible not to chant them as loudly as possible? That was, I imagined, what Sharon had in mind—using rhythmic, predictable text to playfully propel her first-graders into the wonder of language and to ensure they understood something about its repetitive nature. Important objectives for young language learners, to be sure.

What I noticed instead, I told the group of teachers in New York—knowing they had probably experienced a similar scenario—was that almost no one in Sharon's classroom was chanting with her. Fewer still were looking at the pictures or even at the book. And this is not a teacher with a classroom management problem. She is masterful and had given a great deal of thought to her selection of this book.

Sharon tried again. She reread it and asked the children to join her: "Tiki Tiki Tembo, no sa rembo . . ." Sporadic interest and scattered responses met her. I told the teachers in New York that Sharon and I had chatted while the children were in music and decided to go back to the old standard, *Brown Bear, Brown Bear, What Do You See?* when they returned. Same response. Sharon switched gears later that week and used *The Tenth Good Thing About Barney* by Judith Viorst, wondering if their lack of engagement related to the lack of a rich, interesting plot in the predictable, rhythmic books. Same response.

One of the teachers in the New York workshop interrupted my story. "I work with kindergartners and I could tell you a dozen similar stories, especially from the beginning of the school year. It's really as if they don't know that they're supposed to pay attention."

"It's the same in my experience," another added, "but I don't think it's about paying attention. They pay attention beautifully at other times of the day. It seems to me as if they don't know that the books themselves are something to pay attention to. Early in the school year, they don't seem to realize that the words and pictures have stories embedded in them."

"Curious," I said. "When Sharon and I discussed the issue, we drew the same conclusion. Many don't seem to know that they can expect text and pictures to have meaning, and that the meaning is inherently interesting and worth paying attention to."

"I work with fourth- and fifth-graders and I won't tell you that the situation is identical," interjected another teacher, "but the problem is still one of engagement. They read along, independently really, and when we pull response groups together or when I read their reading logs, it's painfully clear that they are not comprehending anything more than superficial meanings. I've often told them that they read the way they watch TV. They just sit there in a daze. I've even watched to see if their eyes are moving." The rest of the group laughed at this image. "They are 'reading,' but they're **so** passive. This spring I asked them to use a highlighting marker to indicate the sections they thought were most important in a science piece I'd copied for them. You won't believe this." She went on with heads nodding all over the room. "They either underlined everything or nothing!"

Several other teachers added their stories, painting a picture of a number of children of all ages who are simply disengaged as they read. The teachers described children trapped by the surface structure aspects of language: sounding out words, never skipping an unknown word, never allowing themselves to form a prediction or develop a reasonable hypothesis about what an unknown word might mean given its context. Others described children who were reluctant to share an interpretation that went beyond the literal, fearful they would be wrong. When I asked them about the questions their students posed about their reading, many said they rarely hear anything but questions about assignments and how many pages their reading log entries should be.

"Maybe the problem I have is a little different," a young teacher perched in the window sill spoke slowly. "My kids are pretty engaged as they read and they do ask great questions, especially in reading conferences." The room was quiet. "But," she paused, "I don't exactly know how to describe this. I get concerned that they don't imagine as they read. They don't, somehow, add to the story as they read, or even when we talk about it as a class. Their retellings are pretty bland. I mean, these are second-graders. Don't you think that they should be imaginative and sort of fanciful when they are retelling a story?"

The anecdotes had an alarming common theme: each described children who were missing out on the pleasures of losing themselves in a book, or learning passionately from its content.

At Teachers College, when we shared our reactions to "Salvador, Late or Early," we wrote and talked about aspects of the piece that were expressed because I asked the participants to share their thoughts and responses. I encouraged the teachers to be metacognitive—aware of their own thinking—and to use that awareness to strengthen and intensify their understanding of what they read.

In some kinds of reading, such as technical or unfamiliar text, we are frequently more aware of our thoughts and more active in forcing ourselves to understand as we read. For example, if someone in my family had been diagnosed with a serious disease, I would head to the medical library and plow through the most up-to-date medical texts. It would be a challenge, but my urgent need would inspire me to work harder to understand it. I might try to mentally link the content to something I already knew, copy and underline some of the important ideas, jot questions, or ask a doctor about the material I read, checking to see if I understood. In other words, when the text is challenging, we have to make a more conscious effort to understand it.

When the workshop participants went through the exercise with "Salvador," we read and then shared what we had been thinking about as we read it. Our thinking followed many paths. Some of the teachers commented about the content of the piece; others had insights about their actual reading process and their ways of making sense of the piece. My first images from the piece were fuzzy and abstract and didn't come into focus until I'd read it several times. Some of the participants said they had a very vivid picture of Salvador the first time through. As the discussion progressed, we became more aware of our thinking processes during our reading.

When thinking about our students, we need to ask whether they are aware enough of their thinking during reading to solve problems they may encounter and enhance their comprehension as they read. Can they stop and take action where needed? Are our emerging and struggling readers learning to be agile, reflective thinkers? What about our older or more proficient readers who find themselves faced with challenging text? If they aren't, we sacrifice the excitement and engagement with text Sharon had so hoped to see in her first-graders. For many young readers, the challenge of reading a complex medical text is equivalent to the challenges they face every time they open a book.

When I first read "Salvador, Late or Early" in preparing for the workshop at Teachers College, I made a conscious effort to monitor my thinking—to be aware of the process I used cognitively to make meaning. "Salvador, with eyes the color of caterpillar, Salvador of the crooked hair and crooked teeth, Salvador whose name the teacher cannot remember, is a boy who is no one's friend, runs along somewhere in that vague direction where homes are the color of bad weather. . . ."

At this point the first time through the piece, I was comfortable with my understanding, but still felt I needed to go back and reread. I had an image of a little boy, Eli, about whom I wrote my master's thesis. A victim of every type of domestic abuse, Eli was a Salvador himself, with three younger sisters and brothers, a father in prison for murder, and a mother with a degenerative muscle disease. As I reread, I pictured Eli's house and the piece took on a startling clarity in my mind: "inside the throat that must clear itself and apologize each time it speaks, inside that forty-pound body of boy with its geography of scars, its history of hurt, limbs stuffed with feathers and rags, in what part of the eyes, in what part of the heart. . . . " Then, my understanding diminished. I was aware that the images were coming too fast for me to keep up with them. I didn't have a fully developed idea about the "geography of scars and the history of hurt" before I was shifting to "limbs stuffed with feathers and rags." And "in what part of the eyes, in what part of the heart" threw me.

I knew then I wasn't comprehending more than at a semantic level. I knew what the words meant, but that was about all. I knew I had to do something about it. I knew I could stop and reread it until the images in the piece were more complete and detailed in my mind.

Now, after rereading it many times, the rapidity with which those images are introduced strengthen, rather than detract from, my interpretation of the piece.

In reading "Salvador," I was aware of when I understood and when I didn't understand. I knew what fix-up options I could use, and how I was going to solve the comprehension problems I had (see Chapter 10). And I knew what I needed to know in order to use this piece with teachers in a workshop.

Far too many of our children, however, don't have an awareness of their own comprehension. They don't have a well-developed sense of what they need to know when reading a piece or what they need to do when their comprehension breaks down. To address these issues, we need to monitor our awareness of our own thinking processes while reading, and we must model those processes frequently. Modeling is an essential, inestimably important step in helping children observe and then use the mental processes used by proficient readers.

In introducing the notion of monitoring one's reading I would think out loud with the students so they can listen to the exact thinking process I used to unravel the meaning as I read. After children have been exposed to explicit modeling, there are a myriad of ways to help them practice the strategies in small groups, in pairs, and individually (see Appendix 6).

Several years ago I walked into Pat Benyshek's first grade, Douglas County Chapter One (now Title I) class. I found Pat cuddled on her couch—a garage sale love seat that rocked on a wooden frame—with three boys, all leaning toward the book she was reading and, alternately, holding up one finger or two. For a moment I was perplexed as I watched them hold up different fingers at different times, until I realized they were indicating when they understood the book (one finger up) and when they did not (two fingers up). After the first reading of the book, Pat reread it. If two fingers went up, the little group stopped and discussed the text until they agreed upon a meaning.

Pat's simple way of asking the boys to physically indicate whether or not they were comprehending engaged them and led to some very thoughtful discussion on the second read. Over time, Pat gradually released responsibility to the boys by asking them to use the one finger/two finger technique when they were reading independently. She also taught them to use small yellow self-adhesive notes in their books when they came to a word or idea they didn't understand. Eventually, they used a coding system on their yellow sticky notes: a question mark meant the reader didn't understand the part (or word), and a *PS* meant the reader had solved a comprehension problem at that place in the text. The codes provided a focus for Pat's daily reading conferences with each child. She began her conferences by asking the child to describe his or her thinking at the time the note was placed in the text. On days she was unable to confer with the child, she could go through the text each child had been reading after class to assess their comprehension and develop a plan for the next day.

The children carried their coding system back to their regular classroom, where the whole class elaborated on the idea by adding different coding symbols: *S* meant this part surprised me, *W* meant I wish I could write like this or I'm going to try something like this in my writing, *T* meant I need to talk to someone (or write about it) to better understand it.

Coding and the finger strategy are just two concrete ways to help children become aware of their comprehension process and remind them that they need to solve comprehension problems actively.

Sharon Sherman-Messinger's students were anything but engaged when she read *Tiki Tiki Tembo* that day in the late summer. Sharon was anything but complacent about the problem. She began by simply thinking aloud about whether she was understanding the texts she read orally or not. In order to share comprehension problems, she thought aloud about difficulties she suspected her children would have in books that were, obviously, easy for her to comprehend.

Gradually, her modeling became more complex. As she thought aloud while reading, she disclosed layers of her own thinking about books, wondering aloud what an author meant, thinking aloud about how she solves comprehension problems, sharing her own interpretations of books and, gradually, soliciting interpretations from the children. For their part, over the course of the fall months, the children literally and figuratively turned toward the books she read, listened as she shared how she struggled to make sense of books, and watched her disclose her love for books. It was a long and sometimes frustrating journey.

Sharon responded to the children's lack of engagement in those early days of first grade not with horror, discouragement, or even sadness; she resisted the urge to attribute their lack of engagement to less than literate home lives; she knew that proficient readers, sometimes automatically, sometimes purposefully, must first be metacognitive: They must be aware of their own comprehension. Then they begin to use strategies such as determining what is important in text, asking questions, inferring, and relating relevant prior knowledge (schema) to the text they are reading. She merely went about the business of *teaching* them.

Sharon's first goal was to teach the children to be metacognitive. She reasoned that if they were aware of when they were comprehending and when they were not (while reading independently or listening to text read orally), they could gradually learn other comprehension strategies and manipulate their thinking independently in order to comprehend more deeply. She taught four more comprehension strategies explicitly and for concentrated periods of time— up to eight weeks per strategy.

When I visited her classroom just before winter break that year, Sharon was six weeks into a strategy session on questioning. She began the day by reading *The Polar Express* by Chris Van Allsburg. By then her first-graders were alert, engaged, and alive to the experience of reading. I remembered wondering if they were the same kids I'd observed early in the school year. They assembled at Sharon's feet, chatting about who had read the book before, and then sat, rapt, as silence preceded the first words she read.

Sharon read the book without interruption the first time. When she reread it, she paused several times in the first pages, looking up at the fluorescent lights of her classroom to indicate she was about to think out loud about the questions she'd had as she read the book the first time.

When she looked up, the children leaned toward her. "I want to stop right here because I'm not sure what is happening. Are they going to the North Pole before Santa leaves to deliver presents? I don't get that exactly. It's already dark and the kids were all asleep. Shouldn't Santa be on his way?"

Several heads nodded. Several wanted to try to answer the question, but she shook her head. "Wait. Let's see if that question gets answered later in the book. Who can help me remember the question and monitor the text for the answer?" The children knew exactly what she meant. A little girl with fifty barrettes in different colors raised her hand and assumed responsibility. Sharon kept reading.

Gradually Sharon's think-aloud questions gave way to the children's questions. Some were literal questions, the answers to which were critical to understanding subsequent parts of the book. Others were more probing, seeking a meaning that went beyond the page. "Do you think the author wants the people who read this to believe in Santa?" asked a little boy with thick brown curls and impossibly long eyelashes, who then quickly added, "If they don't."

Later Sharon mentioned they had been working on developing questions to clarify meaning for over six weeks. She had modeled her own thinking process in developing questions in over twenty different books, in all genres. They had reread many pieces asking more searching questions with each reading. The children had gradually taken responsibility for asking their own questions in the books and articles Sharon read. Now they were practicing asking questions in their own books. At sharing time, instead of discussing only the books Sharon read to them, the class devoted a couple of sessions each week to sharing questions the students had developed as they read independently that day.

David Pearson calls this process the Gradual Release of Responsibility Model (See Appendix, Gallagher and Pearson, 1983). I call it in-depth instruction. Sharon called it successful.

Thinking about one's thinking is a central piece in the mosaic of reading, vital to people who read deeply. Metacognition is a turning inward, purposely at first and automatically thereafter, to reexamine our processes of comprehending, changing interpretations of the text and our reflections in order to elaborate and deepen our own understanding of a text.

We know that many children—including some who can read fluently, sound words out, and use context to identify unknown words—do not think about their own thought processes as they read, and that therefore, they aren't reading text in a critical, analytical, imaginative, or probing way. If we know that thinking about our own thinking and using the strategies that form this metacognitive foundation are associated with the tendency to read more deeply, critically, analytically, and independently, shouldn't comprehension strategy instruction be a major focus of our work with children who are learning to read and reading to learn?

Using Metacognition in the Reader's Workshop: Some Key Ideas

· Proficient readers monitor their comprehension during reading—they know when the text they are reading or listening to makes sense, when it does not, what does not make sense, and whether the unclear portions are critical to the overall understanding of the piece.
· Proficient readers can identify when text is comprehensible and the degree to which they understand it. They can identify ways in which a text becomes gradually more understandable by reading past an unclear portion and/or by rereading parts or the whole text.
· Proficient readers can identify confusing ideas, themes, and/or surface elements (words, sentence or text structures, graphs, tables, etc.) and can suggest a variety of different means to solve the problems they have. (See Chapter 10.)

· Proficient readers are aware of what they need to comprehend in relation to their purpose for reading.

· Many readers must learn how to pause, consider the meanings in text, reflect on their understandings, and use different strategies to enhance their understanding. This process is best learned by watching and listening as effective models think aloud. As developing readers learn these processes, they can gradually take responsibility for monitoring their own comprehension as they read independently.

FOUR

Homes in the Mind
Connecting the Known to the New

I cried then for a while because I wasn't absolutely certain I wanted to spend my life with the boy who lay sleeping next to me. I cried for my bed at home and for my parents. . . . After that, I gave up trying to sleep and decided to sneak into the bathroom to read. Bobbe spotted me when I crept past her door.

"Faygele," she called. "Are you all right? What are you doing up so late?". . .

"I can't sleep either," she said. "Come, keep me company."

She lifted the heavy quilt and patted the bed beside her. I can remember so clearly how gingerly I crawled into the tiny bed, struggling to keep myself at the edge so I would not have to touch the misshapen little bone-bag that was her body. She pulled the blanket up over us both and said, "When you are old, you never want to sleep because there are so many years to sleep soon, anyway."

"I had a dream last night," she told me. "I saw your father-in-law (who had recently died) and I asked, Frank, are you happy where you are? I think he couldn't speak, but he handed me a piece of bread and honey and he motioned for me to eat. You will have a boy," she said firmly, putting her hand on my stomach. A fat little boy and he will have Frank's name. That's what the dream meant."

Still keeping a death grip on the edge of the mattress, I started to tell her how the five-year plan made no provision for fat little boys, but I changed my mind. Instead, I let go, rolling to the hollow where our bodies touched, feeling my firm, moist arms, embarrassing in their ripeness, against her powdery, translucent flesh, fearing my chunky body would crush her brittle, twiglike limbs.

Bobbe threw off the covers and took down boxes in her closet. She showed me her wig, a saucy unexpected auburn, part of her dowry when, as a sixteen-year-old, she had married her first husband. From another box, she drew out a thick brown braid glistening with naphthalene. I had the strangest feeling touching the crumbling hair that if I stretched my fingers far enough I could touch, too, the tender young bride who must have cried so bitterly when the women came to shear her heavy hair.

FAYE MOSKOWITZ,
A Leak in the Heart: Tales from a Woman's Life

It is hot, even at seventy-five hundred feet above sea level. The mid-July forecast calls for one hundred degrees in Denver, so ninety degrees will be the high at Susan's mountain home today. I sit on the deck with the sun on my back, looking out to the Continental Divide, sleeves rolled up, squinting at the screen of my laptop. Helen, Susan's "almost fourteen" year-old daughter, is perched next to me, immersed in her assigned summer reading, *Cold Sassy Tree* by Olive Ann Burns. We allow ourselves to be distracted by each other. She hands me some of her poetry to read. I share these paragraphs from *A Leak in the Heart* with her. I'd rather have a conversation with Helen than most adults I know.

Susan is just within hearing range inside the sequestered room, the studio in which this book is taking shape. She sits at her computer working on Chapter 3, then emerges to check on how things are going, takes stock, and smiles. "I can see you guys are going to get a lot done today. Helen, don't bug Ellin," Susan says. She puts a loose strangle-hold on Helen's neck, pours a cup of iced tea, and returns to the studio, as Helen and I share a conspiratorial look, giggle, and continue our conversation—just more quietly.

Helen stretches her legs, now longer than mine, out along the picnic table bench. With a chorus of birds in the background, she takes my book and points to the page, "This part, 'rolling to the hollow where our bodies touched, feeling my firm, moist arms, embarrassing in their ripeness, against her powdery, translucent flesh, fearing my chunky body would crush her brittle, twiglike limbs,' kind of reminds me of my sister, because Katherine's so thin and seems so fragile and sometimes I feel guilty that I'm strong and healthy and she's so hurt."

Helen's older sister Katherine is brain-injured.

Helen continues. "The braid of hair reminds me of a Sherlock Holmes movie I saw about this girl who looks into a drawer and finds this cut red hair. Cutting hair has to do with the end of things to me. Growing up, moving on. There's something so sad about that, even though the hair could grow back. You know it never will," Helen says.

"Any other thoughts?" I ask.

"It reminds me of so many things, really Ellin. I wrote this poem, 'The Yellow House,' about my mom's great aunts who lived together in an old Victorian house in North Carolina."

Helen pulled the poem out of a folder. "See what I mean."

The Yellow House

She remembers the yellow house
Wrinkled aunts served lemonade and cherries
In flowy summer dresses (peach rose white dresses)

They told stories that left little shadows
In their sun soaked eyes
Then kissed the kids and said go out and play in the lilacs

The city tore the aunt house down
She once went back to see and took a brick from the foundation
Didn't show it to her kids

HELEN PHILLIPS

"The description reminds me of my great grandmother. She has all these wrinkles in her face that show she's lived a lot. She gave me a quilt that her mother made. It has worn-out purple butterflies on it.

One time I brought it down from the top of my closet and spread it out on my bed, but it seemed too tattered to use. I still keep it in my closet though. I picture Bobbe's room as small and cramped in a New Englandy kind of house like my grandparents', with creaking floorboards, and she's wearing one of those filmy old lady nightgowns that looks ridiculous on her. . . ."

This is a child—she hates to be called a child—who reads an Emily Dickinson poem, from a book I gave her for Christmas last year, every morning, and writes a poem of her own every morning. She didn't have much trouble connecting this poem to remembered images—in this case her own life, a movie, and a poem she'd written.

Helen goes back to *Cold Sassy Tree*. I reread these paragraphs silently. A flurry of images bombard me. Sundays throughout my childhood my family went to my grandfather's home for dinner, which was served by two great aunts at exactly noon. My memory of the smell of hot, spattering juices dripping to the pan of the rotisserie as the chicken slowly turned makes my stomach growl even now. Grandpa Bain and I always got the drumsticks, and Great Aunt Lena, whom we called Nonnie, saved the heart and gizzard for me in a paper towel on the kitchen windowsill. They were my dessert—cold, sinewy and tough—absolutely delicious.

The conversations between my parents, grandfather, and great aunts dragged on in slow motion. I often slithered, undetected, out of my chair, crawling under the table where I sat on a small platform at the very center of the table and looked around me, through the dull white light, at the lace tablecloth draped across the Bain knees. The conversation was easier to ignore from this vantage point and I adored my secret, private spot alone in the presence of others.

The knees, shins, ankles, and feet shifted around me and became trees blowing in some imagined wind. The elderly aunts' knees never quite touched as my mother's did, her slender ankles gracefully crossed. As I read of Moskovitz' "death grip on the edge of the mattress," straining not to touch the "bone-bag that was her body," I recall the pains I took to avoid touching any of the Bain knees, especially those of Great Aunt Alice, her hosiery reaching just above her parted knees.

A dry breeze rustles the pile of papers at my side. I look up surprised at how much snow still clings to the summits of the high peaks to the west, then look down and finish rereading these few paragraphs.

I consider, "the tender young bride who must have cried so bitterly when the women came to shear her heavy hair." This image is a moment Moskovitz never witnessed. She was not part of it, yet in writing about it, she infuses it with mourning, the lament of a young woman who looks ahead to a life over which she will have little dominion. The thought of young Bobbe's impending marriage—the end somehow of what little freedom she ever had—tinges Moskowitz' words with uncertainty and sadness.

The journey back to weddings unwitnessed triggers my memory of a photograph. In it my aunt, Mary Ellen, her arm linked through her new husband's left arm, is dressed in sky-blue chiffon, her dark curls folding around her face. She wears a small matching hat with a veil. They descend the steps of a church in Carmel, California. It is 1955. No family members surround them. No rice is being thrown. Who took the picture? The right sleeve of her husband's jacket is neatly pressed and lies flat in the pocket. He had no right arm. Why, I wonder now, had they married alone? Why had my aunt, the eldest daughter, foregone a traditional wedding, a ceremony her family would have valued highly? Why was the setting of the wedding in a town where neither had previous connections?

As I read of Bobbe's tears as she prepared to marry, the photograph of my newly married aunt, a picture I had seen hundreds of times as a child, surfaced. I think of that photograph, the looks of anticipation on their faces, and I think of Moskowitz' earlier line, "I wasn't absolutely certain I wanted to spend my life with the boy who lay sleeping next to me."

Mary Ellen raised three children, virtually alone. She told me recently of the night her second son had required emergency surgery and, when she called her husband at the office to tell him she would meet him at the hospital, he told her he was sorry, he had a meeting that night. Ultimately the marriage unraveled, and at age forty-nine, Mary Ellen returned to Georgetown University to complete an MBA and went to work, carving out new possibilities. These short paragraphs from *A Leak in the Heart* are now linked in my mind to a picture and other remembered images from my childhood; they have an added dimension.

I look up again and for a moment I'm not on Susan's porch, but standing in front of one hundred fifty teachers at a Public Education Coalition summer institute, reading from *A Leak in the Heart* as a way to introduce a week-long voyage we are about to take with Don Graves at the helm. For that week he wanted the teachers and principals to rediscover their literate selves. I hoped Moskowitz' words would allow everyone in that large lunch room at McKinley-Thatcher Elementary School to see the poignancy and power held in the memories that shaped them and in their lives' small details. I hoped Moskowitz' tone—warm, vivid, honest—would help permit them to connect to their creative selves.

If not for these paragraphs, Sunday dinner at Grandpa Bain's, my aunt's life, and a PEC conference—three disparate images—would never have converged into a strand of connected recollections. Now these memories cluster in my mind around the piece that triggered this particular collection of seemingly unconnected images. Another piece would have sparked a completely different array of memories and perhaps one of these, but not the others. My understanding of the piece is different because of my experiences; my experiences are now linked because of these lines. At some level the fabric of my memory is permanently changed because of this scene from *A Leak in the Heart*.

In the last fifteen years reading research has provided valuable insight into the thinking processes of proficient readers, revealing remarkable consistency in the strategies they use to comprehend text. One of the most significant areas of research activity has been in schema theory, a theory that "tries to explain how we store our knowledge, how we learn and how we remember what we have learned" (see Maria, 1990, for a synthesis), not just in reading, but in all areas of learning.

When applied to reading, schema theory provides direction and focus for helping children to enhance their comprehension. It has been known for some time that one of the most effective ways to improve comprehension is to "activate mental files" before reading. For decades publishers of basal reading textbooks have included background information teachers were instructed to share with children prior to reading a story, supposedly to enhance the students' comprehension. Now, in classrooms around the country, it has become common practice to help children recall information from their long-term memory banks (schema) relevant to what will be read, whether that reading is from a textbook, a novel, or an article from *National Geographic.*

As a first-year teacher I remember feeling satisfied that I was activating children's background knowledge if I shared the information provided in the teacher's manual before they began to read. And I probably was activating some background knowledge some of the time for some of the kids. But if there was a mismatch between the way I described the background information and a student's mental file on that topic, all my thoughtful planning and careful exposition may not have been doing a thing to support the complex process of assimilating and storing new information during reading.

As a fifth-grade teacher I had three reading groups. I was given three different teacher's manuals. Each came with three different sets of ditto sheets to run. I was twenty-one years old and had been on the job three days. I went into the teachers' workroom that afternoon and carefully slid a purple master for the next day's lesson into the metal teeth. I started to operate the machine, and mid-crank noticed that the master was crooked. With my right hand still cranking, I laid my left hand on the master to straighten it. I lost two fingernails, and concluded it was a sign that dittos weren't doing me, or anyone in my classroom, any good.

I decided—not for the right reasons necessarily—to abandon the dittos, choose selections from the basal I found interesting, and enjoy the pieces with the children. I still took the stack of teacher's manuals home each evening and made meticulous notations in the margins, wanting my teaching strategies for the next day to make a rich understanding of these stories possible. I still felt I needed the background information provided in the basal, and I began each lesson with a short description of it.

One evening I reviewed the material provided in the teacher's manual for a story on Indians of the Southwest. It suggested that no one knew why the Anasazi had disappeared abruptly from that region in the fourteenth or fifteenth centuries. I read more, convinced this would give me all the background information I'd need to lead a good lesson on the story. Little did I know.

Bryce had been placed in my class by a fourth-grade team that would never do anything like that to a colleague they actually knew and liked. They must have believed that, being new, I wouldn't have been exposed to Bryce's reputation prior to his arrival in fifth grade and, therefore, would be more objective. I'm sure that was it.

As I introduced the lesson on the Anasazi with my sketchy facts, Bryce interrupted. "No way! The Anasazi migrated because of drought. They had very sophisticated agriculture and were growing several different kinds of crops, so when the droughts came, they migrated. Trust me. I've been to Mesa Verde."

I had done my job, I thought, in preparing for the story, but I'd been naive and presumptuous in thinking a little bit of reading would make me the expert. Bryce's schema ran circles around mine, and he shared it aggressively and smugly with his classmates. What he lacked in style, he more than made up for in direct experiences he could apply to thoroughly understand the piece.

How different that experience might have been had I begun with his (and others') background knowledge, had we asked questions prior to reading, and then, together, filled in the gaps. How rich might the students' understanding have been if they'd had an opportunity to express themselves verbally, artistically, in writing, or dramatically (certainly Bryce's choice) before, during, and after they read. How different my students' reading experiences might have been had I known that the process of recalling or activating background knowledge or schema should be taught explicitly, in a variety of texts, over a long period of time. How different our reading classes would have been had I regarded activating schema as one of a mosaic of cognitive strategies readers use to ensure they comprehend.

At the Public Education Coalition, I've participated in dozens of meetings with members of the business community in which we've discussed a broad range of education reform issues and have talked about what aspects of corporate restructuring might apply in school settings. In their high-rise—and the PEC's low-rise—conference rooms, the conversations have touched on concepts such as Total Quality Management, reengineering, reorganization, leadership development, and benchmarking, a process that particularly caught my attention.

In *benchmarking*, companies or processes considered the best in the industry are identified, then carefully studied to determine how they reached their state of excellence. Through that process of scrutiny, others learn from them, and, where applicable, replicate their state-of-the-art practices.

In listening to conversations among educators and business people, I've become more and more convinced that in education, we don't benchmark enough. We find thousands of wonderful classrooms, pockets of excellence sprinkled around the country, but we rarely see those classrooms being studied and replicated. We rarely see the systematic spread of best practices.

In the field of reading, we are fortunate. A great deal of research has been done that shows us what proficient readers do. The benchmark, or standard, of a proficient reader has been thoroughly analyzed and scrutinized. Our challenge, however, is to learn from this research on thinking strategies used by proficient readers, and apply it in classroom settings.

Teaching children which thinking strategies are used by proficient readers and helping them use those strategies independently creates the core of teaching reading. If proficient readers routinely use certain thinking strategies, those are the strategies children must be taught. For the kindergarten-through-twelfth-grade reading curriculum to focus primarily on those strategies, we need a new instructional paradigm: Our daily work with children must look dramatically different from the approaches in wide use in our schools today. We need to find benchmark classrooms where the application of the proficient reader research is up and running and learn from them.

Debbie Miller, whose classroom was described in Chapter 2, has set a standard for reading instruction for many in Colorado. Her instructional practices provide a benchmark for the many teachers who visit her classroom each year. Debbie has capitalized on her knowledge of the research and has carefully observed her students. Working with PEC staff developers, she implemented a new model for instruction that has grown out of the research on the thinking strategies used most frequently by proficient readers.

She knows the reading strategies. She observes meticulously and therefore knows her children well. And she teaches patiently and thoughtfully, one strategy at a time, creating a mosaic of strategies with the children by the time they leave her classroom. Debbie spends weeks, sometimes months, modeling her own thinking processes on a single strategy in a variety of texts, gradually asking the children to assume responsibility for using a strategy independently as they read (see Appendix 3). Following Debbie through a comprehension strategy study focusing on building and activating schema—creating and tapping into background knowledge—reveals the model she uses in comprehension instruction: a model that sheds light on an entirely new way of teaching reading.

The second-graders are gathered at Debbie's feet in her classroom's living room, as she launches the comprehension strategy study on schema. She begins with a description about people known as researchers who study the way people read.

"These researchers were like scientists with a hypothesis. You know, a good guess," she tells them. "They wanted to know what really great readers thought about while they read. And you know what? They really did find out what great readers think about while they read. Do you want to know what one of the most important things is?"

Several "yeahs" filled Debbie's pause.

"The researchers found out that readers think about things they already know, things that have happened to them that are like the things that happen in a book. That means that great readers—like you guys are getting to be—whether they're reading by themselves or listening to someone reading, understand the story better if they think about their own experiences while they read."

"Yeah, that's what I always do," piped Jack. "I think about my family or my pets. I have four . . . If it's the right book, I mean."

"Let me show you how it works," Debbie said, "because all of you probably do what Jack does already, but you might not have thought about it." Debbie pulled *The Two of Them* from the shelf. "First, I'm going to share my thinking as I read, and later, you'll have a chance to share what you think about as you read, or as I read to you."

Debbie's spontaneity made it look as if she'd pulled a book randomly off the shelf. In fact she'd done her homework. Prior to reading a book to the students to model using schema as a strategy to deepen comprehension, she identified the important concepts and key themes in the book, thought about how her own experiences related to those themes, and identified where she might pause and think aloud for the children about the connections.

She had also given a great deal of thought to what she wanted her readers to know about the comprehension strategy. She began by jotting down her own definition of schema. Then she determined that at the conclusion of the six to eight week study, she wanted the children to be able to activate schema—to independently and purposefully recall information and experiences relevant to what they were reading—in four different ways. She wanted her students:

· To relate unfamiliar text to their prior world knowledge and/or personal experience—those connections generally take three forms:

    text-to-self connections
    text-to-text connections, and
    text-to-world connections

- To use what is known about an author and his or her style to predict and better understand a text,
- To identify potentially difficult or unfamiliar text structures or formats, and,
- To recognize when they had inadequate background information and to know how to build schema—to learn the information needed, before reading.

It was early in the school year. The windows were still open wide to the late summer breezes. Debbie held in her lap *The Two of Them* by Aliki, a book rich in connections to her own life. She decided a central concept for the book, and therefore the focus of her modeling or think-alouds, is the idea of oral narrative as a way to preserve a family's history.

Debbie began. "Okay, you guys, this is how it's going to work. When I'm reading, you'll see me looking at the book and showing you the pictures like I always do. I'm going to read the book all the way through one time. Then, I'll go back, and as I reread, you'll see me stop and think aloud about things I know or have experienced that are like the book in some way. I'll probably look up at the ceiling, so you'll know I'm telling you what I was just thinking as I read the book."

Debbie read through the book once and then began to reread Aliki's book about a young child and her grandfather and how their roles reverse as he ages and eventually dies.

She read six pages before stopping to look up. "When I read this part about the grandfather singing songs and telling his granddaughter stories of long ago," Debbie said, "I remember my own grandfather. He used to gather all the grandchildren around him and tell us the stories that were true for our family, just like the grandpa in this book. It was like he wanted us to know those stories before he died, and he was afraid if he didn't tell them, they might be forgotten forever. When I read those words, I could see all of us sitting around him. There were too many grandchildren to sit in his lap like the little girl in this book, but he told us stories about my mom and my aunts and uncles. And you know what? When I had children, I told them those same stories so they would remember all the different people in my family." Debbie closed the book on her lap for a moment to show she was shifting gears.

"When a book makes me think of my own life," Debbie said, "I'm making text-to-self connections—you know, connections from the text or book to myself."

She stopped to write *text-to-self* on the far left side of a six-foot length of horizontally hung chart paper labeled *Making Schema Connections* that hung on the wall nearby. She wrote the title of the book under the *text-to-self* connections heading and put her initials by it.

Debbie continued reading, pausing two more times to think aloud about text connections to herself. By the time she finished, the children stared intently at her, as if she just surgically opened her head so that they could look inside to see how her brain works. They were captivated by this simple demonstration. I believe that many glimpsed, for the first time that day, the thinking processes of a proficient reader.

In the next few days, Debbie was explicit with the children. She used the word schema so they developed a common vocabulary they could use to discuss their reading comprehension. She told them that the purpose of activating schema is to help them comprehend more effectively books they listen to and read. She also began to demonstrate through thinking aloud, that what they already know will change because of what they read.

Referring to *The Two of Them*, she told them that, by thinking about her own grandfather, she could imagine better how the little girl felt when her grandfather held her on his lap for stories, and how the little girl must have felt later when the grandfather died. Debbie told the class, "By remembering my own feelings, I could imagine what the little girl—the character—in this book might have felt. Because I understand the character's feelings, I understand the story better. It makes more sense to me and means more to me. When you go back to your own reading, remember to think about things the book reminds you of in your own life. When the pictures or the story remind you of your life, you're making a text-to-self connection."

Debbie's modeling of the prior knowledge or experience component of schema wasn't over after reading *The Two of Them*. She conducted short (ten to fifteen minute) mini lessons each of the next eight days, modeling with a different book or poem most days, but rereading some well-loved books as a way to prod the children to activate their own prior knowledge and to use their prior knowledge to probe the meanings of a book they had read many times. Each day she added the title of the book she read to the chart paper under the heading text-to-self and put her initials next to it. The list included several picture books, *Koala Lou* by Mem Fox, *Amber on the Mountain* by Tony Johnston, *The Relatives Came* and *When I Was Young in the Mountains* by Cynthia Rylant, *Nana Upstairs, Nana Downstairs* by Tomie dePaola, a poem "Yellow Sonnet" by Paul Zimmer, and a piece about the playground written by one of the children in the classroom.

In each mini lesson, she focused on thinking aloud about her text-to-self connections: her prior knowledge or experience. She made two clear points each time: exactly how her own knowledge or experience helped her understand the book better, and how her schema was changed by what she read.

For mini lessons early in a strategy study, Debbie usually doesn't invite the students' participation. At the outset she wants the demonstrations of her thinking to stand alone, to be clear and precise examples of the thinking process of a proficient reader. She tries to use as few words as possible in think-alouds, letting those she does choose tell the specific story of her thinking. Gradually the children become directly involved. After a few demonstrations she invites the children to share their experiences and knowledge as she stops to think aloud while reading.

When the mini lesson is over each day, the children return to their den, the spot where they read what they've chosen independently or with Debbie's guidance. Debbie confers individually with the children, asking them to think aloud about their prior knowledge or experience, and how that schema helps them to make better sense of whatever book they are reading.

When she pulls up next to the children's desks, she asks them to talk about ways in which their prior knowledge helped them better understand the book they are reading, including the children who are still reading the pictures. She talks with them about how their schema is changed because of the book: how new information added to their mental files will forever alter their prior knowledge. She knows these links will expand and make more complex the network of connections found in the children's long-term memory banks. "See?" I heard her tell a child early in the study, "you'll never read *Where the River Begins* again without remembering your fishing adventures with the Boys Club! Those trips are in your memory and, because you made a text-to-self connection, you know better how those boys felt when they followed the river to its source."

As the study progresses, the class continues to meet and focus on schema as a large group, but each child also learns to apply the strategies in the context of his or her own books. The emphasis shifts from Debbie modeling to the children assuming more responsibility for practicing the strategy themselves.

Three weeks into the schema study, Debbie opens a mini lesson by modeling with the book *Grandfather's Face* by Eloise Greenfield. She reads the book once. When she begins to reread, she stops, looks up, and says, "This book reminds me of the book we read a few weeks ago called *The Two of Them*. Do you remember? The grandfather and his granddaughter are great friends in both books. They do all kinds of things together. The first time I read this, I wondered if the grandfather in this book would die, too."

She continues to read, stopping on a page where the granddaughter, Tamika, puts peas in her water glass and spills it on her grandfather. Debbie says, "This part reminds me of when the little girl in *The Two of Them* gave out the wrong change in her grandfather's store. He didn't get angry at her. The grandfather in this book has a cold, angry face, but he doesn't use it on her, even when she spills green water all over him."

Debbie thinks aloud two or three more times and finishes by telling the children that readers frequently remember another book as they read. "Readers who use this kind of schema are making text-to-text connections," she says, moving to the chart paper once more.

Text-to-text connections becomes another column heading, and as new books remind the students of books they have read, the titles of both are added to the chart, followed by the initials of the contributor.

I have my feet up on Justin's desk. Debbie is inhaling yogurt. We have fifteen minutes to debrief the morning's work on text-to-text connections before the kids reappear after lunch.

"This piece of the study is going so smoothly," Debbie says. "They've been exposed to so many books. The connections between texts are really coming fast. Look at our chart. We're going to have to tape a new piece of chart paper on the bottom because there are so many titles up there. Don't you love the way they're drawing arrows between titles they've connected? I didn't tell them to do that!"

Debbie continues, "I'm really surprised at some of the connections they've made. Did you hear Andrew talking about how *My Grandson Lew* reminds him of *The Two of Them* because the character in each book remembers a grandparent who has already died? Pretty amazing! The other one that got me was when Susanna connected *Amber on the Mountain* to the newspaper article she brought in on illiteracy."

"That's fascinating. That isn't just a text-to-text connection, Deb," I told her, "that's also a great text-to-world connection. I wonder what kind of schema these kids have for illiteracy. This may be a great way to lead into the part of the study on text-to-world connections."

Susanna taught the next morning's mini lesson. She sat in the rocker in the living room and talked about how when her mother read the article on illiteracy from the *Denver Post*, she was reminded of *Amber on the Mountain* by Tony Johnston, a story in which a child living in rural Appalachia learns to read with a friend who temporarily lives in the area. She learns to write through their correspondence after her friend moves. "Do you guys see why this article reminded me of Amber?" Susanna asked. They did.

Debbie, sitting with the children on the floor, raised her hand. "Susanna, what can you tell us about illiteracy?"

Susanna replied, "Well it's when people can't read or write. My mom told me that her father never learned to read or write."

"So even grown-ups sometimes can't read or write?" Debbie clarified. "It's not just little kids who haven't learned yet?"

"No, my mom told me and this newspaper says that there are a lot of people who never learned how," Susanna says gravely.

The discussion that followed revealed this group of seven- and eight-year olds knew a lot about the issue of illiteracy. They had seen television commercials dealing with the issue. Several had been at the school in the evenings when a local community college was conducting classes for illiterate adults. They decided to reread *Amber on the Mountain*. As they read, they talked about how world knowledge enhances comprehension of a book.

The mini lessons that followed in the next few days began, not with books, but with world knowledge the children had about the rain forest. They generated long lists of their background knowledge on topics like the rain forest, and then made connections to books such as *The Great Kapok Tree*. The mini lesson discussions focused on how their world knowledge contributed to understanding the books more thoroughly, and how their world knowledge changed because of the books they read. It seemed they were reaching the end of their strategy study. They were beginning to make text-to-text, text-to-self, and text-to-world connections in their own reading, and many were able to articulate how making those connections permitted them to understand their books more deeply.

On a snowy morning four weeks into the study of schema, the children are restless. They pop up and down out of the living room during the morning rituals of greeting each other and reading the lunch menu. Elan has somehow found his way into a corner behind the rocking chair in which Debbie sits. Her tension is growing as a group of observers, teachers from another school district who are late because of the snow, file into the classroom, shaking the snow from their coats and hats.

Debbie's plan for the morning's mini lesson is to try something new, to shift the emphasis away from her own and the children's prior knowledge about books and focus instead on how developing schema for an author enhances a reader's understanding of other books by the same author. She glances at me. We express unspoken worry about whether or not to go forward with that plan on a snowy, frenetic day.

Debbie takes a deep breath and motions the children closer to her. I can tell she's decided to go for it. Almost in a whisper, she says, "I think you're ready to learn something new about schema today, something most readers don't know until they are much older than you, but I think you're ready."

The room grows completely still as the restlessness drains away. They have learned to take Debbie seriously when she challenges them. The accelerating snowstorm and visitors are forgotten in the children's minds. Debbie pulls out *Mrs. Katz and Tush* and *Just Plain Fancy* by Patricia Polacco. *Mrs. Katz* is a class favorite and has figured prominently in several mini lessons this year.

"We've read *Mrs. Katz* and *Just Plain Fancy* a bunch of times, you guys. We've talked about Patricia Polacco until we know her style as an author very well. You tell me, what does she like to write about? What is she like as an author?" Debbie's eyes flit quickly to mine. The visitors lean forward. Silence.

Roxanne finally ventures a guess. "Well, she likes to write about people from other countries."

Kent interrupts, "Not other countries, Roxanne, people in this country who come from other countries. Mrs. Katz is from Poland, and I know some people who came from Poland. They had a war there."

Debbie says, "You know, Kent and Roxanne, you're both right. Patricia Polacco comes from a family of Russian immigrants and she does like to write about families from other cultures who live in the United States. We're going to read another of her books today. It's called *The Keeping Quilt*. Before we read it, let's list some predictions or expectations we have about this book based on what we know— our schema—for Patricia Polacco."

The list began on the chart paper under a new heading: Schema for Authors. The children decided that, not only did this author like to write about people from other cultures who live in the United

States, she liked to write about older people, often grandparents and their families—or their adopted families, as in the book *Mrs. Katz and Tush.*

Debbie begins reading *The Keeping Quilt.* During the first reading, she stops where the characters Anna and Sasha became engaged while sitting on the quilt.

"You know what?" Debbie looks up, laying the book in her lap, "I'm thinking that since Patricia Polacco comes from a family of people who immigrated from Russia, this might be a story about her own great grandparents."

Elan, out from behind the chair and now fully engrossed, shoots a hand up. "Yeah, I thought that too. It's not like some authors who write like it was their family, but really it's not. She is from Russia, so this probably really is her family."

Debbie laughs and says, "Okay, Elan, what do you think Patricia Polacco is likely to do next in this book? Can you use what you know about her to predict what the rest of her book is likely to be about?"

Elan hesitates before answering, "Yeah, she's going to be in it because she likes to write about kids and old people, like in *Mrs. Katz.* She'll probably be in it only as a little kid."

"Do you mean the author, Patricia Polacco, is going to be in the book?" Debbie asked.

"That's my prediction," he announces confidently.

"Let's read it and see." Debbie returns to the book and smiles as she reads the page where Elan's prediction is confirmed.

The discussion that followed brought a number of additions to the Schema for Authors chart. Based on the three books they'd read, the children added to their list of expectations for books written by Patricia Polacco. Debbie talked with the children about how it was much easier for her to predict what would happen next in *The Keeping Quilt* once she had thought about Patricia Polacco's style.

During the two weeks that followed, Debbie and the children brought in books and poems written by a number of different authors: Mem Fox, Charlotte Zolotow, Judith Viorst, Thomas Locker, Nancy White Carlstrom, and Bill Martin Jr. Next to each author's name on the chart, the students listed expectations and predictions based on their schema for that author. During each lesson, Debbie emphasized how schema for an author helps us understand the book more fully and how our schema for that author changes slightly with each new book read.

In the coming weeks Debbie continued to model her thinking process with books that allowed her to make all three kinds of prior knowledge/experience connections: text-to-self, text-to-text, and text-to-world. And she added a new component: schema for authors. She modeled with more difficult and diverse text: magazine articles, a chapter book, and a variety of books on reptiles as the children entered a new science unit.

As the children read, they added to the chart, creating a chronicle of their study of schema. They added columns for the three kinds of prior knowledge connections: text-to-self, text-to-text, and text-to-world, and for three other kinds of schematic connections: schema for authors, text format, and creating new schema. They listed book titles and the name of the child or adult who described the kind of schema under each.

Gradually, the children took responsibility for the chart, independently adding titles and connections in each column. Sharing sessions at the end of the daily reader's workshop provided the context for the children to share the connections they'd made in their independent reading, add titles to the chart, and for others to ask them questions.

It's been five weeks. Debbie is beginning to feel anxious, wondering whether they should move on to a new strategy. The children are becoming more comfortable thinking aloud and have filled the chart with titles and connections. Mini lessons have incorporated fiction, nonfiction, and poetry pieces, as well as the children's writing. Prior knowledge conversations have seeped into science and math, as well as the morning ritual of greetings, preparing their spaces, calendar, and reading the lunch menu.

Scott, scanning the menu, grimaces, "Ham and baked beans. My schema for that makes me wish I'd brought my lunch today!"

The language of this strategy has permeated every facet of the classroom because Debbie has devoted five weeks of instruction, in-depth modeling, and concentrated follow-up to the study. Now she wonders how she'll know it's time to move on.

Debbie announces sharing time, asking the readers to bring a book to the circle if they used schema that day. Laura begins, using the now familiar sharing process.

"Debbie, I would like to share."

"Go ahead, Laura."

"I read this book today," she says, holding Bill Martin Jr.'s *Knots on a Counting Rope*. "At first I had lots of text-to-text connections with *Grandfather's Face*, *My Grandson Lew*, and *The Two of Them* be-cause the book is about this grandfather who is telling stories to his grandson. But I tried to use author schema. Didn't Bill Martin write *Brown Bear, Brown Bear* and *Polar Bear, Polar Bear*? Anyway, I thought this book was going to be one of those rhyming books, but it's not, so I don't know if it's the same Bill Martin."

Before anyone could get a word in, Laura continued, "The prob-lem with this book is that," she paused, "the problem is that I just don't get it." Laura's frustration was vivid.

"That's why we have sharing time, Laura," Debbie interjected. "Why don't you see if you can show us, in the book, the first place where you really started to get stuck?"

She had no problem identifying where the problem began. Laura opened the first page of the book and said, "Here."

It became clear that Laura's frustration was related to the text structure itself. The action in Bill Martin's popular book is revealed through dialogue between a grandfather and his grandson, but the words are laid out, not in a traditional dialogue form with quotes and references to who is speaking, but using indentations with few refer-ences to the speaker. Laura had lost track of the meaning of the book because the dialogue format confused her and because the format was so unlike the Bill Martin books with which she was familiar. A new instructional direction became clear.

Debbie spent the next day scouring her own library and the school's for books where the format or text structure itself was likely to be confusing to the children. She began modeling with Byrd Baylor's books, *I'm in Charge of Celebrations* and *Everybody Needs a Rock*. Her think-aloud mini lessons revealed her thinking about text structure: how traditional text is laid out; how books like *Everybody Needs a Rock* are different; why the authors may have chosen a different format for the book; and how she goes about solving problems with comprehension when they are due to text structure.

A week later, the class took another look at *Knots on a Counting Rope*. Debbie began reading and stopped on the second page.

> Once there was a boy child . . .
> No, Grandfather.
> Start at the beginning.
> Start where the storm
> was crying my name.
> You know the story, Boy
> Tell it.
> No, Grandfather, no.
> Start, "It was a dark night . . ."

Debbie began, "I know just how Laura felt when she got frustrated with this book a week ago. It isn't written the way most books are and it certainly doesn't sound like Bill Martin's other books. No 'Brown Bear, Brown Bear, what do you see?' here! I started to realize that I was confused on this page and the first thing I did was reread the page. When I was still confused, I thumbed through the rest of the pages of the book like this," Debbie paused, gazing briefly at several pages, "and then I realized that the whole story was going to be told in conversation between the grandfather and his grandson. I knew that because they are in every picture and if I read just a couple of sentences on some of the pages like, '*But I didn't win grandfather. No, but you rode like the wind,*' I could tell that the boy and his grandfather were talking through the whole book, even though the words on these pages aren't written the way conversation or dialogue are usually written. When I started to reread it and I knew it was dialogue, I was able to understand that this whole book is a little boy and his grandfather talking. And the grandfather is telling a story he has told many times before."

Debbie and her class had similar discussions about the structure of nonfiction text. She modeled her thinking process in books like Tomie dePaola's *The Cloud Book*, focusing on his use of bold print, headings, and drawings. They talked about how quickly new ideas are introduced in nonfiction text and how readers' expectations need to be different when they read nonfiction. They talked about how proficient readers read more slowly and do a great deal more rereading when they read nonfiction, especially in areas where they don't have a lot of knowledge or experience. And once again, they talked about how understanding different kinds of text structures helps them to understand the book better, and how their schema for nonfiction text had been changed by what they have read.

Their discussions moved from nonfiction to text structure in poetry, newspapers, and magazines. Debbie modeled with a poem, "Elephant Warning" from Georgia Heard's book *Creatures of the Earth, Sea, and Sky*, talking about how authors like Heard write poems differently than they write stories.

Following her mini lesson, the children broke into groups of four. Each child had a copy and the group thought out loud about the poem.

"There aren't so many words. That's why I like poetry," Alice began one small group's conversation.

"Debbie says it's because poets have to use fewer words to make pictures in the reader's mind," Casandra grinned following her revelation.

Debbie and I, standing nearby, wondered in whispers whether Casandra had any idea what that meant. It didn't matter for now. Our goal was to get them to think aloud in a group, each adding to the group's growing schema for text structure. The discussions were rather superficial that day, alerting us that we needed to stick with the schema strategy study rather than indulge our restlessness to move on. There was clearly more to be done.

Debbie and I decided I would conduct one of the last mini lessons on schema. Our goal was to consolidate the children's knowledge of all aspects of schema: using prior knowledge and experience (text-to-self, text-to-text, and text-to-world connections), capitalizing on prior knowledge about authors and their style, and building schema for different text structures and formats. This time Debbie sat among the children with a notebook and I gathered them around me.

"You guys amaze me," I began. "Debbie told you seven weeks ago that great readers use their prior knowledge or schema to understand what they read better." I glanced at the gargantuan wall chart that charted their progress in understanding schema. "You have used your prior knowledge and experiences to make text-to-self, text-to-text, and text-to-world connections. You now use your prior knowledge about authors and their writing style to predict what their next books are going to be like. And you know how to recognize different text structures to help you understand different genres. Can you believe what you know how to do?"

The kids nodded. Elan shook his shoulders and put out his arms, "Yeah, yeah."

"But," I said, throwing the budding rock star a direct look, "today my goal is to really confuse you. I'm here to get you in a really big comprehension mess, because I think you can solve it. You have been reading a lot of books about families in this strategy study because those are the kind of books that are great when you're practicing schema. The book I want to read today is about families, too, but it's very different from the ones you have read so far. It's called *My Grandpa and the Sea* by Katherine Orr." I showed them the colorful cover featuring Caribbean drawings and a grandfather with a boat. "Let's talk a little about this before we read it today. I'll list your prior knowledge and experience on the board under three ideas I think are pretty important to the story."

I wrote *passions*, *fishing as a job*, and *life on an island* on the board.

I said, "Okay, let's brainstorm. Think for a moment about any prior knowledge or experience you have that I could list under these headings."

The offerings were scant: "My dad took me fishing once;" "I'd like to live on an island;" "fish stink;" "I like trout, except for the bones." Passions didn't come up.

I gradually added more detail from the book to the brainstorming session. "The book is about a grandfather who had a great passion—

that's like an interest that you almost have to do you love it so much—for fishing. He lived in a region called the Caribbean his whole life. The Caribbean is a sea the color of the Colorado sky on a clear day. Its water is full of coral reefs and wild colored fish. You know, fish that look kind of like tropical birds. They're so bright you can't believe it. The sea's dotted with small islands, like the one where the grandpa lived. Are you getting the picture?" Some nod.

"Well, the grandpa always felt he was terribly important to his friends and the other people on the island because he was a fisherman and brought food for them from the sea," I said.

Before I read *My Grandpa and the Sea* to the class, I tried to paint an image of a life and a set of pursuits vastly different from those of these urban children. I attempted to create schema for a way of life dictated by water, rather than highways and mountains.

When I read *My Grandpa and the Sea* aloud, I became aware that, for most of the children seated around me, there weren't any incomprehensible words. Yet their lack of schema for the setting—a setting that was critical to understanding the key themes in the book—would have kept the key ideas in the book just out of reach for many. Without building or creating a new schema for them, their understanding would have been stunted.

My idea was to begin by activating any schema they did have around what I felt were the key concepts in the book. Another teacher might, very legitimately, have chosen different concepts. I didn't want to make any assumptions, nor did I want to start with concepts like ocean or boats. They were too broad and related too generally to the story. I chose the concepts of fishing as a job, life on an island, and passions because they were critical to understanding this story.

After we read the story once, I went back, reread, and thought aloud about how my schema for the three areas was changing because of the story. "When I read this part, I can see how different Lila's grandfather's work is from the work I do or my father and grandfather did. When I think of going to work, I think of leaving in the morning, going to a school or office, and coming home in time for dinner with the rest of the family. In this book, the grandfather is gone before sunrise and he isn't back until everyone is in bed. This book really changes the way I think about work."

Then I said, "There is something that is really like my schema, though. I have a great passion for my work. I really love and believe in the work I do, and that is very much like grandfather's passion for his work, fishing."

The following day we read the book for a third time and added to the list of schema for the three key concepts I'd listed on the board. This time many children had connections: an uncle who'd been a river guide, a parent's vacation to the Bahamas, a boy's passion for rollerblading, a girl's love for soccer. The board filled quickly.

The children's ideas about passions, fishing as a job, and life on an island were activated and in many cases created by reading the book. In effect, they created new memory networks to which subsequent readings and experiences about life on a Caribbean island could be linked. They connected their existing schema to the new schema from the book—a vital linking that helps them permanently store the new schema in their long-term memories.

In the final days of the strategy study on schema, Debbie focused on integrating all four components of schema when reading independently. Debbie modeled the kind of flexible, adaptable thinking used by proficient readers as she read in a variety of genres, including *The Trumpet of the Swan* by E. B. White, which she read aloud each day after lunch. She moved fluidly from text-to-self connections to author schema, to creating new schema for unfamiliar content in text, to using schema for different text structures.

In her demonstrations the types of schema blended together. The four components of schema were taught separately initially, but in the final stages of the strategy study, they were used interchangeably.

There was no defining moment that told Debbie it was time to move on to another strategy. Some children still struggled to activate author and text structure schema. Together, though, they had taken a complex thinking journey. The eight weeks devoted to schema had left the children with a kind of independence, a kind of power in their thinking that engaged them in reading more thoughtfully, critically, and enthusiastically.

There were, and are, times when my awareness of my own reading processes and my use of a strategy like schema are so prevalent that they annoy and distract me from my reading. There are books, like Faye Moskovitz' *A Leak in the Heart*, that take me down dozens of rambling paths, lined with memory and experience and knowledge. The PEC staff developers have heard dozens of stories from teachers and other friends who became obsessed with making schematic connections once they consciously learned to do so.

I have come to believe that this hyperawareness may be a necessary and inevitable stage in coming to know oneself as a reader. It may be that as we reintroduce ourselves to our own reading processes, we need to make conscious the strategies our minds have used subconsciously for so many years. It may be that, in order to empathize with the frustrations of our developing readers, we must spend a few extra hours lost in the words, considering, simultaneously, the stories we read and the way we read them.

FIVE

The Essence of Text
Determining Importance

I am not free of the condition I describe here. I cannot be certain how far back in human history the habit of denial can be traced. But it is at least as old as I am. In our common history, I have found it in the legends surrounding the battle of Troy, and in my own family I have traced it three generations back, to that recent time past when there had been no world wars and my grandparents were young. All that I was taught at home or in school was colored by denial, and thus it became so familiar to me that I did not see it. Only now have I begun to recognize that there were many closely guarded family secrets that I kept, and many that were kept from me.

When my father was still a small boy, his mother did something unforgivable. It was a source of shame as many secrets are, and hence kept hidden from my father and, eventually, from me. My great-aunt would have told me this secret before she died, but by that time she could not remember it. I have always sensed that my grandmother's transgression was sexual. Whatever she did was taken as cause by my grandfather and his mother to abandon her. They left her in Canada and moved to California, taking her two sons, my father and his brother, with them.

My father was not allowed to cry over his lost mother. Not to speak her name. He could not give in to his grief but instead was taught to practice the military virtue of forbearance and to set an example in his manhood for his younger brother, Roland. In this way I suppose my grandfather hoped to erase the memory of my grandmother from all of our minds. But her loss has haunted us.

How old is the habit of denial? We keep secrets from ourselves that all along we know. The public was told that old Dresden was bombed to destroy strategic railway lines. There were no railway lines in that part of the city. But it would be years before that story came to the surface.

I do not see my life as separate from history. In my mind my family secrets mingle with the secrets of statesmen and bombers. Nor is my life divided from the lives of others. I, who am a woman, have my father's face. And he, I suspect, had his mother's face.

There is a characteristic way my father's eyelids fold, and you can see this in my face and in a photograph I have of him as a little boy. In the same photograph there is a silent sorrow mapped on his face, and this sorrow is mine too.

I place this photograph next to two others which are on my desk. Tracing the genesis of the bombing of civilians, I have come across a photograph of Dresden taken in 1945. A few dark figures hunch over a sea of corpses. There are ruined buildings in the background and smoke from a fire. The other photograph was sent to me by my cousin, after I asked her if she knew the name of my paternal grandmother, or if she might have a picture of her.

The photograph my cousin did send me has a haunted quality though it was taken in Canada before the erasure of my grandmother. It is not a picture of my grandmother. It is a picture of my grandfather with my father. It was taken a few years before masses of soldiers died on the battlefields of World War I, and over three decades before the bombing of Dresden, the concentration camps, Hiroshima. And yet, my grandfather's face bears an expression of grief just as if he were looking over a scene of senseless destruction, a field of bodies. What was his sorrow? . . .

If I tell here all the secrets that I know, public and private, perhaps I will begin to see the way the old sometimes see, Monet, recording light and spirit in his paintings, or the way those see who have been trapped by circumstances—a death, a loss, a cataclysm of history—grasping the essential.

SUSAN GRIFFIN,
A Chorus of Stones: A Private Life of War

My assistant, Stephanie, is leaning against my office door frame. She is not happy. She holds the office calendar in one hand and my calendar in the other. I'm talking with an assistant superintendent from Boulder and checking my watch. It's clear I need to hang up fast to get to my meeting across town and squeeze in time to explain to Steph how I have double booked myself again. Steph's eyes tell me this time she means business. I feel like a child sitting in the principal's office following a playground altercation.

I hang up, deciding to take a philosophical stance. "Let me explain," I say trying to look a little pathetic. "This is one of my worst shortcomings, but at least I know it! I'm not like an addict who refuses to admit the problem!" I think I see the shadow of a smile, but she's not buying. "I knew I was double booking but I couldn't say no to the teachers at Sabin, Steph. We've been working so hard on this assessment stuff. Maybe if I leave a little early I can still get to most of the Urban Teaching Corps meeting?" My expression changes from pathetic to hopeful, but still no smile from Steph.

"Ellin, I'm taking your calendar away until further notice. I'm putting you in calendar time-out. Don't dare to schedule anything on your own. Do you understand?" Now, her eyes dance and finally a smile. "Which meeting is essential, Ellin?"

Essential. Which is essential? Susan Griffin's words from *A Chorus of Stones* "grasping the essential" ring in my mind. How do I grasp the essential?

The all too familiar list unfolds in my mind. Maybe it's more essential to say no to both meetings and be at the front door when Elizabeth's carpool drops her off after a day at kindergarten. Maybe it's essential to plow through the pile on my desk (but I don't think so!) or to spend a day writing, swimming, hiking, writing a letter to my friend in Portugal who has written twice. Maybe it's time for me to spend a few days at home reading the pile of newly published books on reading and writing in my little downstairs office where the constant ring of the phone won't disturb me. Maybe it's important to write a grant proposal for the PEC Scholar's Project that has been so effective but remains so sparsely funded.

I know I need to spend more time with the other staff developers in their schools and more time in the schools in which I am the staff developer. I need to take Elizabeth to the library more and visit her former nanny who isn't well and is confined to her home. I need to have my dad and his wife to dinner. "You tell me, Stephanie," I thought. "What is essential?"

It's late afternoon. Steph has moved a meeting and, for once, I've arrived home before Elizabeth, who is off on an adventure with her nanny. This once she doesn't have to wait with another adult until mommy and daddy come home. I'm at the door waiting for her. She leaps onto the front porch, yelling, "Mom, you should have seen the ball room at the Children's Museum. It was like going in a swimming pool, but better because you didn't get water up your nose."

Moments after her arrival, the phone rings. One of the staff developers is describing a conflict in one of her schools that's accelerating and must be dealt with before the next morning. "Ellin, she's so angry that I'm not working in her classroom that she's sabotaging my work in the school. What can we do? She's a good teacher. I just can't work with everyone at the same time." Her voice is filled with anxiety.

I watch Elizabeth as she begins to amuse herself with the basket of dress-ups in the corner of the den. She stuffs a flowing piece of silk under the rubber band in her hair and starts dancing around. "Mom, pretend I'm a princess," she chirps, as I try to concentrate. It crosses my mind that she'll have to postpone her stories of today's adventures. I realize the phone conversation will not be short. I think about good leadership. I think about good parenting. How to grasp the essential?

In *A Chorus of Stones*, Susan Griffin juxtaposes the global with the current and familiar. She connects the historical realities of war with the realities of family struggles, secrets, and loss. When I read the chapter "Denial," I was literally breathless. I couldn't take it in fast enough, but I wanted to read slowly enough that I wouldn't miss a critical concept.

Later I tried to tell Anne Goudvis, a friend and colleague, about the piece by stripping it down to its essence. I wanted her to get a sense of how significant I thought this chapter was. "Anne, it's like trying to understand the evolution of modern civilization by reflecting on your dinner conversation. It's incredible. She links her own family's history of denial to the Dresden firestorms of World War II. She connects the denial we all use to cope with our own suffering to the history of human suffering and global conflict." My thoughts blur for a moment. I slow down. "It's as if she's saying that the ugly little truths of our lives have the same weight and significance as cataclysmic events in history. It blew me away."

> I am beginning to believe that we know everything, that all history, including the history of each family, is part of us, such that, when we hear any secret revealed, a secret about a grandfather, or an uncle, or a secret about the battle of Dresden in 1945, our lives are made suddenly clearer to us, as the unnatural heaviness of unspoken truth is dispersed. For perhaps we are like stones; our own history and the history of the world embedded in us, we hold a sorrow deep within and cannot weep until that history is sung.
>
> Long before the firebombing of Dresden, the German government knew about the terrible effect of firestorms. Late on the night of July 27, 1943, and in the early morning hours of July 28, the first firestorm was created. It was a new phenomenon, even to its makers, who dropped 7,931 tons of bombs, almost half of these incendiary, over the city of Hamburg. . . .
>
> We forget we are history. We have kept the left hand from knowing the right. I was born and brought up in a nation that participated in the bombing of Dresden, and in the civilization that planned the extermination of a whole people. We are not used to associating our private lives with public events. Yet the histories of families cannot be separated from the histories of nations. To divide them is part of our denial. (Susan Griffin, *A Chorus of Stones*)

Ironically, when text is well written, I have a more difficult time deciding what is most important or essential. Elegant diction and a tight compression of ideas combine to persuade me that everything is equally important. I engage in an absorbing intellectual game. I reread excerpts and ask myself, consciously and subconsciously, what is most important here, what is essential to remember?

In the chapter "Denial," I am engaged in an intriguing tug-of-war. Is the essence of this piece the denial Griffin describes as certain of her ancestors were deliberately erased from the family memory or permitted to slowly kill themselves with alcohol? Is the essence a comprehension of the horrific secrets hidden by both the Axis and the Allied powers in the Second World War? Is the connection between these two ideas essential to understanding Griffin's point in this chapter? Inevitably, I'm led back to reread the text for answers.

> How many small decisions accumulate to form a habit? What a multitude of decisions, made by others, in other times, must shape our lives now. A grandmother's name is erased. A mother decides to pretend that her son does not drink too much. A nation refuses to permit Jewish immigrants to pass its borders, knowing, and yet pretending not to know, that this will mean certain death. The decision is made to bomb a civilian population. The decision is made to keep the number of the dead and the manner of their death a secret. (Susan Griffin, *A Chorus of Stones*)

Anne Goudvis and I consider using the chapter in an upcoming study group of teachers and librarians from Boulder. We speculate about the group's reaction and wonder if the piece will evoke emotions they are reluctant to share with colleagues. In the end we opt to mail the piece in advance and live with our anxiety about their responses.

The six study group members were still gathering in the hall outside the library at Louisville Elementary School when the debate that structured the entire discussion began. What was this piece actually about? Was it about war? Was it about families burying their ugliest truths? Was it merely the ravings of a daughter badly bruised by the generations that preceded her? Is it an indictment of society's mores that oblige individuals to conceal their dilemmas rather than confront them? What notions were most important if the piece as a whole was to be understood?

Opinions among the members of this study group weren't sparse, and as they settled in the library and leaned toward each other across the small table, they defended those opinions thoughtfully and logically. They returned to the copy of the chapter, pointing out their highlighted sections and imploring the group to listen to the sections they found most important, most essential to their conviction about what the piece was really about.

"I, too, have my father's face," one woman said, "and I'm not at all sure I like that. He was so cold and I'm afraid that means I share his detachment."

Another remarked, "My great aunt Louise committed suicide when her children were four and eight. The children weren't told what had happened until they were grown up and had children of their own. I'd never heard of Louise until a few years ago. Now I can't get her off my mind."

Another said, "I was an adult when my parents told me about my brother who'd spent his life in an institution. He was severely brain-injured and died when he was eighteen, but I felt so angry and left out. I might have loved him."

The stories went on and on—stories that illuminated the devastating, or in some cases salvational, effect of denial. Some found the author's personal stories most essential to understanding the text. Others believed that the piece was a treatise about war. The conversation focused for a long time on what Susan Griffin intended as her key themes as opposed to what we, as readers, believed to be most essential. Most revised their beliefs about the piece based on the opinions of others and their suppositions about the author's intent. All participated in the debate based on what they had determined was most important or essential for them. All defended their beliefs. None agreed absolutely with any other.

At the end of the session, as Anne and I picked up the last of the styrofoam cups and tossed them in the trash can, she stopped midstream, slumped like a rag doll into a metal folding chair, and said, "Jeez Ellin, this is what they call constructing meaning! What a workout."

That afternoon, driving toward Denver on the Boulder Turnpike in the surge of rush hour traffic, I felt simultaneously invigorated and exhausted from the "Denial" discussion. The range of opinions and life stories brought energy and fatigue. The piece had been more provocative than we imagined. It had unleashed an array of thoughts and memories usually kept buried. I knew and respected those people in new ways. They may not have agreed, but together, through the sharing of their stories and revealing what each found most powerful, they created layers of new meaning. In order to decide what the piece was about, they had to decide what ideas and themes were most important to each of them. The cognitive processes the study group members used to make those decisions are the same processes they use each day, to make decisions in the grocery store, or in life and death situations.

Listening to music I hoped would quiet my mind, I wove through clogged traffic. But, my mind wandered to the session just ended and the classrooms I'd be in later in the week. How often, I thought, have I come to new insights about teaching children following a potent adult learning experience? For me, and many other teachers, I suspect, rediscovering our own subconscious processes of learning led to our most important progress in working with children.

This discussion led me to wonder how we could create more open, frank discussion opportunities for children, opportunities for children to question, defend, rethink, and ultimately draw conclusions about the essence in a given text.

I thought about how critical it is to help children make decisions about important themes and ideas in what they read based on evidence in the text, as well as their experience, knowledge, and beliefs. For me the Boulder discussion confirmed that if we want children to be deeply engaged in conversations about issues of great significance in books, we must not only teach them how to read, but show them how to reason.

Summit Elementary was one of the early schools in the PEC's Literacy League. I was fortunate to be its staff developer, working with a group of highly skilled teachers hired to open this new suburban school. Because of the group's luster, at the outset I was more intimidated than usual. The sleek coldness of the new building—not yet broken in with children's paintings and voices—didn't help.

At my first meeting with the staff, we gathered around tables in the stunning new library which was filled with natural light, an amphitheater, and half bookshelves that allowed the children to reach all the books. Mimi DeRose was the teacher whose direct gaze and sense of humor I most remember from that meeting. During the session with the staff, she asked a number of challenging questions. I had a slight sinking feeling, unsure of what I'd bring to the already stellar team.

At the end of the session, Mimi calmed my concerns. "I really look forward to working with you, Ellin," she said. "It'll be helpful to have a fresh pair of eyes and some new ideas."

Weeks later, after the chaos of getting the school up and running, Mimi and I started working together to set up a reader's and writer's workshop in her classroom.

Several years later, after the PEC's Reading Project was underway, I returned to Mimi's classroom for another round of co-teaching and coaching. By then Summit felt very lived in. Children's pictures lined the walls. The carpets had a few stains. The new school smell had been replaced by scents from the cafeteria.

"Something has been bothering me for a long time, Ellin. You know these kids head off to middle school next year, and they're expected to read and write expository text immediately. In the past, I don't think I've done enough to prepare them. Reading textbooks and writing reports are so different from what we typically have kids read and write in elementary school. It's really more of a fiction and narrative focus here so I want to concentrate on helping them develop their expository skills."

"Don't think you're alone with those concerns, Mimi. Our staff developers are struggling with the same issues. Let's see what we can do together," I said.

Mimi walked across the room to where she kept the students' writing folders and flipped through them as she talked. "I also want to focus on my reading conferences with kids. My writing conferences are pretty effective and I've seen real growth in the kids, but conferring in reading is tougher. I feel like I sit down with kids and say, 'How is your reading going? What do you like about the book?' and it just doesn't go far enough. The conferences rarely get beyond the superficial."

For several weeks during my day-a-week visits to Summit, I spent time in Mimi's classroom. We stood back and observed the students with Mimi's two goals in mind. We watched, took notes, and jotted questions about their reading and about ideas for mini lessons. To the casual observer, these kids were reading well. They chose books effortlessly. They read and shared in conferences and during sharing times. They were enthusiastic about the novels they read, and yet, when they read the texts Mimi had chosen to set the stage for social studies and science learning, we watched many struggle to understand and then discuss what they read. Most were competent oral readers. They pronounced words correctly, missed few words, and sounded out words they didn't know. But many were so disconnected from the meaning of the text, especially expository text, that they were often unaware of the essence of what they were reading.

"Why does this happen, Ellin? These kids are fluent readers and many of them really like to read, but it's as if this fog bank rolls in when they're hit with challenging nonfiction. They're in a kind of daze and for many of them, it's almost impossible to find any clarity. They're going to be eaten alive at Horizon Middle School."

One morning, after several weeks of observing and conferring with the students, Mimi and I stood to the side, leaning against the room's built-in teal-coated laminate cupboards. We scanned the class, sitting side by side on the counter top, and quietly discussed our two conclusions: First, explicit instruction in reading expository text would be critical if the children were to learn the social studies and science content through their independent reading; and, second, conferences would become a critical venue for reading instruction because there was such wide variance in the students' needs.

We decided to undertake a comprehension strategy study focused on determining importance in text to coincide with a planned quarter-long study of the colonial and Revolutionary War period in social studies. Based on our observations of the children's needs, this linkage made sense. We could provide explicit instruction in determining importance by modeling with expository text written about the revolutionary era. Mini lessons would focus on how Mimi, as a proficient reader, made decisions about what content was most important, most essential in a nonfiction passage. She would follow up by conferring with individual students as they made their own way through the expository text they needed to read for the group presentations that would bring the unit to a close.

One of the first snows of the season distracted us one morning as Mimi and I cupped our hands around the mugs that held our last sips of coffee. The cooperative learning groups that had met to plan their presentations were gradually disbanding, with students pausing at the window to see if there was any hope for an early dismissal. That hope dashed, some of the fifth-graders were reading and taking notes, as others worked on the early stages of their colonial projects.

Mimi and I leaned against the counter and watched, looking for a place to begin our conferring for the day. Mimi's goal was to infuse conferences with more instruction based on the child's needs as a reader. We watched as Jeremy took an extra long gaze out the window, his longing to be somewhere else clearly written on his face.

As we pulled alongside Jeremy, he refocused on a printout from a computer encyclopedia entry on the Revolutionary War. Mimi leaned toward him. "How's it going Jeremy? Are you starting to shape a plan for your part of the presentation?" she asked.

Jeremy's reply wasn't inspiring. "Not really." He stared at the page.

"How can we help?" I asked.

"Not sure," came the reply.

"Why don't you read to us a little bit and let us get the gist of this text," I suggested. With no reluctance Jeremy launched into reading the page.

The first armed encounter of the American Revolution took place in Massachusetts, where the British force in Boston numbered some 3500 men. General Gage was aware that the militia members of the outlying towns were being trained and reorganized into active elements known as minutemen, ready for immediate service. Ammunition and military stores were being gathered under direction of a Committee of Safety acting for the provincial assembly. (*Microsoft Encarta Encyclopedia*)

Jeremy pronounced every word accurately. His inflection was good. He paused appropriately at the end of sentences. We glanced at each other over his head, silently puzzled by his lack of direction. He certainly was *reading* this text.

Mimi interrupted Jeremy, who stopped, hunched over the page. "Thanks, I think we're getting the picture. Tell me, Jeremy," she paused, long enough that he turned his head to look at her, "Tell me what, if anything, you are going to use from that passage in your group's presentation." The silence that followed became uncomfortable for me, but Mimi was wiser. She waited patiently, knowing Jeremy needed time to collect his thoughts.

Finally, he said, "I really can't decide. It seems like I should use everything, but Mr. Ricker told us in fourth grade we had to put things in our own words for reports and I don't want to put everything in my own words, . . . you know?"

"What parts do you think are most important here, Jeremy?" I ventured. "Can you show us in the text you just read what you believe are the most important ideas? Look back over this section. See if you can decide what is most essential to you."

Jeremy looked over the page and, lackadaisically, pointed to the sentence that began with the words ammunition and military stores.

"Can you tell us why you decided that was most important?" I asked.

"I like guns and stuff. My brother wants to go into the army after high school." Mimi shot me a knowing glance.

Then I said to Jeremy, "Thinking about how the text reminds you of your own life is one way to decide what's important. Great readers often do what you just did, Jeremy. They let their own interests and experiences creep into their minds as they read. Then they focus on certain parts of the text they believe are most important to understanding the whole piece. Very often great readers decide something is most important because they have background knowledge in that area. That's one way to decide what is most important or essential in a text." I paused and reminded myself that Jeremy might need to hear what I'd said a number of times before really understanding it. "Let's try something together, Jeremy," I suggested. "We're going to break this passage down a little to make it easier to decide what's important. You need to decide what's most important for two reasons: so you don't have to put the whole thing into your own words, and so you can choose what you're going to put into your part of the presentation. Great readers are thinking all the time as they read, 'What's most important in this part, what's most important?' I'm going to read that sentence you just pointed to. You listen, and I want you to tell me what you think is most important in that one sentence, okay?"

He looked at me quizzically, but said, "Sure."

I read slowly, " 'Ammunition and military stores were being gathered under direction of a Committee of Safety acting for the provincial assembly . . .' What d'ya think, Jeremy?" Silence. I resisted the urge to pose another question.

"I don't understand anything after this word." He pointed to committee. I reminded myself that when he first read to us, he had read each word perfectly with the exception of provincial, which he had sounded out adequately. Then Jeremy said, "But I think this thing about gathering is really important, 'cause if they were gathering, that's like stockpiling weapons, then they had a plan of attack."

"Stockpiling, wow, I didn't think of that." Mimi's response led to a visible change in Jeremy. He sat up in his seat and a faint smile crept across his lips. He launched into a short monologue on stockpiling for Mimi's benefit.

I slipped in as he took a breath. "Jeremy, let me tell you something I've noticed about people who are trying to understand text like this—text that is trying to teach the reader something. It's hard to decide what is most important when there is a new idea or two in every sentence and that's how nonfiction is often written."

"Yeah, and it is borrrring," Jeremy said, rolling his eyes.

"Yeah, sometimes there's a voice in your head that says 'Ugh, this is boring' or 'I don't get this' or 'I love reading about this,' you know?" I asked.

I got a little nod from him.

Then I said, "When great readers are reading this stuff that has so many ideas in it, they have to listen to that mental voice tell them which words, which sentences or paragraphs, and which ideas are most important. Otherwise they won't get it. Great readers really listen to the voice saying 'I think this word or this idea is most important.' Then they're able to decide which ideas are most important in the piece."

I reached into my bag and retrieved a highlighting marker to hand to Jeremy. "Try something for us, okay? Take this marker and highlight the words or phrases in this passage that you really think are most important to understanding what the whole passage is about. Be sure to use it only on the words or phrases you think are essential for you to understand the whole thing. Deal? We'll stop back in a few minutes."

Mimi and I moved away. "I don't know, Mim, whether that was the right direction to go with him. His stockpiling interest was a good step. But, in general, he isn't discriminating important from less important ideas too well."

She agreed. "This isn't the first time I've had that kind of conference with him. It's like pulling teeth. I'm a little surprised that he isn't comprehending more than he is, because he reads so fluently orally. There are so many unfamiliar concepts in that passage and somehow the ideas seem to run together for him and he isn't able to sort out what is important."

"I gave him the marker to make it easier for him to focus on identifying important words or sentences before he tries to identify important concepts, though he might highlight everything the first few times he uses it."

"That could happen," Mimi laughed. "I'll buy a bunch of them."

The conversation with Jeremy reminded me that there are three levels at which proficient readers make decisions about what is most important in any text: They decide what is important at the whole-text level, the sentence level, and the word level. After we read, we make rational judgments about what was essential, but even as we read, we make continual decisions about what sentences or phrases are most essential in a paragraph and even which words are most important in any given sentence.

We know from eye movement studies that the eyes of proficient readers focus longer (by milliseconds) on words that carry the weight of the meaning in any given sentence. Linguists call those key words *contentives*. Sometimes they're nouns and verbs, sometimes not. Contentives are words that hold the meaning in any sentence, given the overall meaning of that sentence in the passage being read.

With Jeremy I had the sense that if we encouraged him to identify important words (contentives) and important sentences first, he might start to monitor his own understanding more and work toward identifying important ideas in longer passages and text.

"It's interesting, Ellin," Mimi said, turning serious, "but I think Jeremy and the great majority of kids in this room, from what I've been able to tell so far, are much better able to decide what is important in fiction or even in nonfiction that is written in a less didactic way, but they seem to lose that ability to discriminate when they pick up a textbook."

Mimi's concerns are common among intermediate-grade teachers. Reading theorists distinguish between *considerate* and *inconsiderate* text. Text is considerate when it is written in a way that its content and format are familiar or predictable to a particular reader. Writers of more considerate text take the intended audiences' probable background knowledge into consideration. Text is inconsiderate when it is written in a way that its intended audience has difficulty comprehending it.

For Jeremy and many others like him, fiction is more considerate. In fiction, characters interact in a setting and encounter some conflict. The action rises and falls around that conflict and their actions until some sort of resolution presents itself. Those fiction plot elements and sequences allow the reader to make reasonable predictions (see Chapter 4). This helps make the text considerate or readable. Considerate text for one reader may be inconsiderate to another.

In American schools children generally learn to read in predictable fiction and story books, making them more considerate forms of text for most learners. Nonfiction that is more narrative or story-like tends to be more considerate than pedantic, expository text.

Jeremy had encountered text that, for him, was inconsiderate. The paragraph from which he read was fifteen sentences long. There were no characters. There was no bold print to draw the reader's attention to important ideas. The sub-heading "Lexington and Concord" referred to towns that weren't mentioned until the fourth and fifth sentences. Words such as forestalled and tactics weren't defined contextually in the passage. It was a far cry from Beverly Cleary's *Dear Mr. Henshaw* Jeremy had recently read.

It wasn't inappropriate for Jeremy to read that text; we all have to tackle inconsiderate text. But Jeremy needed some specific instruction to help him pay attention strategically, to help him focus on the most important ideas.

Mimi and I might have had some success by asking Jeremy to reread the text and "really concentrate this time." Essentially that is what we did, but with one key difference: Rather than merely telling him to concentrate, we were specific. We began to teach him a strategy known to be used by proficient readers that will be applicable in many other reading situations. We helped him to know specifically on what he should concentrate. Although it is a strategy used in many reading situations, proficient readers must focus on what is important as they find their way through inconsiderate text.

"I don't think I've ever seen Rachel wear the same hair bow," Mimi whispered as we passed Rachel's corner desk, stacked with organized piles of paper, open books, and spare pencils, sharpened and resting in the crevices between her desk and those on both sides of hers. She didn't even look up when we walked past to confer with other students. All we saw was her long blonde pony tail and her head bent over the neat array of tools on her desk.

Rachel was a fifth-grader with a mission. She didn't want to be interrupted. Later we overheard her open a meeting with her presentation team members, "Okay, you guys, here's the plan . . ." We didn't worry too much about Rachel. She was engaged and conscientious. Children with more pressing needs generally drew us to them.

After some time moving around the room, conferring with several children, Mimi and I pulled back and stood near the door to observe the interactions and activity. We wanted to be sure we didn't solve problems for the students but allowed them to use their knowledge of strategies to solve them for themselves.

"Look at Rachel," I said, shaking my head with awe and relief. "She's amazing. What organization! I can't wait to hear what she's going to present."

"Didn't I tell you her idea?" Mimi asked. "She's going to relate the Revolutionary War to modern military conflicts. She's researching patterns and similarities between the Bosnian and Revolutionary wars. I overheard her tell her group that she'd try to make all the research they'd done on colonial times more relevant to the audience by comparing it to Bosnia."

"Impressive," I said, looking more carefully at Rachel and catching the titles of a couple of books propped on her desk: *I Dream of Peace*, a collection of written and artistic images by children of the former Yugoslavia, and *Zlata's Diary*, a memoir written by a thirteen-year-old Sarajevo child.

Rachel read for a couple of minutes, then jumped up and scurried to a nearby corner where she'd stashed a story board—three large pieces of tagboard bound together by clear tape so that the board can stand alone. On the story board Rachel had taped newspaper clippings, sketches, poetry, and envelopes that said "Open Me."

"That's her part of the project," Mimi told me. "It's starting to look a little crowded on that story board. It represents all Rachel's research on Bosnia."

"Let's confer with her," I suggested.

As we moved in her direction, Rachel looked up with her index finger tucked into *I Dream of Peace.* "Mrs. DeRose, I need to make a copy of this poem for my story board."

"Hmmm," Mimi glanced at the book and then at Rachel. "Why?"

"It's a great poem and it makes me feel what it's like to live in a place that's in a war. Listen." She read from a poem written by a child Rachel's age whose experience with war allowed her to write in a painfully accurate way.

"It's so sad and so real and the girl was about my age so I can really understand how lonely and worried she would have felt. I hope her dad's okay."

We agree the poem is powerful. I make a mental note about the importance of using primary sources in the research process.

"You're welcome to make another copy, Rachel, but you've made a lot. You can't use every poem in this book, so you're going to have to make some tough choices," Mimi told her.

"Yeah, I really like all of them, or almost." Rachel twisted her finger through her pony tail and squinted in concentration.

"Maybe you need to ask yourself why you're using them, Rachel. What do you think your audience is going to learn from them?" Mimi paused. "We've been working on this research for over five weeks now. During that time we've also done a comprehension strategy study on determining importance in text. Maybe we're talking about the same process in reading and in putting together a presentation. Let's think out loud a bit. How do you decide what's important enough in your research to include in your presentation?"

Rachel answered quickly, speaking with energy and confidence. "Well, I've read all these newspaper articles. There are articles in the newspaper every day, and I've read these two books by kids. You really get to feel what it's like to live there. And I've interviewed our neighbors whose grandparents are Croatian. They worry all the time if they're okay especially if they don't get any letters for a while. I've read the computer encyclopedia entries and it was all really important, you know? It was all about the war in Bosnia and that's my part, you know, to connect it to the Revolutionary War." I was certain she hadn't taken a breath so far, but she went on. "The presentation is two weeks from Thursday and I really think those fourth-graders need to know how all the kids who wrote these poems feel, living in Sarajevo."

"Whoa, Rachel!" Mimi laughed and put her hand on Rachel's shoulder. "You've found so much that's important. You've found out so much about Bosnia. Let me ask you again, though, what exactly is your role in this presentation?"

"To compare the Revolutionary War to wars today."

"Okay, if that's your purpose, how do you decide what to leave in and what to leave out of your part of the presentation? How did you decide what to include on the story board, for example?"

"Well, not much more stuff will fit." Rachel's statement turned into a question right around the word fit.

"Let's talk a little about your presentation, Rachel," I offered. "Who's going to see your story board and listen to your presentation?"

"The fourth-graders, right?" She shot a glance at Mimi who nodded.

"You were in fourth grade once a long time ago, Rachel! What did you know about the Revolutionary War, and how wars in this century compare, when you were in fourth grade?"

"I don't think I knew anything," Rachel said.

"And now you know a lot, right?" I leaned forward and whispered as if we were, at that moment, surrounded by fourth-graders. "Rachel, they're not going to really learn everything you know about these two wars. Look at your story board. It's crammed full of information. Your presentation notes are, how many, six pages long? Think about the fourth-graders and what they know. Think about what Mrs. DeRose just asked you about your role in the presentation. If you could have your audience remember just two really important ideas, what would those be? Are there two ideas you think are most important when you compare these two wars?"

"I don't know," then her voice revved to full throttle. "I really want them to know . . ." and she was off again.

When the litany had concluded, I said, "Rachel, we're going to leave you for awhile so that you can identify what two things you think are most important to your part of the presentation. Take some quiet time, look over your great work so far, read through your notes, but when we check back in, say fifteen minutes," I glanced at the clock, "I want you to tell us the two ideas here that you think are most important for the fourth-graders to learn."

"Two, not twenty-two, Rachel," Mimi winked at her as we left. "And we're going to ask you to defend your choices."

"I figured that," she said.

We retreated between conferences to our place on the counter. "You know what I just realized? She doesn't discriminate, Ellin. She comprehends all kinds of text, including the newspaper, beautifully. But she thinks *everything* is important. You know, we've been in this comprehension strategy study for weeks. I've really modeled, thought aloud about how I make decisions about what is important in narrative and expository text, but she's not following through on any of it. She doesn't seem to have any criteria in her mind to help her select a few key themes and leave the rest out. She has an incredible memory. She remembers everything and she must figure if she can remember it, it must be important to include."

I agreed with Mimi, saying, "I think Rachel and probably a few others in here need to understand that it's the purpose for the reading, along with personal beliefs, experiences, prior knowledge, and knowledge of the audience that govern our decisions about what is important in any given text. Rachel has a lot of background knowledge, and she has a clearly stated audience and purpose. The problem is that she isn't really considering her audience and purpose as a way to discriminate between important ideas to include on her story board, and interesting but unimportant facts that don't match the purpose or the needs of the audience."

"That's right," Mimi nodded.

"I think they may need some mini lessons on how proficient readers actually use purpose, beliefs, prior knowledge, and audience to make decisions about what is important in text."

"Yeah," Mimi said. "I've done so much modeling in this strategy study where I read aloud and pause to think out loud about what I think is important, but I don't think I've been explicit enough about how I decide, why I decide—you know, what criteria I use to make those decisions. I guess I wasn't consciously aware of it before now.

Just when you think you're done," Mimi joked. "But I know that's right. If we have a kid like Rachel who is comprehending so much, but can't prioritize, I worry that she'll have a tough time in middle school doing assignments like writing a summary or a persuasive piece. I also worry that she'll believe everything she reads. Through this comprehension study, I've discovered better what I mean when I talk about determining importance. One big piece of it for me is the ability to read critically, to mentally throw out propaganda or stuff that is just plain inaccurate according to my background knowledge, opinion, and beliefs. When you focus on what's important, you're also deciding what isn't worthy of being remembered. I want these kids to discriminate that way, too."

In *A Chorus of Stones* Susan Griffin writes that "all that I was taught at home or in school was colored by denial, and thus it became so familiar to me that I did not see it. Only now have I begun to recognize that there were many closely guarded family secrets that I kept, and many that were kept from me."

Determining importance, finding the essence, in text or in life is the antithesis of denial. Determining importance means revealing that which may be denied or ignored—those key themes and ideas that hide beneath the surface and may go unnoticed if we don't bring them to our conscious attention. The events denied in Susan Griffin's family became those most essential to her as she came to understand her life. The firestorms in Dresden during World War II provide essential insight into our nation's psychology and, if studied, may lead to prevention of such horror in our collective future.

In our classrooms determining importance implies that we go beyond what becomes so familiar to us we can no longer see it. It means that we initially become aware of our own processes of determining importance—when we read, when we converse, when we shop, when we make profound decisions—and then we reveal our thinking for children. They may, like Jeremy, have difficulty identifying anything of importance, or they may, like Rachel, need to learn about the criteria we use to discriminate from a myriad of important ideas. They may find focusing on the essence effortless in some texts only to be confounded by the process in others. Our task is to reveal the thinking that is part of grasping the essential.

Determining Importance in Text: Some Key Ideas

Proficient readers make instantaneous decisions about what is important in text at the following levels:

Word Level: Words that carry the meaning are contentives. Words that connect are functors. Contentives tend to be more important to the overall meaning of passage than functors.

Sentence Level: There are usually key sentences that carry the weight of meaning for a passage or section. Often, especially in nonfiction, they contain bold print, begin or end the passage, or refer to a table or graph.

Text Level: There are key ideas, concepts, themes in the text. Our opinions about which ideas are most important change as we read the passage. Final conclusions about the most important themes are typically made after reading the passage, perhaps several times and/or after conversing or writing about the passage.

Decisions about importance in text are made based on the following:

the reader's purpose;

the reader's schema for the text content (ideas most closely connected to the reader's prior knowledge will be considered most important);

the reader's beliefs, opinions, and experiences related to the text;

the reader's schema for text format (text that stands out visually and/or ideas that are repeated are often considered most important);

concepts another reader mentions prior to, during, or after reading.

Frequently, pointing out non-examples (what is unimportant) helps children to distinguish importance more clearly.

Interesting discussion emanates from dispute about what is most important—children need to work toward defending their positions, but there is rarely a true set of most important ideas.

A Sample Comprehension Strategy Study Using the Gradual Release of Responsibility Model: Determining Importance in Text

- The teacher begins by modeling: thinking aloud about his/her own process of determining importance during reading. Modeling should occur frequently using short selections. The teacher should focus not only on conclusions about importance, but on how and why he or she arrived at those conclusions. It is important to think aloud about how the focus on what he or she believes to be important enhances comprehension.
- In small and large group mini lessons, students are gradually invited to share their thoughts about what is important at the whole-text level, and later at the word and sentence level. Students should provide some evidence or reasoning to support their judgments.
- Students may meet in small groups or pairs to compare ideas about what is most important in text and how they came to that conclusion. They should be asked to discuss how their comprehension is enhanced by focusing on themes they believe to be important.
- Book clubs focus on determining importance during the strategy study. They discuss different conclusions about important ideas if all are reading the same text, or ways in which the members of the book club drew conclusions about importance if each is reading a different book.
- In reading conferences with students, conversation can focus on what decisions the child is making about important

ideas in a variety of texts. Think-alouds are an effective way to assess the student's use of the strategy.

· Invitational (needs-based) groups are created for children who need more modeling and explicit instruction.

· Text sets can be used to invite children to draw conclusions about important themes found in all (or most) books in the text set. Note: Text sets are collections of books with a common characteristic, i.e., books by the same author, or books about the same topic, books with poetic language, books with strong lead sentences or passages, books written in a particular style or format, etc.

· Sharing time at the conclusion of the reader's workshop should focus on ideas individual children found important in their independent reading for the day, how they arrived at their conclusions, and how thinking about important ideas enhanced their comprehension.

· Connections between this strategy and other strategies the children have learned should be made throughout the study.

· Modeling in a variety of texts—genre and difficulty—is critical. Modeling is most concentrated at the beginning of a strategy study, but does continue throughout. Students may gradually assume responsibility for modeling their own conclusions about importance in texts they are reading.

SIX

Delving Deeper with Questions

An Unspoken Hunger

It is an unspoken hunger we deflect with knives—one avocado between us, cut neatly in half, twisted then separated from the large wooden pit. With the green fleshy boats in hand, we slice vertical strips from one end to the other. Vegetable planks. We smother the avocado with salsa, hot chiles at noon in the desert. We look at each other and smile, eating avocados with sharp silver blades, risking the blood of our tongues repeatedly.

TERRY TEMPEST WILLIAMS,
An Unspoken Hunger: Stories from the Field

When I read "It is an unspoken hunger," I wonder, is this lust, repression, a search for meaning or for answers to unanswerable questions? Last year I read Williams' book *Refuge* in which she writes of her mother's death from cancer at about the same age my mother died of cancer. Does the unspoken hunger relate to the pain and loss a motherless daughter faces? Is the hunger the need to break down barriers and open oneself to a friend, a lover, a husband?

Is the "deflect(ion) with knives" the pain they cause one another? Is it the anger they've held inside too long? Is it their fear of one another? "Knives," the image is sharp and violent; yet I feel these people are terribly controlled. Is the need to control part of the hunger?

What is this tension, "one avocado between us, cut neatly in half?" Is this intimacy sliced in two? What questions float between them in the hot, dry air? Is one shared avocado a symbol of their marriage, friendship, affair? Are things so neatly cut in their relationship that they're unable to get to murkier, messier areas of their lives? "Twisted then separated." Is it their intimacy that has been torn apart? Why? "From the large wooden pit." Pit is such an empty, hollow word. What does it reflect in this piece? A pit can also be a seed, something from which new life will grow. Does she mean both things, an emptiness and a chance for new life? Who are these two people? Are they in love? Were they once?

I read on. "With the green fleshy boats in hand." Is this as sensual as my mind is making it? Why is it that green speaks to me of growth, but here the feeling is of death, endings? "We slice." Is this a physical separation or is their slicing an emotional cut? "Vertical strips from one end to the other." Why does it sometimes seem our lives are torn from one end to the other? Is this what she means? "Vegetable planks." Why the abrupt language? Why contrast vegetable, which sounds soft, earthy, nurturing, with planks, which remind me of hard, straight wooden boards? Why does the sliced avocado image remind me of a Georgia O'Keeffe painting?

As I read, the tension grows. "We smother the avocado with salsa, hot chiles, at noon in the desert." I love salsa, chiles, but this is too hot. Why do I feel I want to run from the heat, both the heat from the outside—the sun—and the heat that will burn in my body as I eat?

"We look at each other and smile." Is this a distant, awkward smile, or an intimate, knowing one? Is it the resigned smile of an ending? "Eating avocadoes with sharp silver blades." Is it a smile masking rage—a cutting, narrow smile? What is the source of this hot anger?

"Risking the blood of our tongues repeatedly." The line replays slowly in my mind. Why does this language still me? Why are they afraid to speak? Why do their words cause such wounds? Risk. Repeatedly. We risk as we enter relationships. We risk the almost unimaginable pain of loss when we choose to raise children. We risk each time we step into our cars, each time we head out for a bike ride, each time we hop on a plane. We risk any time we love unconditionally. Will we ever be loved as we love? We risk when we stride away from the past and venture into uncharted territory. We risk when we give voice to questions.

The weight of an early September snowstorm has snapped trees all over Denver and left 50,000 people without power for more than three days. Susan and I sit, afghans tucked around our legs, thankful that the power outage on Lookout Mountain where Susan lives was brief. Our fingers fly over computer keyboards. We take a Mocha Cafe break in her writing studio, watching the snow fall. It's a Friday afternoon and we are just beginning work on Chapter 6—a chapter about questions formed in the mind while reading.

"I've been reading through the most recent summaries of reading research," I say, pulling a copy of the *Annual Summary of Investigations Relating to Reading* (IRA) from the plastic file basket I keep at Susan's. "The research shows that children who struggle as readers tend not to ask questions at any time as they read—before, during, or after. It confirms what I've seen so many times in classrooms, particularly with upper-elementary and middle-school kids. They're inert as they read. They read—or I should say they submit to the text—never questioning its content, style, or the intent of the author."

"It's disturbing, but it makes sense, doesn't it?" Susan responds, "Because they're not really reading, not really getting it, not really connecting with the text enough to interact with it. We've talked about that passivity again and again. I wonder why. Why some kids and not others?"

We shake our heads. The question floats in the air between us, swallowed by the silence of the snow falling. One more question between us. We've reveled in a continual flow of questions over the course of our friendship and work together. We've learned more about each other from our questions than from any answers we've stumbled upon. We ask the same questions over and over, puzzling and laughing at our own searches and the journeys we've taken together. "Just tell me one thing," Susan will begin, "why do I . . . ?"

Of all qualities, questioning is fundamental to being human. It is how we dispel confusion, probe into new areas, strengthen our abilities to analyze and deduce. It is how we learn about other people and deepen friendships. We've all known people who never asked us questions. At some level we felt they didn't really care about us, didn't want to know us better. Those who take the time to ask thoughtful, provocative questions are those who help us learn about ourselves. Through their questions we learn, also, about them.

Questions weave through the fabric of each day: Why are you sad? What would you like for dinner? How can I fit in my haircut and pick up Elizabeth's carpool on time? Why do wars persist? Why do I have such a hard time understanding the issues in countries an ocean away?

Some of our questions are trivial, get-through-the-day questions; others go to the fundamental underpinnings of our society; others to issues about what motivates people to love, hate, kill, persevere, or destroy.

Questions help explain our ever-changing understanding of children and teaching. Why do some learn to read so effortlessly, while others never do? Why do they choose certain books? Why do they choose to reread some books so frequently? How does language develop? How can we help children who come to us with underdeveloped oral language? Our questions help us formulate our beliefs about teaching and learning, and those beliefs underlie our instructional decisions.

Questions lead children through the discovery of their world. They want to know everything: "Why are there clouds, Mom? What happened to the dinosaurs? Why do leaves fall in the fall? Is that why they call fall fall? Why do flowers have all different colors? How does a light bulb make light?" Children offer an endless stream of questions that delight us and drive us to distraction.

I remember Susan's early questions at the PEC—around conference tables, in classrooms. "Why isn't public education working for so many kids, I mean really why? Why aren't more of our children reading and writing well? We all know how naturally curious kids are. Why are some teachers less than competent? Why don't university teacher-training programs work as well as they might? Why can't we just go around the country and see what works and model it here?

Does it really matter how a child learns? Does it matter which educational philosophy we use to teach? Isn't there research on all sides of every question? Can our work really make a difference for children?"

Initially, I was a bit defensive. Maybe as a lawyer she didn't understand the complex realities of working with children. Perhaps she didn't realize that people all over the country were trying to address those issues and that change takes a long time. Susan's questions worked on me. They crept into my thinking at odd moments: driving between schools, under the nozzle of the shower. I began to realize that asking the tough questions and providing a venue for conversation about them is, perhaps, our most important work.

Looking back, I wish I'd read *An Unspoken Hunger* at the time I met Charline Mize, a first-grade teacher at Denver's Sabin Elementary School. I believe its residue of questions would have meant something to her, perhaps even comforted her.

Char was overwhelmed but compelled by the prospect of dramatically changing her classroom. The tension of Williams' short piece would have matched her uneasy state of mind in our earliest conversations. A skilled, veteran teacher, she had a vague longing to transform her classroom, to do things differently, to implement something of the new theory in reading and writing she'd been hearing about. She knew she had more questions than answers, and was stepping into uncharted territory.

Char was one of many teachers with whom I've worked who was searching to satisfy an unspoken hunger that came from her work. Those with the unspoken hungers, those with the incessant questions, are the lucky ones. They know they do good work, but they also have a deep intuitive knowledge that their classrooms and schools could be better.

Williams' words, "Eating avocados with sharp silver blades, risking the blood of our tongues repeatedly," reminds me that the most critical questions imply we must take risks, leave our comfort zones, and embrace the questions. The questions we have about changing the world, our lives and loves, and our classrooms begin in our minds and hearts. They emanate from a twinge that can't be ignored—a realization that children aren't learning as deeply, remembering and applying as much, or engaging as completely as we'd like.

Char Mize and I met after school in her first-grade classroom at Sabin Elementary. She walked her students to the bus as I wandered around her room, darkened by half-closed roller shades and a gray winter sky. Hands-on science materials were stacked in plastic tubs and stored neatly in a learning center at the back. The children's desks sat in clusters of four, with their chairs resting upside down on top and their books and folders piled neatly within.

A sense of organization and order permeated the room with everything in its place. It reminded me of the sense of satisfaction I have when my house is dusted and cleaned, counters wiped, and dishes stacked neatly in the cupboards.

Several minutes later Char returned, breathing heavily after a sprint down two long hallways. She collapsed into a first-grader's chair. In her warm, gravelly voice, she dove in. "Where do I start, Ellin? What do I do? How do I do it? I've been going to a (reading/writing) study group for six months. I hear all the great teachers talk about the things they're doing in their (readers'/writers') workshops. I've observed in Ann's classroom. She's so good. I just don't know if I can make mine that good. I know I want to do things differently, but I want to make sure the kids have the skills they need. I don't know how to cover everything to get them ready for second grade and still help them learn to love to read and write. I've always thought of myself as a teacher with high expectations. What do high expectations look like now? I think I may be too old and rigid to do this."

Char laughed, and as her laughter faded, she paused. Her face grew more solemn, "I have a really tough group this year. A lot of them, too. What do I do? I need a change. They need a change. It's overwhelming, Ellin. I have so many questions." Char's gaze remained steady and I knew she meant business.

I thought back to the hour earlier in the day when I'd observed in Char's classroom. Indeed, she did have a big group—I guessed twenty-eight—with some very challenging children. As I circled around the desks and looked over shoulders, I saw children with a wide range of needs. Kevin's volatile temper intruded frequently, disrupting the classroom. It took Char five minutes to move Mary in and out of her wheelchair and set up her communication board or a new activity for her every time there was a transition. The PA system cut harshly into the children's hushed work too many times. Six children were pulled out for work in special ed or Title I classrooms during the hour I observed.

The classroom had all the hallmarks of a well-organized ship. The room was immaculate and uncluttered. The schedule ran down to the minute. The desks were neat. Materials sat in flawless piles ready to hand out. The classroom was organized in a way that permitted Char to manage an array of variables. She was acutely aware of, and annoyed by, the stream of disruptions and children who were off task. She resented the distractions that cut into learning time. And there was an edge to her interactions with the children that suggested a restless dissatisfaction with the status quo.

I liked Char and didn't want to offend, but there were difficult questions begging to be asked. During my observation time in her classroom, I sat down to focus my thinking in my notebook. I wrote, "In her zeal for a well-managed, efficient learning environment, do the structures she has in place ensure order but necessarily limit the children's ownership and participation in this classroom? When do children ask questions? What are they curious about? How to begin to tackle the issue of control here? How can I directly, but respectfully, ask questions that will help her see the need to share responsibility for learning with the children?"

As I wrote, my mind returned to the critical concepts of time, ownership, response, and community articulated in *When Writers Read* by Jane Hansen. Issues of control are really questions about ownership in a classroom. Who is responsible for the learning? Who is doing the work of learning? Who monitors the learning? Who makes the choices?

It was tough to know where to start. Char's honesty, her obvious frustration, her beseeching look, and the images from my short time in her classroom made me want to find the answers. Her questions made me want to hand her a to-do list, but I knew that if change were to last, she would have to draw conclusions about her classroom based on what she observed in her children. She needed to see the possibilities. If we could create conditions in which children's voices emerged and their questions were honored, a direction would become clear.

"Char, I don't have the answers for you, but I have a thought about where we might start. You told me you wanted to see the children more engaged and excited about writing. Let's show them how writers use questions to choose writing topics. We both know first-graders are a volcano of questions. If we can get them to articulate their own questions, they'll be on their way to imaginative writing and their passion will be directed."

One morning the following week, I gathered the children around me in Char's classroom and pulled out my writing notebook.

"You know," I told them, "I've been thinking about so many questions lately, and you know what else? Often my own questions lead me to write my best pieces."

As they watched, I jotted questions in my notebook. "I've been wondering what will happen to this cat that has been roaming around our neighborhood for a couple of weeks. Does she have a home? How does she eat? Where does she sleep? Did someone abandon her? Should I take her to the Dumb Friends League? All those questions could become a piece of writing—a story or maybe a poem."

Char recorded my questions on a large sheet of chart paper. As they watched, I wrote a couple of lead sentences in my notebook that formed the beginning to a first-person piece about the cat.

"I wonder about other things, too, and I want to write them down in case I want to write a different piece later. Our friends told us recently they've decided to divorce. I have so many questions about it and I may write a piece that I won't share with anyone else just to help myself understand this. I wonder what will happen to their son. Who he will live with? Will they sell their house? Will they ever get back together? Why did they decide to separate? Will they remarry?"

We switched roles and Char generated questions for her own writing while I recorded them for the children to see. We paused frequently to talk about how the questions could become pieces of writing—stories, nonfiction, or poetry.

When we sent the children off to share questions with a partner and later to write, ideas flowed. Some began by simply writing the questions. Others were able to take ideas inspired by the questions and write longer pieces. Others drew pictures related to their questions. No one had to be told what to write.

"I've worked so hard," Char told me later, shaking her head, "to try to ask children good questions. I try to keep them diverse. I try to use great wait time—I can just see myself counting quietly to myself to avoid calling on someone before the fifteen seconds someone told me to wait." She laughed. "But I never once stopped to think about whether or not I let them generate questions. Not just whether I let them generate questions, because we saw today they have a million, it's really that I haven't heard the questions. I must have asked ten thousand questions so far this year. Imagine the questions I ask them after we've read a story from the basal. I skip the literal questions because they bore me, but I ask all these inferential questions, count, and then tell them what I think. They must know by now they don't have to think, because as soon as I'm done counting, I'll answer! But really, I have no idea what their questions are—about their lives, their writing, or their reading."

"Do you really need the list of questions out of the teacher's manual?" I asked. "These kids have loads of real questions—things they really want to know about the stories. And you have your own questions. What do you think about letting those questions, rather than the questions from the basal, guide your discussions in reading, as well as in finding writing topics?"

We decided to expand our focus to reading. We knew we could build on the children's success in using questions to generate their writing topics and began with a comprehension strategy study on questioning.

In our planning conversations we discussed whether the students would read books of their own choosing, or stories from the basal readers. We decided to use the basals as one source of short pieces. The children could choose something from the basal or any other book to read. The basals were taken out of the desks and placed on bookshelves. A series of mini lessons on how to choose appropriate text (see Appendix 7) was taught in the two weeks prior to the beginning of the questioning study.

During those weeks Char and I talked about how her reading instruction would differ from the weekly routine of working through stories in the basal. Instead of teaching a series of skills in an order determined by a basal publisher, she would capitalize on research that tells us proficient readers ask questions as they read. She would teach one strategy—asking questions—for many weeks to her first-graders. She would model her own questions in a variety of texts and, through reading conferences with the children, monitor their developing use of questioning.

The enormity of the change, predictably, sparked many questions for Char. She wondered if asking kids to generate questions would actually improve their comprehension. What about the kids who weren't reading unfamiliar print yet? Would their questions provide insight into what mini lessons should be taught during the comprehension strategy study? How could she sustain instruction on one strategy for weeks? Would the children's questions about books link in any way to the questions they were using for writing topics? Where would we begin?

The morning we launched the strategy study was filled with the standard fare of interruptions. The faculty meeting ran late. The children were standing outside in a fierce wind, waiting to be brought in the building. We walked into the classroom to find a new volunteer from the local senior citizen's center who needed to be oriented to her work reading to children. The mini lesson had to end by 10:00 when the fourth-grade play was scheduled to begin in the auditorium. Two announcements were made over the PA system at two different times.

Nonetheless when the children finally came together around Char's new author's chair (a cozy burnt orange cast-off from her mother's basement), I looked into eager faces and felt the familiar surge of energy and purpose. They were ready.

Char turned off the overhead lights so that only the floor lamp next to the author's chair lit the pages, and I started to read. *"Tell me the story again, Grandfather. Tell me who I am. I have told you many times, Boy. You know the story by heart. But it sounds better when you tell it, Grandfather. Then listen carefully. This may be the last telling. No, no Grandfather. There will never be a last time. Promise me that. Promise me. I promise you nothing, Boy. I love you. That is better than a promise."* I read slowly in a voice no louder than a whisper.

I read *Knots on a Counting Rope* by Bill Martin Jr. and John Archambault, slowing as my voice moved across the words, *"Will I always have to live in the dark? Yes, Boy. You were born with a dark curtain in front of your eyes. But there are many ways to see, Grandfather. Yes, Boy, you are learning to see through your darkness because you have the strength of blue horses."* I looked across the six- and seven-year-old faces, curious to see if they understood that this author, writing about a Native American child's developing internal strength, had just revealed that the child in the story is blind.

I saw hands raised and faces brimming with questions. I resisted the urge to call on them. I wanted to preserve the solemn tone and let the questions linger in the children's minds a few moments longer.

I read the book without interruption, closed it and let the silence fall around the children. After a long minute Char stood and moved to the chart paper taped to the chalkboard behind us. She spoke and wrote in large red letters, "Why a counting rope? Where are the boy's parents?"

I added, "Why are some children born strong and others born with physical challenges that last a lifetime? Where does strength inside a person come from?"

Char recorded as the children watched, still bathed in the mystery of the book. I reopened it to a page in the middle and read, *"I see horses with my hands, Grandfather, but I cannot see the blue. What is blue? You know morning, Boy. Yes, I can feel morning. Morning throws off the blanket of night. And you know sunrise. Yes, I hear sunrise, in the song of the birds. And you know sky, Boy. Yes, sky touches my face . . .*

soft, like lamb's wool . . . and I breathe its softness. Blue is all of these. Blue is the feeling of a spring day beginning. Try . . . try to see it, Boy."

I turned to Char, "Mrs. Mize, would you add another question that is in my mind? I want to ask myself, have I ever felt sky on my face? What did it feel like? How can I help myself remember it without seeing it?"

We didn't tell this group of first-graders, "Today we'll talk about asking questions. What questions do you have as we look at the cover of the book? Now let's see if we can answer them as we read." We paid careful attention to the questions that spontaneously took shape in our mind as we read. We tried to model that process, thinking aloud about our own real questions. They were not questions that led to answers in the book. They were questions that hung in the air and replayed themselves in our minds. They were questions that led to other questions.

When we looked back at the children, ten hands were in the air. "Is his real name Boy? Can horses be blue or rainbow? Did his parents die? Why is he blind? I think I would have been scared in that race if I couldn't see. I wonder if he was scared." Occasionally, another child would try to respond to the questions that were gradually filling the chart paper, but we would hold up a hand or shake our heads and say, "Let the questions live for awhile without any answers."

"I don't get why it's called that, *Knots on a Counting Rope*," Eric wondered. Char recorded his question, added another of her own, "Why does this author write this way?" and then said, "Look at the way the words are placed on the page. It's so different from other books. It's so different from other books by Bill Martin Jr. that we've read. Can you guys believe that this is the same author who wrote, *Here are My Hands* and *Barn Dance?* This book is more like poetry to me."

Chancy, a tiny girl with red hair and a million freckles, had been squirming, her hand dancing in the air. She could stand it no longer and burst out, "Why did the boy keep asking his grandfather to tell him that story when he had already told him it a bunch of times?"

All the questions were carefully recorded in the language the children used and, as we sent them off to the fourth-grade play, the words of a question were the last words they heard. "Do you listen to the questions in your minds?" I asked them. "Do you hear your own questions?"

Initial mini lessons set an important tone and reveal the ultimate goals for a comprehension strategy study. Char and I had numerous hopes. We agreed that we wanted to create an aura of mystery, curiosity, and wonder around the concept of questioning during reading. We wanted them to experience the insight that comes from questions, and to learn to love unanswerable questions. We wanted them to experience the absorption we'd felt when reading a text that filled us with questions.

We knew that modeling our own—typically unspoken—questions would be vital if the children were to become aware of the questions they naturally ask as they listen to or read text. We wanted them to give voice to those questions and to remember them as they continued reading. We wanted one question to lead to another and on to a search for information. We wanted the questions from one book to remind them of other books. We wanted the children to use the questions they have about books to begin discussions with each other about what they read. We wanted their questions to lead them to engaged and passionate reading.

We also wanted the group to get into the habit of recording their questions before, during, and after they read, and sharing them with each other in pairs and groups. A tall order for six- and seven-year-olds? Knowing how naturally and continuously young children ask questions, we didn't think so.

Knots on a Counting Rope read dramatically in a semidarkened, quiet room had been a perfect send-off. We knew we would return to it several times in the course of the study to see how the children's questions changed. Now it was time to create a plan. It wasn't hard to see how we could spend six weeks or more on questioning, given our hopes for these children.

Char and I met after school to articulate some overarching goals for the study. Our list included hopes that the children would do the following:

- become aware of questions they have about text before, during, and after reading and/or listening to a book;
- use questions to clarify meaning, wonder about forthcoming text, speculate about an author's intent, style, content, or format;
- understand that some questions are answered specifically in a text, but others must be inferred based on the reader's background knowledge, and;
- discuss ways in which questions help them focus on and understand text.

We laughed at our own litany of questions. What about the daily routine for the study? What about the students who didn't yet understand the concept of a question as opposed to a declarative statement? Would there be children who would become so consumed with recording the questions that they would lose track of the content of the book they were reading? What about the children who were reading simple books like *Mrs. Wishy Washy* that didn't inspire thoughtful questioning? Would we kill the beauty of rich, interesting books by generating questions ad nauseam? Which books were most appropriate to use for the study? The class had already undertaken a social studies exploration of Native American culture. Was there a way to integrate the two studies? We agreed we needed to wait for answers to be revealed to us by watching the children throughout the study and keeping careful records of their progress.

The next morning wasn't as frenetic and fraught with interruptions. Once again we gathered the children around us and dimmed the lights. Almost instantly a stillness came over them.

I opened *The Way to Start a Day* by Byrd Baylor and watched the illustrations, poetic language, and unconventional diction seize the children's attention. I read all the way through the book slowly, quietly trying to capture a sense of awe in the words. I wanted the first reading of the book to reflect a sense of sweeping light, space, and wonder. I've found that a room's ambience affects the quality of the questions generated.

Without a word I closed the book, paused, went to the chart and wrote, "What did Byrd Baylor want me to feel as I read her book?" Then instead of inviting answers or rereading the book from the beginning, I sat down and started from the middle of the book with the words, "*People have always known that. Didn't they chant at dawn in the sun temples of Peru? And leap and sway to Aztec flutes in Mexico? And drum sunrise songs in the Congo? And ring a thousand small gold bells in China?*" I closed the book and didn't need to say anything to these first-graders. Hands shot up and questions were added to the chart.

Char laughed as she struggled to record the avalanche of questions. "We're going to need a new roll of chart paper!" she said.

The children's questions were as diverse as they were. Maria, usually a silent presence in the classroom, listened to a question about why Byrd Baylor wrote her words more vertically than horizontally on the page, and raised her hand tentatively, and said "She likes questions."

Char knelt beside Maria, "Tell me more about that."

Maria looked as if she might not respond at all, then paused and said, "and ring small gold bells in . . . ?"

It took us a moment to realize Maria was referring to the author's use of questions as a way to tell this story. As Char recorded Maria's insight, I reread the litany of questions Byrd Baylor uses in her picture book about the morning rituals of cultures around the world.

We then turned on the overhead lights and asked the children to return to their desks for the independent reading portion of their daily reader's workshop. "Listen to your minds at work. Do you have questions before, during, or after you read? In a little bit, we'll be around to confer with you about your books, and we want to hear the questions your mind creates about your books."

So that we could measure progress, Char and I decided to gather data about the children's current use of the questioning strategy. We used questions from the Major Point Interview for Readers (see Appendix 4), an assessment instrument I developed with the help of colleagues Jan Dole, Anne Goudvis, and Roseanne Schwartz. We wanted to obtain baseline information so we could track their development.

As we went around the room that morning early in the study, we stopped and asked the children to read from or tell us a little about the book they were reading. For children who were not yet reading unfamiliar text, we reread part of *The Way to Start a Day* or asked them to tell the story from the pictures in their books. Then we asked the following questions:

A. What questions did you think about before you started to read this story (or tell the story from the illustrations)?
B. What questions did you think about while you were reading this story (or telling the story from the illustrations)?
C. What questions do you have about this book now?
D. Does it help you to understand the book when you ask questions like you asked just now? How do those questions help you understand the book?

Jotting their responses was anything but a time-consuming process. Many had few, if any, questions about books they were reading—in most cases text far less complex than the two books we had used in the mini lessons.

Our original concerns came flooding back to us. Are they too young to undertake this process? How will they ever ask great questions when the text they can read limits them? Does it matter if they ask great questions about uninspiring text?

We decided to press forward. Within two weeks Char had baseline data on all the children. We pored through it, and recognized a clear direction for instruction. Most of the children weren't aware of any questions they asked as they read and couldn't say how questioning would help them understand a book better. The memory of their spirited questions in writing and mini lessons kept us going.

The data told us that modeling for the children—the real crux of the instruction—had to include explicit descriptions of how asking questions before, during, and after reading actually helped us to better comprehend text.

Char continued to model in a variety of texts each day. In an effort to integrate their social studies unit into the study, many of the books had Native American themes. Char used books like *I'm in Charge of Celebrations* by Byrd Baylor, *The Girl Who Loved Wild Horses* and *The Friendly Wolf* by Paul Goble, *The Rough-Face Girl* by Rafe Martin, and *Boy Who Doesn't Fall from Horse* by Virginia Stroud. Initially, the questions she modeled focused on clarifying portions of the text she suspected might be unclear to the children. As the chart of questions filled, the class decided they could keep track of the questions better by grouping them on a table like that in Table 6.1 below.

	Before Reading	*During Reading*	*After Reading*
with answers in the text			
with answers I must find by thinking about the book and my own experience			
with no certain answers			
to clarify meaning			
about what's coming next in the book			
about the author's intent			
about the author's style			
about the author's format			

TABLE 6.1 *Questions We Ask . . .*

We created another chart-paper list of ways questions helped us comprehend more fully. Char and I made the first contributions:

Asking Questions . . .
helps me focus on the parts of the text that are most important to understand . . . Mrs. Mize
makes me aware of the parts of the text that are toughest for me to understand . . . Ellin
helps me to stop reading long enough to see pictures in my mind about the book . . . Ellin

By the second and third week of the study, in the daily large group mini lessons, the children were generating more diverse and interesting questions. The table began to fill out. Most of the children's questions, and certainly their most thoughtful ones, were from the books Char read aloud to the group, rather than the books they were reading independently. This told us that we had to help children focus on applying the strategy in their own reading. Reading conferences and small group instruction would become an increasingly important venue for instruction.

Char taught the children to use small self-adhesive notes, write a question mark on them, and place them in books wherever words or an illustration caused them to ask a mental question. They loved this scheme, and for a few days a hurricane of yellow notes whirled around the room. Soon the novelty wore off and they began to use the notes more judiciously.

During their reading conferences we asked the children about their question marks, but realized we'd made a strategic error. Char laughed as she described conferences with children whose books were filled with question-marked notes, but who were unable to remember the questions they'd had.

Going back to the drawing board, we decided to pause several times during the workshop and ask the children to share one question with their nearest neighbor and to make sure they marked that question with a note in their books. By this process the children's memories were enhanced, and Char was able to focus her conferences around the questions they remembered. She also jotted down some of their questions to help them remember, so they could share with the large group and add to the table at the end of each reader's workshop.

Within a week the room became a hive of questions. The process of generating questions about books became a routine part of reading—before, during, and after. Many children shared questions about their books spontaneously with each other. Large group sharing time frequently turned into small group sharing time because so many children had questions they wanted to share. For all of two weeks, we had a sense of satisfaction about the way the strategy study was going.

One day three weeks into the questioning study, Char said, "I'm frustrated, Ellin. I don't really know whether all the kids are aware of the questions they have as they read."

She ran a hand through her short blonde hair as we walked to her classroom after leaving her students in the lunchroom. "Some of the kids I confer with are aware of their questions and beginning to understand how those questions help them understand. But there are a few kids—around six or seven—hovering around out there. I'm afraid they're not connecting with what we're doing at all. They don't share much during large group sessions or when I confer with them. Sometimes I think they're just mimicking what I say in the mini lessons.

Char continued. "Manuel is a good example. I say, 'Manuel, what questions do you have as you're reading *William's Doll?*' And he'll say something like 'Why did this author write this book?' or 'What would have happened next in the book if the author had kept on writing?' Those are really questions I or other kids have asked during mini lessons or sharing time. Brian asked the question about what would have happened next if the author kept writing and I made a huge fuss over it because I thought it was such a great question. The problem is, I don't know how to tell if Manuel really has that question. He doesn't seem excited about his questions and they don't seem to be authentic for him. How can I find out?"

Char's question was one that had troubled the PEC staff developers for some time. What if the children were merely echoing the language they'd heard their teachers using in mini lessons and think-alouds? What if they didn't have a true understanding of the strategy and weren't, therefore, using it automatically as they read?

I suggested we try a technique used masterfully by a colleague, Colleen Buddy. In her first/second-grade classroom, when faced with similar concerns, Colleen calls for an *invitational group* meeting.

Invitational groups are needs-based groups which meet for a specific instructional purpose. Children are invited to join the group for a short, intensive mini lesson or lessons that serve to reinforce or extend a concept—like a comprehension strategy—that they've discussed in large group instruction. Invitational groups enable the teacher to gauge a child's use of the strategy more quickly, and to tailor instruction for a group of children with similar needs.

A group may disband after one session or meet several times during the course of a comprehension strategy study. Occasionally, children who already understand and are adept at applying the strategy are invited to join the group. Sometimes several children who are adept at using the strategy call their own invitational group to work on it in more difficult text or in a more in-depth way.

Other times when telling the whole class that an invitational group will meet, Colleen announces the names of those who will be part of the group and also tells the class that there are two or three open positions. If any children other than those she has named believe they would benefit from more in-depth instruction on the strategy, they too are welcome to join the group. Colleen convenes several invitational groups during a given strategy study, each with a different purpose.

Invitational groups meet for a short (ten or twelve minute) period during the workshop or independent reading time—the time when a teacher would typically confer with individual students. The teacher models or addresses specific instructional needs and the children talk about their understanding and use of the strategy.

Char and I started out by convening an invitational group of five. We offered two open spots which were quickly filled by children eager to join the group, but who were asked to tell us why the group would be helpful for them.

We discovered quickly that the children Char had invited didn't seem to be fully aware of the questions they asked during reading. They were able to generate questions before and after reading, but seemed not to pay attention to their questions while reading. The children could read independently in predictable, rhythmic books with controlled vocabulary. Their independent reading books, while appropriate for them to use in practicing their newfound decoding skills, had little story development that inspired genuine questions during reading.

In the invitational group Char modeled in books more likely to inspire questions. She focused on the questions she has during reading, particularly those which helped her clarify portions of the text that were more difficult to understand. After two short invitational groups in which Char modeled, the same children were asked to come back to the group with an adhesive note marking a question they had during independent reading. As a group they generated possible answers to the questions, but the reader was always left to make the final determination about the meaning of the piece.

Delia was typical. "I brought *Just Me and My Babysitter* (Mercer Mayer) today," she announced, "And I have a question. Why does Lil' Critter say 'I always eat all my dinner' when right here he's pouring his food out on the floor?"

Char immediately knew the answer to Delia's question was critical to understanding the book. "Delia, that's the kind of question great readers ask. While you were reading this page, you had a question and you stopped, and thought, 'This doesn't make sense. The picture shows Lil' Critter throwing his food on the floor, but the words say he always eats all his dinner. How can both be true?' If they're really confused, great readers have to figure out some answers before they can really know what the book is about, right? Let's tackle Delia's question together."

The group read the pages before and after the page that confused Delia. The children concluded that the text and illustrations differ throughout the book and that the author intentionally created the contrast to make the book funny.

Through a series of meetings this invitational group solved a variety of comprehension problems that they'd identified by asking questions. Gradually, the group members generated their own questions before, during, and after reading. They continued to ask better questions about the more complex texts used during mini lessons, but each became more aware of his or her own questions and began to use questions to clarify the meaning in a text if they were confused.

Six weeks after the chaotic day when we began the study, Char and I sat together after school. "It's amazing, Ellin. It's as if we're really looking into their minds," Char marveled as we reviewed the interviews Char had given at the beginning and end of the study. "They're using questioning to solve problems on their own and for each other all through the day. They talk about asking questions in Math and Science."

I looked around Char's class. The roller shades were tossed away, letting in a stream of natural light; floor lamps lit reading and writing areas; the burnt orange chair had become the heart of the classroom. More important, asking questions had become part of the culture of Char's classroom, a classroom that looked very different from the too-organized room I'd walked into that winter day months before. A transformation had begun when children were allowed to ask their questions.

Char's voice trailed off and she looked up briefly. "Before this study I bet I asked eighty-five percent of the questions in this classroom and they asked fifteen percent. Now I think that's turned around! It adds such energy to the day."

"It is an unspoken hunger . . ." How powerful are our unspoken hungers, those yearnings in life we can't quite understand. They drive us. They teach us, if we allow ourselves to open ourselves to them and hear their subtle messages. How many days have Susan and I sat writing together, the silence punctuated only by our questions about life, relationships, children, learning. Our questions help us find meaning, help us define our life quests. They enrich our lives and our friendships. We must honor our questions. They are our unspoken hungers.

Some Key Ideas

Proficient readers spontaneously generate questions before, during, and after reading.

Proficient readers ask questions to

- · clarify meaning
- · speculate about text yet to be read
- · determine an author's intent, style, content, or format
- · locate a specific answer in text *or* consider rhetorical questions inspired by the text

Proficient readers use questions to focus their attention on important components of the text; they understand that they can pose questions critically;

Proficient readers understand that many of the most intriguing questions are not answered explicitly in the text, but left to the reader's interpretation;

However, when an answer is needed, proficient readers determine whether it can be answered by the text or whether they will need to infer the answer from the text, their background knowledge, and/or other text;

Proficient readers understand how the process of questioning is used in other areas of their lives, academic and personal;

Proficient readers understand how asking questions deepens their comprehension;

Proficient readers are aware that as they hear others' questions, new ones are inspired in their own minds.

A Sample Comprehension Strategy Study Using the Gradual Release of Responsibility Model: Some Key Ideas

- · Model your questions with picture books or other short text over several days—record questions on chart paper that has categories for each of the purposes and times readers ask questions (see above), e.g., questions before reading that relate to author's intent;

- Make clear the distinction between reading aloud and thinking aloud as you model;
- Talk to the children about why readers pose questions, how questions help them to comprehend more deeply, and how they use questions in other academic areas and in their lives outside school;
- Gradually invite the students to share their questions, adding them to appropriate places on the chart in the children's language—continue to model, gradually diversifying the genre of text you use;
- Invite children to meet in small groups or pairs to share and compare questions—encourage them to list new questions generated through these discussions;
- Continue modeling with invitational groups of children who might benefit from more explicit instruction;
- Remind book clubs to focus on questioning in their conversations throughout the strategy study;
- In reading conferences, focus on their questions before, during, and after reading; ask students to identify places in the text where they had questions and ask them to use the class chart to categorize their questions; invite them to pose types of questions they haven't tried yet; use think-alouds to assess their use of questioning; ask the children to identify ways in which posing questions helps deepen their comprehension; model how posing questions helps deepen your comprehension;
- Focus sharing sessions on questions children discovered while reading and can add to the class chart—add new categories to the chart if necessary;
- Continue large and invitational group modeling in a variety of texts—modeling is most concentrated at the beginning of a strategy study, but continues throughout;
- Make frequent connections between questioning and other strategies on which the children have already focused;

· Use the Major Point Interview for Readers to assess children's use of questioning as a tool for deepening comprehension before and after the strategy study;
· Use a variety of tools such as coding, highlighting markers on copied text, self-adhesive notes, question maps, story maps, and double entry diaries (see Appendix 6) to help children become aware of and record their questions.

SEVEN

A Mosaic in the Mind
Using Sensory Images to Enhance Comprehension

Three Small Oranges

My old flannel nightgown, the elbows out,
one shoulder torn . . . Instead of putting it
away with the clean wash, I cut it up
for rags, removing the arms and opening
their seams, scissoring across the breast
and upper back, then tearing the thin
cloth of the body into long rectangles.
Suddenly an immense sadness . . .

Making supper, I listen to news
from the war, of torture where the air
is black at noon with burning oil,
and of a market in Baghdad, bombed
by accident, where yesterday an old man
carried in his basket a piece of fish
wrapped in paper and tied with string,
and three small hard green oranges.

JANE KENYON,
Constance: Poems

The elbows are butter soft in their threadbare state. The top button (is it supposed to button down the back or front?) is splintered and slides out of its button hole. On cold winter evenings, I hug my legs under my nightgown, stopping the chill as I connect the warmth of my body to my well-worn flannel.

In my mental image Jane Kenyon slices through her flannel with my orange-handled scissors, slightly rusted. She cuts diagonally upward from sideseam to sideseam. She cuts across the fabric spread out on the dining room table where I ate as a child.

The immense sadness, I can't help but think, is related to the author's leukemia, a disease from which she ultimately will die. I feel the sadness wrap around my shoulders, the subtle pressure of a shawl of grief provoked by reading this poem. Seconds later as I read the dining room image lifts from my mind and is replaced with another: the first day of the Gulf War in January, 1991. I am lying under the white afghan on our den couch, riveted to the television coverage of the events, weakened by stomach flu but unable to stop watching.

As I read the poem, my own grandfather's face appears on the humped body of the old man in the Baghdad marketplace. The man is stooped and dry. The light burden of fish and oranges he carries is unbearably heavy for him. In my mind the fish wrapped in paper and tied with string rests in a shoe box, not a basket, and is carried by a string and handle, like the ones I used to get at the shoe store in my hometown.

Black air shrouds and eventually consumes the old man. The cloud of dense, dark, putrid air thickens in my mind. The juxtaposition of the warmth of well-worn flannel and the stench of burning oil draws my eyes back to reread the poem.

This time aware of the key ideas in the poem, I listen for the sound of scissors bisecting fabric, but the sound never comes. The fabric has grown too soft. The damage has been done. Instead, in the background, I hear urgent voices reporting from the Middle East, a cacophony of sound from the television resting on a counter in Kenyon's kitchen. No, it's my kitchen, the one my family left when I was seven, the one with shiny, speckled counters and pink metal cabinets.

I see those cabinets and hear the sound they made when my mother snapped them closed, as she simultaneously prepared breakfasts and lunches during my childhood, years before her leukemia. I see that kitchen, the vinyl covered chairs, the metal table, the brown and white placemats. At my place and my brother's, I see mounds of scrambled eggs, two strips of bacon, and orange juice in blue plastic glasses. Then I see my father and me, sifting through mother's closets after her death, sending most of her clothes to Goodwill, turning some into rags.

The film unfolding in my mind takes me back to Jane Kenyon's poem. I see her face as I read. A deep channel of concern runs vertically between her eyebrows and leads me into the thoughts she captures in the poem. She has a mental image: She sees her home following her death, her dining room table without her, the television in the kitchen silent . . . suddenly an immense sadness.

An odd collection of images have merged in my mind. Jane Kenyon, a poet whose face I know only from the back of the book, stands using my orange-handled scissors in the dining room and kitchen of my earliest years. Knowing she died of cancer brings my mother into this picture, a presence literally standing to the side, watching . . . suddenly an immense sadness.

Weeks later I am in my writing room, my basement office. Alone in the house, I go back to read the poem with this chapter on my mind. This time my eyes move over the last word in every line. My friend, poet Georgia Heard, suggested this technique as a way to look at a poem through a new lens. A very different collection of images arises: Out, up, opening, breast, rectangles, sadness, news, oil, air, bombed, fish, string, oranges. Small words.

The old man with my grandfather's face comes to my mind again, this time surrounded by chaos and movement, but no sound. He shuffles silently through the street, the string of his shoe box cutting into the fingers of his cracked hands. People dart about him, intent, fearful, silent. He is not afraid. A siren's wail three blocks from my home enters my image—the only sound—then disappears. The weight of those three, small, hard, green oranges rests somewhere in my knuckles as my fingers move across the keyboard of my computer.

An amalgam of images influenced by the two weeks between the readings creates my personal meaning for this poem. The poem starts to feel like an old friend. I picture myself revisiting it. Its familiarity will be soothing, like an old flannel nightgown, cozy but laden with indelible images, some comforting, some disturbing.

One of my great passions is to sit on benches in museums—the Metropolitan or Frick in New York, the National Gallery in Washington—in front of a painting that touches my soul. I look and write and look and write and look again. During those museum forays, I find a different rhythm.

I've concluded that the sensory images that surface as we read are a type of Impressionism of the mind. The images are like dabs of paint on a canvas. Just as each brush stroke is meaningless until the viewer stands back to regard the whole painting, each image created in the mind while reading has little meaning unless we associate it with words on the page and with other images and memories in our lives.

If we stand very close to an Impressionist painting, we see a blur of dots and abrupt brush strokes that leaves us with no sense of form or character. As we move back, we gain perspective and clear images arise for our interpretation. When we view the painting for a prolonged time or return for a second look, our response deepens to something more profound and lasting. When we remember it or try to describe it later, the meaning is more fully developed still. Similarly, the images that spring to mind as we read are a part of understanding the whole text, but the perspective gained from rereading, writing about, or discussing that text adds to the images from the first reading and enhances the meaning.

Standing back from a book to reflect on images as we stand back from a painting permits us to create an amalgam of the printed word and our own images. That amalgam—the conclusion we draw, the interpretation we create—is our very personal rendition of text.

An image, like a paint stroke, means little alone but becomes a memory associated with a text in the mind of a reader. My orange-handled scissors and well-worn nightgown—images in my mind as I read "Three Small Oranges"—mean little alone, but when associated with this poem, they anchor a meaning for the poem in my memory. It becomes personal. Images of my flannel nightgowns are forever altered by Jane Kenyon cutting hers into rags. For me her poem also holds a permanent space for the faces of my grandfather and mother.

I collect museum catalogs—the vast, heavy inventories of exhibits I have seen and want to remember. My collection began in 1982. Jan Dole and I spoke at an International Reading Association conference in Chicago. Jan introduced me to the Art Institute of Chicago and, after that introduction, I saw little of the conference. The book Jan gave me is filled with beautiful representations of Impressionist paintings from the museum's vast collection.

It rests on my desk now, open to a painting, *Uncle and Niece* by Edgar Degas (Portrait of Henri and Lucy de Gas–c. 1870). Like the words in Jane Kenyon's poem and the images triggered in my mind as I read it, the fragments of this painting—a child's ear, papers laid on the table, a window with green just outside it—are indistinct and appear unfinished. The vibrancy and meaning of the painting, like the meaning in a text, only become clear after considering and reconsidering the whole.

The child and her uncle are dressed in black that blends into one garment as the girl pauses behind his chair. They both look toward the viewer, but in different directions, as if their minds were occupied by different thoughts, though they are within a foot of each other. They seem accustomed to the presence of the other, but not completely comfortable with it. There is the sadness of age in the red around the uncle's eyes and a wistful boredom in the tilt of the child's head. According to the catalog, she is an orphan, he a bachelor raising his brother's child.

In looking at the painting, I hear the rustle of his newspaper, smell smoke from the cigar he holds in his left hand, feel the smooth, curved wood of the chair the child leans tentatively against and the chafing of her neck under her stiff white collar. There is longing implied in both sets of eyes—perhaps that is what occupies them at this moment captured by Degas. There is a resignation in the still air around them. They are each other's life now.

The painting conjures images from the senses and from emotions. When we view a painting again, new images and meanings are added to our existing impressions. So it is with images from text. Images originate in our senses and our emotional fabric. And they are altered each time we read or reflect on a text, if we pause long enough to pay attention to them.

Curious that some of my most vivid recollections of teaching children to use images to comprehend text come back to me in impressionistic smatterings. I remember a mini lesson I've taught in several grade levels, conferences I've had with children about their images, times I've pushed children to articulate their images and talk about how that process helps them understand text more fully. I recall watercolors children have painted to represent their images from books and moments when children have written vividly about their images.

What I remember most is that—for children and adults—text comes alive through the creation of sensory images. Those images take on a three-dimensional character in our minds and connect us personally, often permanently with the text.

When I was a staff developer in the Douglas County Schools, Enid Goldman, a teacher at Parker Junior High, asked me to conduct a demonstration lesson on evoking images as part of a comprehension strategy study her eighth-graders were beginning. I decided to use a picture book, *Where the River Begins* by Thomas Locker, to help the students describe sensory images I was sure they'd had, but to which they probably hadn't paid conscious attention. *Where the River Begins* starts with a young boy asking where the river that runs near his house begins. With his brother, father, and grandfather, he explores the question and hikes to the river's source.

The morning of my visit to Parker Junior High, I awoke before five, tortured by my own sensory images of a class of eighth-graders responding to the oral reading of a picture book. At Parker I watched as twenty-five eighth-graders shuffled into the room, dragging their feet over dirty linoleum, and flopped into their chairs, studies in lethargy.

I asked myself, "Am I really going to read a picture book to these kids?" "Why did I agree to do this?," while at the same time, they posed their own questions: "Who's she?" "Is she a sub?" The elementary teacher in me marveled at the size of the feet that shot out in front of all those desks in rows; I got out my picture book, anticipating the students' comments.

They did not disappoint. "That book is for little kids," "C'mon, what's this for?" and "Do we have to sit here and listen to you read; we can read, you know," lasted only a moment, though. I removed the jacket from the book and held it close so none of the illustrations, each an original oil painting by the author/artist, were visible. While the students concentrated on looking like they were not listening, I read the whole book; then reread a few pages before looking up and beginning to think out loud about the images Locker's words had created in my mind. I tried to be as detailed as I could in my think-aloud, and tried to include sensory images from the hearing, tasting, and touching realms as well as the visual.

A few pages later I invited the students to share their images. The offerings were pretty meager. I glanced at Enid, who raised her eyebrows dispiritedly. I read on and again asked the students to describe the pictures that came to their minds, knowing that the propensity to create vivid images during reading correlates highly with overall comprehension.

Roberta raised her hand and said, "Well, I see them by the river, they're walking along and they have backpacks."

I paused. "What are they wearing?" I asked.

"Ummm. Shorts."

"What color, length? Do they have belts on? Are they wearing hiking boots, hats? Do they have sunglasses on? Are the three dressed the same? Do they have T-shirts or sweatshirts?" As I took a breath, the snickering died down.

"Oh . . ." Roberta said, as if she had never thought about elaborating her image. "Well, the grandfather is mostly bald and he's wearing, you know, those old army pants . . . fatigues, that's it and the boys are around twelve and fourteen and the older one is mad at the younger one all the time. They have on shorts and tennis shoes, but their grandfather has told them (this wasn't in the book) that it was dumb to wear shorts and sneakers because their feet will get all wet and their legs will be all scratched up, but they didn't listen and now their feet are wet because the ground near the river is all marshy and stuff."

Enid and I exchanged another glance. I let out a quiet sigh of relief.

Other students followed with their images. I challenged them to hear, touch, taste, and smell, but mostly to pay attention to the emotional content of the images.

Mark began a little sheepishly, "I'm making this up, you know."

"We know, Mark," I said, "But it's really not making it up. You're taking what you remember from the book and pausing to focus on what's really happening. The more detailed your images, the more the book will stay in your memory. Since you can't create detailed images for everything in the book, really focus on the parts you consider most important to the overall meaning. Create images for those sections of any book you read."

"Okay," he began, "I think that this grandfather maybe took this same hike when he was younger. Now he's, like, getting old and he wants his grandsons to see what he saw before he dies. That's really not in the book, but that's something my grandfather would do. Is that an image?"

"Yes!" I assured him.

These kids showed us that images come from the emotions as well as the senses. Readers take the words from the page and stretch and sculpt them until the richness of the story becomes the richness of a memory replete with senses and emotions. Words on the page become recollections anchored in an unforgettable image of one's own making.

It was a brilliantly sunny morning. I had hoped for rain. Colorado's piercing blue sky framed new green leaves as I looked out the expanse of windows that line Paige Inman's kindergarten classroom in a southwest Denver school. Many of the older Denver schools have wonderful kindergarten rooms that are full of light, encircled by whimsical paintings of book characters on the walls, and big enough to create cozy learning nooks all around the room. Paige has made the most of hers.

Her twenty-eight students burst through the door full of the energy of spring, delighting in one of the first days of the year that they didn't need coats.

Without any instruction from Paige, the children headed for the center of the room and formed a circle, sitting on the floor in the meeting area. Paige and I joined them.

The children knew each day begins with books. Charts of the books they've read and language they have loved from those books hang on the walls—testaments to what is valued in this classroom. On this day, we added a book, *What Does the Rain Play?* by Nancy White Carlstrom, to the growing spring list. I had hoped for rain.

I began the mini lesson that day by reading the book from beginning to end once, sharing the pictures and reading slowly. "When the little boy walks home up the steep steep hill high above the bay, and fog hides the bridge as boats rock in and out of mist, what does the rain play? Swish swish swiffle swish. When the little boy gets home and carries the drips inside to his careful cat, Albert who purrs by his side, and bread bakes in the oven, steaming up the kitchen windows the little boy writes his name on, what does the rain play? Tippita drippita tippita Jon."

We read the book again, together this time. Paige and I turned to face each other and sat cross-legged, modeling for the children what we would ask them to try. I read three or four pages and stopped for Paige to think out loud about the images that surfaced in her mind. She read another three or four pages, then paused to let me think aloud.

"When the little boy practices piano and his mother reads and drinks tea and his father sketches pictures of the sailing trip they took last summer, what does the rain play? Plink, plink! Sip sip! Slipper slip!"

I looked up and said, "I love the part you just read, Paige, because I used to play the piano and I can sort of hear, in my mind, the notes the little boy is practicing and I can smell his mother's tea and sort of picture her mug steaming on the table as she reads. And even though the book didn't exactly say this, I'll bet sometimes she looks up from her book and says, 'Try that again, Jon' and then he has to practice that one song again. And, quietly in the background, I can hear rain and it feels sort of cozy, like when you really want it to rain or snow because your whole family is safe inside and all the pets are safe and you know you don't have to go outside at all."

Paige nodded and we switched roles, working our way through the book.

As we read, we modeled by thinking aloud, referring to each kind of image as we went. When I mentioned an image I could smell, Paige responded very explicitly, "Ellin, you had an image you could smell! I could smell the bread baking a few pages ago." She made clear that images emanate from all the different senses, as well as from emotion.

When we described an image anchored in our own past, we spoke explicitly about it, showing the children that images are spawned by the text, but are linked to our experiences. After the little boy in the book crawls into bed hearing, "Ping! Ping! Ping in the pan on the bedroom floor. Ping in the singing pan!" Paige spoke of the sound of rain on the tin roof of a cabin in her childhood.

For the third reading of this short book, we asked the children to sit as we had, facing another child, knee to knee. Paige read, without showing the illustrations, and paused twice to let the partners close their eyes as we had found ourselves doing and think aloud about the images in their minds. Some children simply retold what they had heard or seen in the book; others talked about the sounds of rain, ingeniously revealed through Carlstrom's onomatopoeic words, "tap, tap trickle slide" or "clink clink gurgle drip."

As we heard individuals move away from the literal text and describe images of their own, we stopped the group and shared the successes on the spot. Michael saw the boats in the sea. "They're like white ships," he told Brandon and then the group.

We pushed him. "Michael, where are the boats in your mind? Where are they going?"

"They're not!" Michael replied indignantly. "They're parked!"

Mandy and Tenesha added to each other's images. Mandy told Tenesha that her image at the beginning of the book was "just gray, lots of gray."

Tenesha picked up where she left off, "It's gray and the little boy is walking through puddles."

"Yeah, I do that, and my mom gets mad because I get soakin' wet," Mandy said, looping back to her own life. "I wonder if this little kid gets in trouble, too?"

Gregory saw the little boy painting in the classroom. "He's painting just blue and the other kids are doing rainbows," he said seriously.

"Do you picture the little boy in this classroom?" I asked him.

"Nope, he's in the room where I had preschool, painting with blue watercolors."

We quickly pointed out to the rest of the children that Gregory's preschool classroom had found its way into his image and, therefore, his interpretation of this book. We emphasized that good readers add to what they hear in books with remembered images from their own lives. We asked Gregory to describe the room where he pictured the boy using watercolors. As he described tables around the room and a big rocking chair in the center, other children interrupted to share different images of the classroom in the book, all based on the classroom settings of their own lives.

As the kindergartners headed back to paint their images with watercolors, tousle-haired Sammy said, "Paige, I like that upside-down part. For me it was like there was this big, giant space guy and he had this little tiny ball which was our earth, where we live, and then he tipped the world upside down!"

Paige and I looked at each other a bit puzzled. It was Paige who remembered the words on the first page of the book, "When the sky is heavy as lead and the whole world turns over, gray." Sometimes children's images aren't what we expect and they bring a new way of seeing, a new richness.

"We've just finished reading *Shiloh* and I'm not sure where I want to go next," Todd McLain told me as we sipped coffee while his fourth graders were preparing for the holiday program with the music teacher. "I really want them to select their own novels and read independently, but I know I can't read all of them and I don't know how I'm going to know if they are comprehending . . . or even reading them!"

Todd began our first conversation by telling me that he was feeling overwhelmed. He was in his second year of teaching, his first year in fourth grade. He had been tucked into an improvised and rather dismal interior room at Cottonwood Creek Elementary in the suburban Cherry Creek school district. No windows and only a flimsy partition separated his class from the next fourth grade. His head was full of creative ideas; his desk was stacked with incomplete paper work.

As we talked, I learned that Todd's class had read *Shiloh* as a group, taking turns reading orally to the whole group, discussing the book as they went, completing independent projects from a list of extension activities at the end of the unit. As he talked about it, he grew more uncomfortable. The whole process had taken too long. Some children didn't pay attention as their classmates read. Others had little personal connection to the book. Others seemed to have a difficult time following the plot. A few shared very sophisticated interpretations. Todd wished more children had found depth and meaning in the book. Those whose final projects revealed thoughtful effort were few and far between. Todd described a lethargy most students had shown toward their projects.

"The worst part of it," Todd began, and I knew what was coming, "is that during *Shiloh*, I didn't feel like I was teaching reading, and I'm beginning to realize these kids really need it. I've always heard that kids learn to read in the primary grades and read to learn in the intermediate grades. Now I realize that they are still very much learning to read and I've got to teach. I'm not sure if discussing one novel with the group is the kind of teaching they need. I want them to choose their own books next time, but I've got to have an instructional focus."

Two weeks later, after several mini lessons and demonstrations about selecting books and a great deal of book selection support from Ann Zimmer, the school's library media specialist, the students each had a novel to fly (read), and one in the hangar (a fallback in case the one they chose was inappropriately easy, difficult, or uninteresting). We set a clear, daily structure for reader's workshop.

And we set an instructional focus: Todd had decided to undertake a comprehension strategy study on evoking images during reading.

He had noticed that too many of his students didn't stick with a book long enough to develop an interest in it, and if they did, didn't notice much more than the most literally stated events in the book. There had to be a way, he reasoned, to help them engage deeply in reading, immerse themselves in language, and create vivid interpretations.

Todd wanted the children to pay closer attention to their reading, to make the characters and events real in their minds, and to be able to share their interpretations with others. He knew he couldn't just tell them to engage deeply and create vivid images; he had to model explicitly how he creates images as he reads. He knew that, over time, they would need to take responsibility to do the same thing, to take possession of the books they read by creating, being aware of, and describing their own mental images.

The mini lessons in the early weeks of the strategy study focused on teacher modeling. With the class gathered around him, Todd read from a wide variety of texts: picture books, *National Geographic* magazine, poems, even the social studies textbook. As he read, he paused to think aloud about his mental images, both sensory and emotional. He included a great deal of detail in his descriptions and emphasized how pausing to stand back and reflect on his images helped him understand the text better. He talked about how his images changed as he read further in each text and how his images helped him create his own meaning for the text.

He thought out loud about how fiction and poetry gave him more latitude in creating images and forming interpretations than the social studies text, but how visualizing events from the westward expansion chapter made it seem more real, almost like a movie in the reader's mind. He talked about how being aware of his spontaneously formed images and purposely forming other images helped him comprehend and engage more fully in what he read. He stopped to think aloud when the images ceased, pondering reasons for the breakdown in comprehension.

During these weeks the children gradually assumed responsibility for monitoring, paying attention to, and elaborating their own mental images as they read, marking the text with self-adhesive notes when they became aware of an image, and marking again when that image changed as they read further. They began to differentiate between sensory and emotional images and talked in pairs and small groups about the details of the images they saw and felt as they read.

The large group sharing time at the end of most readers' workshops focused on how awareness of images deepens comprehension and engagement. The students talked about how being aware of mental images helped them experience the detail in the books they read. They told stories about rereading sections with a particular image in mind to see how their comprehension changed with the perspective of rereading. They laughed at how wildly different students' images were about the same text.

One morning, toward the end of the sharing session, Todd noticed that Kent, one of the larger children, had a pencil sketch in front of him on the floor where the class had gathered in a circle, permitting them to see each reader who shared. Kent seemed to be deliberating about whether to volunteer to share.

On numerous occasions Kent had declared his aversion to anything having to do with reading. When visiting teachers came to the room, Kent was quick to tell them how much he hated to read. In fact he had spent many days at the beginning of the school year avoiding reading altogether. Now he actually seemed to want to share.

"Kent," Todd looked at him curiously, "what is that paper in front of you?"

"I don't know. Something I drew." A long pause followed. Kent looked down.

"I can't really see from here. Can you tell us about it?" Todd asked.

"It's from *Where the Red Fern Grows*," Kent stared at the drawing of one of the dogs from the novel. "I don't like to talk about images, so I drew mine."

When Todd and I huddled after the fourth grade trooped off to lunch, we knew we had to build on Kent's idea. "Is there life beyond sticky notes?" he laughed. "There have got to be other ways for these kids to mark and express their images."

Undoubtedly there were others in the room who would love to

sketch or create watercolor or oil pastel drawings of their images from the books they were reading. Todd was concerned about those who were reluctant to draw and preferred to discuss the images.

"Okay, we know that it's going to help their comprehension if we can get them to stand back and be aware of the images they have while they're reading," I said. "Most of them are really doing that now. We also know that, if we can get them to express the images somehow, they will develop them even further. Kent drew his. Other kids are less comfortable with drawing. So the question becomes, what are all the ways we can encourage them to describe their images?"

We decided to create literature response areas that, once the children learned how to use them, could be used throughout the rest of the year during all of the strategy studies the class undertook. During the fourth week of the evoking images strategy study, Todd created four small areas near the four corners of his classroom. Each area provided the space and different materials students could use to express images evoked during the reading of their own books. There were a limited number of spaces available in each area. Todd's goal was to set aside a thirty-minute time slot during the workshop portion of reader's workshop two to three days per week. He hoped that, eventually, the students would choose the area to represent their images based on the content of the book they were reading and the images it evoked. Todd prepared a simple form and asked the children to complete it when they finished in a literature response area. It was a half sheet of paper describing how the image they had articulated in that area enhanced their comprehension.

The Theater Corner was designed for groups of children who had read the same book or poem to dramatize images or scenes from the text. The area included a small staging area and chairs in a semicircle. There were long sheets of chart paper to use for scenery backdrops, markers, and a box of fabric scraps. Copies of poems, allegories, and picture books were available so that small groups could have a common reading experience. The Theater Corner could accommodate four actors and up to four audience members.

The Book Talk Zone consisted of six chairs clustered around a small beat-up table Todd found in the school's storage area. A cast-off table cloth was thrown over it and a small lamp provided a softer light. Up to six children could gather there to discuss images from their books. A basket of pretzels and a carton of juice and cups were available as a way to make students' visit to the book talk zone authentic and more intimate.

The Artist's Studio had different sizes of unlined paper, markers, crayons, oil pastels, watercolors, and brushes. The class easel was set up in a corner and the walls in the area were stripped of everything so that paintings could be hung in the area. Children who did not want to paint at the easel took art materials back to their desks.

The Writer's Den had all the equipment needed by writers—different kinds of paper, staplers, hole punchers, pencils, pens, lined and unlined paper, etc. As written responses to books accumulated, they were framed with construction paper and hung around the den, letting students read the responses of other students, as well as write their own.

Todd introduced each area by dividing the class into four groups and stationing them in each area of the room while he read scenes from Cynthia Rylant's *Appalachia* aloud. He paused and asked each group to begin by sharing images with the other members of the group. Once the images had been shared and elaborated, each group went about responding to the book and the shared images.

The dramatic group performed a theatrical interpretation of the scene; the artists went to work to represent their images with paint, pencils, or pastels; the book talk group shared and expanded upon each other's images; and in the writer's den, images were recorded and shared. Todd repeated this process each day for four days until all of the children had a sense of how each area would operate. After the practice sessions the groups talked about the rough spots: what additional materials were needed in the area, how to involve students who didn't participate fully or handle those who tended to dominate, how to keep the activities closely linked to the book, and whether to share with the whole class.

By the conclusion of the strategy study, most of the kinks had been worked out of the literature response areas. Todd was able to assess the depth of students' use of images as a tool to better understand text. He was also able to observe and draw important conclusions about the children's overall comprehension through their periodic representations of images in the response areas.

The literature response areas did require a great deal of time in the early going. Not only did the materials and resources have to be gathered, organized, and introduced, the procedures for using each area had to be amended several times. The class finally formed committees to draw up procedures lists for each area, and in time, the four areas became part of the everyday fabric of the classroom—not so much an activity as a means for expression and exploring the meaning of books. The children's work from each area was sent home following each comprehension strategy study, providing parents with a glimpse into the authentic ways in which children in Todd's classroom represent what they understand when they read.

We have all walked into a movie made from a favorite book and been overcome with disappointment. They just didn't get it right. It's hard to stay seated. The visual images are too far from those we carried in our minds—and cherished—as we read.

Boris Pasternak's *Doctor Zhivago* and Katherine Anne Porter's *Ship of Fools* are two of my favorite novels, books that create poignant, tangible, gritty visual images. For me Omar Sharif and Julie Christie were perfectly cast as Yuri and Lara. They captured the passion, the complexity, of the characters and the era depicted in Pasternak's epic work. My strong mental images were confirmed, even enhanced, by that movie.

In the movie version of *Ship of Fools*, however, my images were thwarted. Among other things, the older, too brittle, Vivien Leigh didn't work as Mrs. Treadwell, and the blonde, by then stocky, Simone Signoret was miscast as the Spanish Condesa. The movie destroyed my imaginary characters. Its portrayal clashed too much with what I'd carried in my mind. I couldn't finish it.

We each have examples of movies of favorite books that work or don't work for us, some that actually leave us with an "aha" of deeper understanding, and others that dampen our imaginations and stifle interpretations.

In reading, our images take on a life of their own, a three-dimensionality, a meaning, a vividness—often without our consciously knowing it. The images are evolutionary, changing over time, developing organically like a tree whose trunk thickens and branches spread.

Sometimes we've read a book too quickly or without full attention. Years later we reread it only to be amazed at the depth and range of our response to words that before meant little to us. Or we read something and at first see only one aspect of it, but find our eyes opened through a discussion with others that gives us much more vibrant and profound images.

We have all known students who, as they grow older, begin to censor and limit their images as they read. They focus only on literal meanings—narrow, dictionary-type definitions of each word read. It is as if they have been taught to think that only the dabs of paint and brush strokes matter; though when they were younger, their imaginations were intact and they were full of vivid images. Too often in school they've been conditioned to pay attention only to the literal interpretation of text. When that happens, something critical is lost.

Understanding, attending to, and developing a personal awareness of the sensory and emotional images that arise from reading give students the flexibility and capacity to experience an added depth of interpretation. It allows a passionate, individual response and makes the text memorable by anchoring it to personal experience.

If Jane Kenyon had chosen to end the lines of her poem, "Three Small Oranges," with different words, if I didn't know she died from leukemia, if my own experiences were different, my images would have been different, and therefore, my comprehension of the poem different. The act of writing about my images—specifically for this book—altered and enhanced them. I considered them purposefully as I constructed a meaning for the poem, yet that meaning is dynamic. When I reread the poem the next time, new images will be assimilated into those I have described.

For writers, images allow infinite possibilities of expression; for readers, the mental images derived from what they've read connect them personally to the texts, over time coalescing into a self-awareness, complexity, and depth which is at the core of being human.

Evoking Images in the Reader's Workshop: Some Key Ideas

- Proficient readers spontaneously and purposefully create mental images while and after they read. The images emerge from all five senses, as well as the emotions, and are anchored in a reader's prior knowledge.
- Proficient readers use images to immerse themselves in rich detail as they read. The detail gives depth and dimension to the reading, engaging the reader more deeply, making the text more memorable.
- Proficient readers use images to draw conclusions, to create distinct and unique interpretations of the text, to recall details significant to the text, and to recall a text after it has been read. Images from reading frequently become part of the reader's writing. Images from a reader's personal experience frequently become part of his or her comprehension.
- Proficient readers adapt their images as they continue to read. Images are revised to incorporate new information revealed through the text and new interpretations as they are developed by the reader.
- Proficient readers understand how creating images enhances their comprehension.
- Proficient readers adapt their images in response to the shared images of other readers.

A Sample Comprehension Strategy Study Using the Gradual Release of Responsibility Model: Evoking Images

- The teacher begins by modeling—the goal is to help students understand and witness ways in which evoking images enhances comprehension. The teacher should be very specific about how standing back to reflect upon his or her images helps the reader to understand more and to understand the text deeply.

· The teacher begins with short, probably fiction, selections and limits the mini lessons to her or his own thinking aloud and explanations about how evoking images improves comprehension. The process of modeling should be almost entirely teacher directed in the early mini lessons.

· Gradually the teacher invites students to share and expand their own images created as he or she reads. Most mini lessons at this stage will be done with interesting, but relatively unchallenging text with the whole class. The emphasis for students is on awareness of their own images, elaborating upon them, and developing a sense that reflecting on one's images enhances comprehension.

· In conferences, the teacher begins to focus on images children have when reading. He or she asks children to read and think aloud about their images and helps them to distinguish between images that are critical to understanding the text and those details in images that may be interesting, but not critical to understanding the text as a whole.

· In sharing sessions children begin to share images evoked as they read independently and how those images helped them to comprehend.

· The teacher continues to model in the large group mini lessons, demonstrating how reflecting upon images is different in different genres.

· The teacher meets with small invitational groups to support children who need more instruction and modeling in order to make the connection between awareness of their images and comprehension.

· Students may use different response options (artistic, dramatic, written, or spoken) to depict their images.

· The teacher should collect depicted images (in any form)

from each child over the course of the six to eight week study and assess changes in the images. Key elements to assess are images that are central to understanding key points in the text rather than peripheral details; images that are detailed and richly descriptive; images that extend and enhance the text; images that come from all the senses and the emotions; images that are adapted and revised as the child reads or on the basis of conversations with others; and images from text that find new life in the child's writing.

EIGHT

The Intersection of Meaning
Inferring

Inferring

We who lived in concentration camps can remember the men who walked through the huts comforting others, giving away their last piece of bread. They may have been few in number, but they offer sufficient proof that everything can be taken from a man but one thing: the last of the human freedoms—to choose one's attitude in any given set of circumstances, to choose one's own way.

A thought transfixed me: for the first time in my life I saw the truth as it is set into song by so many poets, proclaimed as the final wisdom by so many thinkers. The truth—that love is the ultimate and the highest goal to which man can aspire. Then I grasped the meaning of the greatest secret that human poetry and human thought and belief have to impart: The salvation of man is through love and in love. I understood how a man who has nothing left in this world still may know bliss, be it only for a brief moment, in the contemplation of his beloved. In a position of utter desolation, when man cannot express himself in positive action, when his only achievement may consist in enduring his sufferings in the right way—an honorable way—in such a position man can, through loving contemplation of the image he carries of his beloved, achieve fulfillment.

VIKTOR E. FRANKL,
Man's Search for Meaning

I lay in bed, throwing the covers off as I broke into a sweat, only to shiver moments later in the 95 degree heat—the hottest June on record. I stopped taking my temperature when the mercury refused to descend below 102 degrees. I slept fitfully, whole days dissolving without a memory. David and Elizabeth's movements in and out of the room left only peripheral images in my mind.

A misdiagnosis had led to treating what turned out to be pneumonia with the wrong medication for two weeks. I sank deeper and deeper into the illness and began to lose track of time. When a correct diagnosis was made, I had lost four weeks of the summer and it was six more weeks until I fully recovered.

As I lay in bed battling with myself over the loss of those weeks—the time I'd wasted, the work I should have been doing, the fun I was missing with my family—Susan suggested I read Viktor Frankl's *Man's Search for Meaning*, a book published after Frankl's release from Auschwitz.

This was not a serendipitous suggestion. Susan saw how frustrated and depressed I was. She had recently reread the book and it had, she told me, given her a deep sense of hope and comfort. Since first reading the book in the early seventies, Susan's life had taken many turns. Rereading it created deeper and more lasting impressions. A new meaning of the book, directly tied to her life as a mother, had taken shape.

"When I read it the first time, it was powerful, but hypothetical. I remember trying to put myself in the position of an inmate in a concentration camp, but having no success really. This time, I read it differently. I could intimately feel what Frankl was saying. I didn't try to experience what he'd gone through, but felt it from what I'd gone through. At times the book sounds almost simplistic, but it's a simplicity wrought from unbelievable sorrow and loss. Frankl's outlook is inspiring." Susan handed me her battered copy. "It'll give you a different perspective."

That summer day Susan wanted me to think about Frankl's underlying message: that even under the most horrendous conditions, one has the power to choose one's own attitude. No one can take away that power, no matter how horrific the situation, no matter how extreme the pain and loss. While very different, Susan's experience had given her a personal understanding of Frankl's words.

Susan's oldest child, Katherine, now sixteen, has Rett syndrome, a debilitating condition that has left a child, who developed normally until around her first birthday, profoundly handicapped. Her simplest needs must be met for her. She is one of the most helpless people I've ever met; but, because of her family's response to her, one of the most powerful.

At the time of my illness, Susan was writing a book about her journey with Katherine. Searching for meaning in her life experience, she wrote of the sorrow, the shattered dreams, and the intense efforts she and her family undertook to help Kat recover. She wrote of periods of despair and helplessness, of the heroic strangers who came into their lives to work with Katherine, of how, after great struggle, she came to understand Kat's gifts, and of how Kat's unpredictable and life-altering condition gave added meaning to the rest of the family.

For fifteen years the reality of feeding, bathing, changing, and carrying Katherine from room to room provided a sobering backdrop to Susan's life. Slowly, by acknowledging that Katherine has a profound and powerful effect on those who interact with her, Susan began to extract a larger meaning from her daughter's life. Through the process of her own writing, a new interpretation evolved—one that did not in any way match the hopes and dreams parents have for their children, but one that permitted a deep understanding of the power of love and the dignity of all human life.

So it is with reading. We are bound, to an extent, by the print on a given page, as Susan and her family are bound by the constraints of Katherine's life. Katherine will never walk, talk, or feed herself. That is the literal reality. Yet her gifts are significant and the interpretation of her life through Susan's book, *Grief Dancers: A Journey into the Depths of the Soul,* is a contribution to all who have experienced loss. When we read, we stretch the limits of the literal text by folding our experience and belief into the literal meanings in the text, creating a new interpretation, an inference.

Inference is part rational, part mystical, part definable, and part beyond definition. Individuals' life experiences, logic, wisdom, creativity, and thoughtfulness, set against the text they are reading, form the crux of new meaning. Because each person's experiences are different, the art of inferring takes the reader beyond the text to a place only he or she can go.

At the time Susan reread *Man's Search for Meaning*, she went to it for a reason: She was just starting to write about Kat and was feeling terribly trapped. She'd remembered the wisdom of the book and thought it might help her come to terms with the prospect of a lifetime of caring for her handicapped daughter. At that time she wrote:

> I have thought a lot about the word freedom recently and it took me back to *Man's Search for Meaning*. When I read it, I was struck by how a man could be in the most confined, evil place ever imagined and yet feel free in his mind. The book is beautifully written because it is close to the bone. There is nothing extra there, because in the concentration camp everything was stripped away, everything except that rare ability one has to shape one's own attitude. Freedom is a state of mind and nothing more, I think. And in our minds we can be as free or as trapped as we decide we want to be. I am enslaved by Katherine if I allow myself to view Kat that way. I am also freed by her—freed to see life differently, to love differently.
>
> I suppose those who really recognize Frankl's truth shape the reality around them on a minute by minute basis and are enlightened in the true sense. Maybe that's what Christ and Buddha did, and why they were so unutterably magnetic to others. (1993)

Frankl's message—that in deepest despair, we have a choice; we can search for a slender hope, one bright memory, one beloved person, one joyful moment, and in doing so, create a positive and valuable meaning for ourselves—is elegant, simple, and profound when considered in light of some of life's greatest challenges. When Susan reread his book in a different life circumstance, she had new connections, new conclusions, new inferences.

When we read, we can limit our interpretations to the dictates of the text, the literal reality of the text. But there is more. In *Man's*

Search for Meaning, we find a personal strength through learning how others coped with suffering—in Frankl's case the ultimate suffering of a concentration camp and the deaths of those he most loved.

To infer as we read is to go beyond literal interpretation and to open a world of meaning deeply connected to our lives. We create an original meaning, a meaning born at the intersection of our background knowledge (schema), the words printed on a page, and our mind's capacity to merge that combination into something uniquely ours. We go beyond the literal and weave our own sense into the words we read. As we read further, that meaning is revised, enriched, sometimes abandoned, based on what we continue to read.

That summer as I read Frankl's words, "to choose one's attitude in any given set of circumstances, to choose one's own way," my first thoughts were literal and cynical. I was so sick and there was little I could do to rush my progress. I had to wait and as I waited, I could almost hear my mother talking to me about "maintaining a positive attitude at all times." Mentally, I snarled at her, indulging my frustration and self-pity, but I read on. "In a position of utter desolation, when man cannot express himself in positive action, when his only achievement may consist in enduring his sufferings in the right way—an honorable way—in such a position man can, through loving contemplation of the image he carries of his beloved, achieve fulfillment."

I read with horror of Frankl's most desperate moments when day after day he was forced to do back-breaking concentration camp labor—labor so excruciating and unrelenting that many of those around him died from it. I read on as he described how while working, starved and exhausted, he could turn deep within himself and actually create joy by recalling past images of his family.

In those weeks of my pneumonia, I also read the drafts of Susan's book, *Grief Dancers* (1996). In it, Susan tells her story through the images of her life with Kat, those things she could not forget: a floppy blue doll Kat had once loved, a plastic activity center, a potty high chair, their first camping trip, Kat's thirteenth birthday. Between the images, she weaves her learnings from Kat.

She writes, "When we are in the depths of pain and everything around us has become tasteless, we try to bury the images that remind us of our loss, to force them back into the box that holds our sorrow, but they erupt at unexpected times and leave us shaking. If we help them out, if we bring them forth and make them a part of our stories, finally, with time's passing, we are able to see the drama and beauty of our lives."

As I lay in my bed reading the words "the box that holds the images of our sorrow," my eyes left the page and rested as if for the first time on a small wooden chair that has been in my bedroom for years. At that moment, I also left the literal meaning of that page and found a meaning of my own. My eyes followed the curves of the chair and I recalled pulling it to the side of my mother's bed where she lay in the final stages of her battle with leukemia. The funny little chair that came from my grandparents' home, found its way to my parents' home and later to mine, is part of the image of sorrow I carry. Susan's words opened that box.

My memories of sitting in the chair with my feet on my mother's bed, talking for hours or sitting in the same position listening to her halting breaths as she drifted in and out of sleep bring to my reading of this passage an entirely original interpretation—one that no other reader will create.

Good writing does that. It permits the reader to create an original, and therefore memorable, interpretation of the book. If my comprehension of Frankl's book or Susan's passage had been limited to a literal interpretation, chances are good that I wouldn't have remembered the passage. If I had thought, "Okay, this is about making the best out of whatever life hands you and trying to be positive in difficult circumstances" and that was the extent of my comprehension, I wouldn't have remembered it. But my thoughts, winding around a little wooden chair and my own experiences, took me far beyond the literal and made both texts unforgettable.

The passage containing the words "the box that holds our sorrow" (and where I was when I read it) brought to mind a visual image and prior knowledge—me sitting in a chair talking with my mother—that caused me to remember the tone and substance of my final conversations with my mother. That recollection linked back to

Susan's words, "the drama and beauty of our lives" which made me realize I had created an entirely new interpretation for the short passage she had written. There was drama in those final days with my mother. The conversations we had would be our last and we knew it. It added an intensity and strangely slowed the pace of the conversations.

There was also beauty. Susan's words permitted me to recall the intimacy, the humor, the joy, even the hope I had felt during those conversations. I realize now that I didn't hold out hope she would survive the cancer, but came to believe I would have a life after she died. I knew I was learning the most important lessons of my life as we talked.

Now, years after I first read Susan's book, I know I would have remembered it no matter who wrote it because my mind soared beyond the obvious and used the words and their literal meaning to propel me into inference—an opportunity to sense a meaning not necessarily explicit in the text, but which derives or flows from it. Each time I read that little passage, my mind works with it and I learn something more, something new. It helps me reinterpret and learn from my life experiences. It helps me to infer.

I remember now the combined effect of reading those two books and turning inward to quell my own much less significant anger and restlessness with a new interpretation, a conclusion, a prediction—all inferences that made it possible to endure my frustration, consider the experience in a way that restored my typical high energy, productive manner, and move toward healing. Frankl's monumental experience and Susan's daily challenges put my illness—from which I knew I would recover completely—in perspective and left me with a sense of gratitude and calm.

Knowing this about my own reading leads me to wonder if we create learning situations in which children can infer and, therefore, learn and remember. Not everything that is read can or should be remembered. Often learning is embedded in the process of determining importance (Chapter 5). The reader makes judgments about what must be remembered, what can be forgotten. As a society, we may disagree about what we want children to remember, but none would disagree that there is critical content to be learned, recalled, and reapplied in new situations.

Inferring is a tool we use to go beyond the text, to leverage prior knowledge and create connections among various details and concepts we have learned, to draw conclusions based on the text and our full array of life experience and knowledge. Without inferring, we may be condemned to remember only phone numbers, padlock combinations, and plant names.

When I visit classrooms and observe teachers who ask children to recall endless literal detail from what they've read, I ask myself, what is the consequence when children comprehend (and listen) only for the literal meaning or just the facts? The price may be nothing less than the inability to recall important content. We wring our hands over children who seem to remember and reapply little of what they have read. Yet how often do we create the context for them to discuss, ponder, argue, restate, reflect, persuade, relate, write about, or otherwise work with the information we consider critical for them to recall? To push beyond the literal text, to make it personal and three-dimensional, to weave it into our own stories—*that* is to infer.

I recently read Benjamin Bradlee's autobiography, *A Good Life: Newspapering and Other Adventures*. A portion of the book chronicles Bradlee's experiences as executive editor of the Washington Post (1968–1991) during the Pentagon Papers and Watergate controversies. As I read, I became enthralled. I couldn't stop. I read during breakfast and while friends spent New Year's Day at our home. I pretended I wasn't home when the phone rang.

Why was I so captivated by this book? I love newspapers, but have never been a journalist. I was fourteen in 1972 and remember little of the Watergate scandal. I grew up in a politically active family, but there are few direct connections between this book and my life.

In addition to being captivated by the man, I slowly began to realize that Bradlee's recollections were a study in leadership. The book is about an old-fashioned kind of leadership that is authentic and unselfconscious. It is about gritty, honest leadership built upon Bradlee's knowledge, experiences, and his uninhibited search for truth in journalism. His bold and impertinent style, egotistical and brash, nonetheless inspired and empowered those around him.

The word leadership was probably not mentioned in relation to him once in five hundred pages, but as I reluctantly read the last pages, I knew that Bradlee's words expanded my views about leading and stretched my understanding and practice as a leader. I recognized part of me in him and smiled to myself as he got himself into and out of quagmires that sounded all too familiar. The inferences I made as I read would have a lasting effect on my work.

I also argued with Bradlee as I read, another type of inference. I doubted, was skeptical, and recognized what I believed was too much poetic license here and there throughout the book. I mentally sparred with Bradlee as I read about his relationships with women, his three marriages, the way in which one wife conveniently folded into history as the prospect for a new relationship arose.

As I read, I felt I knew this man, that I could predict his course of action in different situations, and see errors in judgment coming before he made them. I literally stopped and reflected on choices I might have made in his circumstances. I read paragraphs aloud to David and used information from the book to build my arguments when we engaged in our (frequent) political conversations.

Inferring has many facets and great books provoke us to consider and use them all. An inference can be a conclusion drawn after considering what is read in relation to one's beliefs, knowledge, and experience. Inference can be a critical analysis of a text: a mental or expressed argument with an author, an active skepticism about what is stated in the text, or a recognition of propaganda. Inference is, in some situations, synonymous with learning and remembering. It is the process of taking that which is stated in text and extrapolating it to one's life to create a wholly original interpretation that, in turn, becomes part of one's beliefs or knowledge. But an inference is also the play of imagination as we mentally expand text. Predictions are inferences. We base a prediction on what has been stated in the text, but we add to it an informed guess about what is to come.

Inference is a mosaic, a dazzling constellation of thinking processes, but the tiles available to form each mosaic are limited, circumscribed. There must be a fusion of words on the page—and the constraints of meaning they impose—and the experience and knowledge of the reader. In an inference the whole is greater than the sum of the (literal) parts. Inferences result in the creation of personal meaning.

I recall a conversation about inferring with a group of teachers in an after-school study group. Several teachers argued for a hierarchical approach to teaching children to infer. Children need to comprehend at the literal level first, they asserted, then we can teach them to read between the lines. Other concerns surfaced: Are young children developmentally capable of the abstract thought of inference? What about all we've heard about the *literal* young child?

Whether children must literally understand before they can infer, is, I think, the wrong question. For me, the question is how do we use the literal—the words printed on the page—to propel children to conclusions, predictions, and unique interpretations? The conversation reached an impasse.

I suggested we explore, together, what young children can do. We decided to bring a first-grader from the school's extended day program into our next study group meeting. We could observe the child and teach her explicitly how proficient readers make inferences. Together, we would have the opportunity to explore a number of questions: Can young children predict? Can they imaginatively expand a story in their minds thereby creating their own meaning? Can they argue with the facts as they are stated? Can they question the conclusions drawn by other readers?

"Christina is unflappable," her teacher had assured me. I hoped so, as Christina and I sat at a table encircled by more than a dozen teachers. The after-school air in the library was stagnant, late February air which made me long for the first spring breeze that would permit the windows to be thrown open. Christina looked wary and weary. It had been a long day. We chatted as the teachers gathered around us,

154

notebooks in hand. They would jot down examples as I assessed Christina's current use of inferences and then began to teach her how proficient readers infer. Later, we would see if there had been changes in the types of inferences Christina made independently. We were condensing six to eight weeks of instruction into an hour to get a microglimpse into a young child's ways of inferring.

"Okay, Christina, we're going to start today by having you listen as I read this book, *Stellaluna*, by Janell Cannon. I want you to listen as I read several pages of the book and, when I stop for a moment, tell me as much as you can about it. After I read every two or three pages I will ask you to think aloud, and that means that I want you to tell me everything that is in your mind about the book while I was reading, even if some of your thoughts aren't exactly about the characters and events in the book. What do you think?"

Christina sat as straight as she could on the wooden chair and listened intently as I read. When I stopped the first time, I asked her to tell me what she had been thinking while I read.

"I don't know, I couldn't think. I had to pay attention to the book. The owl knocked Stellaluna out of the air." Indeed, that event was explicitly described in the text and she recalled it accurately. There was no connection, however, that permitted a deeper conclusion. I continued to read. Several pages later, I stopped again and asked her to predict what was going to happen next.

"She's kind of like turning into a bird, but she's a bat?" The prediction came in the form of a question and indicated that Christina was comprehending the sequence of events in the story.

"Does that make you think of anything, Christina?"

"No."

"Okay, let's keep reading."

Christina's responses bordered on frustration as I stopped at several other points in the book. I asked her what she thought the author meant by phrases such as "the three anxious birds went home without [Stellaluna]." Focusing her attention on one section of text led to slightly more successful inferences, but she still wasn't using background knowledge and context to draw a conclusion about the word anxious.

"Oh, that means they thought, 'oh well, she's a bat, she can take care of herself, but we need a mom,' " Christina said.

At the conclusion of the book, I asked Christina if she thought there were any important messages the author wanted her readers to understand—messages the author thought were important, but hadn't stated directly in the book. Christina thought a moment and replied, "The author liked bats and birds and he thought it might be good if bats and birds got together and made friends to make a book."

Christina had been so absorbed with understanding the gist of the text, she had devoted little thought to drawing conclusions, making judgments, predictions, or otherwise thinking critically about the text.

After a snack break, we reconvened. I told Christina I was going to teach her something that great readers do and that I expected it would change what she thought about as she read.

"Christina, I want to show you something that great readers do while they're reading. It's called making an inference. An inference is a new idea that happens when a reader thinks about something that is probably true about a book. The reader can decide what is probably true because of things she has read in the book and what she already knows, her background knowledge. Inferring is a great thing for readers because inferences really help you remember what happens in a book. Inferences are like lifting ideas out of a book and adding your own ideas to them. When you do that, you really remember the idea.

"I don't exactly understand," Christina said.

"Let me show you. I'm going to read a few pages of this book *Tar Beach*. When I make an inference in my mind, I'll stop and tell you what I did, so you can see how another reader infers, okay?"

I read a few pages from *Tar Beach* by Faith Ringgold, and paused after the phrase, "the bridge was my most prized possession." I stopped and put the book down so there would be no question that what I was saying was not read from the book. The first inference I shared was in the form of a simple conclusion, yet one that children Christina's age sometimes fail to make in *Tar Beach*.

"I just made an inference, Christina. I was thinking that when Cassie says that thing about the bridge being her most prized possession on this page back here (I leafed back through the pages), she was just talking about looking around her at all she could see from the rooftop and wishing it were her own, but not really flying around and owning it. I remember thinking when I was little and my family drove down the highway that all I could see on either side of our car belonged to me. I've decided that is what she is feeling and thinking as she lies and looks around her into the night sky."

Christina replied, "Oh, you mean that you know she can't really fly because nobody can really fly, but she is probably just lying in her bed and sort of dreaming, awake dreaming you know, about flying around?" She hadn't yet grasped the concept of a tar beach—a city rooftop—but I wanted to focus on the inference she had made.

"Exactly, Christina. Do you know how we were able to make that inference? We used the actual events in the book—this little girl soaring over the bridge—and our own knowledge—people can't fly, but often want to feel like they own all they can see—to decide that she was daydreaming. What else can we decide about her? Like, can we decide from what we've read so far what kind of person she may be?"

"Yeah, I think she's a dreamer and she likes the city," Christina said.

"What else?"

"She likes to dream and she likes to imagine, like her flying around the city?"

"Wow, Christina, did the book say that she was a dreamer who likes the city?" We looked back through some of the pages. "Nope! You drew that conclusion. You listened to words like 'giant diamond necklace and sparkling beauty' to decide she likes the city skyscrapers and bridges and 'free to go wherever I want for the rest of my life' to decide that she is a dreamer. Remember when you said 'awake dreaming'? You have probably done that yourself, haven't you? When you put the words in the book together with something you have done, that's an inference." I literally told her the words from the text and the background knowledge she probably had that might have formed her inference.

"Now that you have decided what the little girl in this book is like, let's read a bit further and see if either of us has any more inferences," I said.

I paused several pages later after reading, "And mommy won't cry all winter when he (the father in the book) goes to look for work and doesn't come home."

"I have one!" Christina said.

"An inference?" I asked. Laughter from the now forgotten audience.

"Yeah. They're poor," she said.

"Christina, show me where we were in this book when you decided that." She pointed to the page where I had stopped. "How did you decide they were poor? It didn't say that in the book. How did you decide it was probably true?" I asked, using the language I used originally to define inference.

"When it said he was looking for a job and her mom was always crying."

I wasn't sure where to go next, so I said, "What else?" A long pause followed while both of us collected our thoughts and then Christina burst out, "I think she thinks he's never coming back!"

"Hmmm. How did you infer that?"

"Well sometimes when parents don't have jobs, they just go away and they never come back," Christina said.

"What does that tell you about this character, Christina?" I asked, still grasping a bit for direction.

"Maybe that her dad doesn't work in the summer so he has to get a job for the winter so they won't be so poor," Christina concluded.

An inference, to be sure, but one that began to take Christina away from the central concepts of the story. I resumed reading.

We shared several other inferences. After each I talked explicitly with Christina about what part of her conclusion had come from the book and what part from her background knowledge. I reinforced the creative aspect of inferring, assuring Christina that great readers love books even more when they can make up part of the meaning. Not only was it okay to do so, inferring would make whatever she read more interesting and easier to remember.

I asked her if she would like to try inferring on her own. I would read a book and she could stop me when she thought she had inferred. I chose Eve Bunting's *How Many Days to America?* Christina was listening rather than reading independently and I wanted a challenging enough text that would suggest a variety of inferences.

"Okay, Christina, I'll just read and pause a little after each page so you have a chance to tell me if you have an inference, but remember, great readers don't necessarily have inferences on each page."

It didn't take long. I had only read to the first sentence on the second page, "My mother hid my little sister and me under the bed" when Christina said, "Stop—I think because of the way he talks, I think he was kind of poor and didn't have a very good vocabulary."

"Can you tell me what you mean?"

"Hid my little sister and me under the bed, that doesn't sound right. He doesn't have a good vocabulary."

"Is there anything else that helped you make that inference, Christina?"

Christina paused and finally said, "The pictures?"

"The pictures made you conclude he is poor?"

"Yeah, because look at their clothes and they live in a village?"

"Are people poor if they live in a village?"

"Yeah."

I decided not to push these points. Grammatically the sentence she had referred to was correct. And, ironically, she had drawn a conclusion that was probably what the author had wanted the reader to conclude, but she had done so using inaccurate information—that people in villages are poor. Nonetheless, it was an inference. I kept reading. At the conclusion of the second page in which soldiers storm into the characters' home in an unnamed, but presumably Central American country, Christina said, almost to herself, "It could be true—there really could be soldiers." Another inference. I nodded and continued.

When the family in the book turned to look for the last time at their home, Christina interrupted, "when they had to leave their house and all their things behind, the mother was so sad, she looked like this." Christina transformed her face into a sad, lonely stare.

As I read, Christina continued to share her inferences, sometimes telling us explicitly how she had made them. "You know how the sister keeps asking questions? It's because she's real little and little people ask a lot of questions."

When at last the family in the story sighted land, Christina shared an inference she must have been holding for several pages. "They were probably tired of fish because they've been fishing a long time and they have fish every day on that boat. They are going to be glad to have something else to eat." Laughter broke the silence around us.

Christina drew several inferences from the illustrations, something I would encourage in children her age, particularly if they have difficulty inferring from text. On the second to last page, the illustration shows the family's arrival in America and a group of people waiting for them. Before the text indicated that those awaiting the boat yelled "Welcome to America!", Christina interrupted with another inference.

"They might have thought that the people there were going to hurt them or something, because of their own land." With this statement, Christina demonstrated a subtle kind of inference. She recalled information from an earlier passage and applied it to subsequent text. She understood the gravity of the situation the family left behind and worried that the same circumstances might be true in their new country. Though she didn't have background knowledge about immigration to this country that would have altered her inference, she showed empathy with the characters and, for her, a very reasonable prediction.

When we had finished the book, the teachers asked her about her inferences. To one query she responded, "You know what else? I made a whole inference for the whole book. It could all be true—I think that soldiers—I know that there have been a lot of wars and I think that this was a war against the people 'cause there really were a lot of wars so it's probably true."

Teaching children to infer often begins with a journey into our own reading, stopping ourselves when we infer, and analyzing our process as we do. Man's Search for Meaning, Grief Dancers, and A Good Life provoked dozens of inferences for me. Reading them enabled me to consider different types of inferences and their impact on my life. When considering ways to work with children, I first look to my own experience, reminding myself of the effect of inferences on my ability to recall content and to remember the life lessons I've learned from the books.

We must pay attention to the conditions in which we infer and go about creating classroom structures that permit children to discuss, ponder, argue, restate, reflect, persuade, relate, write about, or otherwise work with the words and ideas they read. And we must think about the most effective ways to entice children—especially those whose oral and written language is just developing—to express their inferences.

Why did I, when sitting down to write a chapter on inference, think of Viktor Frankl's words, "Then I grasped the meaning of the greatest secret that human poetry and human thought and belief have to impart: The salvation of man is through love and in love"? What makes an image, a passage, a book memorable? What anchors it in the mind and causes it to slip into consciousness or the conversation in a book club at the most probable or improbable moment? Is it a powerful character who stays alive in our minds, an author's style that draws us in, a conversation about the book where another's insight revealed added meaning we hadn't before contemplated?

To infer is to manipulate, to sculpt, to shape, to argue with the themes, concepts, or characters. To infer, in a pure sense, is to build meaning. We build meaning by doing something with the text. Whether that something is a quick, almost subconscious prediction, a conscious sense of outrage and indignation, a vigorous discussion in a book club, a letter to the editor, or a subtle change in one's outlook during an illness, to infer is to make text our own.

Certainly much that children read in classrooms is never sculpted and shaped, discussed and written about. Much of what we read passes through the lenses of our eyes to our brains, is comprehended superficially, and never considered again. However, as teachers we have the challenge to make sure children have the cognitive agility to consider what is worth savoring, what portion of a text has the potential to change a life, what merits discussion, what should be lingered over, argued about, and anchored in memory, because to comprehend only literally would be too great a loss.

Drawing Inferences in Text: Some Key Ideas

· Inferring is the process of creating a personal meaning from text. It involves a mental process of combining what is read with relevant prior knowledge (schema). The reader's unique interpretation of text is the product of this blending.
· When proficient readers infer, they create a meaning that is not necessarily stated explicitly in the text. The process implies that readers actively search for, or are aware of, implicit meaning.
· When they infer, proficient readers

draw conclusions from text;
make reasonable predictions as they read, test and revise those predictions as they read further;
create dynamic interpretations of text that are adapted as they continue to read and after they read;
use the combination of background knowledge and explicitly stated information from the text to answer questions they have as they read;
make connections between conclusions they draw and other beliefs or knowledge;
make critical or analytical judgments about what they read.

· When proficient readers infer, they are more able to

remember and reapply what they have read;
create new background knowledge for themselves;
discriminate and critically analyze text and authors;

engage in conversation and/or other analytical or reflective responses to what they read.

- Inferences are revised based on the inferences and interpretations of other readers.
- A wide variety of interpretation is appropriate for fiction text; a narrower range of interpretation is typical for nonfiction text. Teachers should allow great latitude for inferences, provided that the reader can defend his or her inferences with a description of relevant, prior knowledge and specific text.

NINE

The Contour and Substance of Meaning
Synthesis

Lost in the Stars

The operators of the Hubble Space Telescope announced last week that by taking photographs in deep space they have discovered the existence of forty billion galaxies (though one scientist allowed that this figure might be "somewhat imprecise"). This discovery, in turn, has led the nation's leading launderers to speculate that they have solved the still more ancient riddle of where all the socks go when they disappear from the dryer.

Dr. Robert E. Williams, director of the Space Telescope Science Institute, in Baltimore, seemed to confirm this conclusion, however cryptically, when he was quoted in the *Times* as saying that of the myriad galaxies now visible "there are large ones and small ones, red ones and blue ones." Launderers speculate that the telescope could soon pull into view an Argyle galaxy and, quite possibly, with greater focus, some sheer knee-highs.

Across the nation, formerly flummoxed consumers of hose stopped searching under beds and hampers. Indeed, experts allowed as how the new discovery could revolutionize a field in which they have invested countless hours. Linda Haddock, the manager of Immaculate Hand Laundry & Dry Cleaning, on West Seventy-second Street, declared herself amazed. "Our theory before was that the socks were stuck inside people's pants and they got lost in the dry-cleaning process," she said. "But maybe this is right. This could be the answer."

Surely the discovery of forty billion galaxies will make Alvy Singer (late of *Annie Hall* and Coney Island) the front-runner for next year's Nobel Prize for Physics (or whatever). It was Singer who, decades back, told his mother that the source of his anomie was rooted in his firm knowledge (the profound insight!) that the universe is expanding—rendering homework near to meaningless. Singer's mother was heard to respond, "What is that your business?!"

Now we know.

DAVID REMNICK,
The New Yorker, January 29, 1996

"The operators of the Hubble Space Telescope (I'm thinking, do I know much about this? Do I even care? I may not keep reading . . .) announced last week that by taking photographs in deep space they have discovered the existence of forty billion galaxies."

(Okay, I say to myself, I've heard about this. National Public Radio did a report. But how can they possibly know that it is forty billion? Does Susan really think we should use a piece about galaxies in our chapter on synthesis?) "Though one scientist allowed that this figure might be 'somewhat imprecise.'" (I like this guy's wit. I may keep reading . . .) "This discovery, in turn, has led the nation's leading launderers (What, launderers? Reread, yep, launderers) to speculate that they have solved the still more ancient riddle of where all the socks go when they disappear from the dryer." This guy is going to connect forty billion galaxies to **SOCKS**? What is he trying to say? What is his point?

"Dr. Robert E. Williams, director of the Space Telescope Science Institute, in Baltimore, seemed to confirm this conclusion, however cryptically, when he was quoted in the *Times* as saying that of the myriad galaxies now visible 'there are large ones and small ones, red ones and blue ones.' (Sounds like a jingle, sounds like bouncing balls, sounds like a nursery rhyme about . . . yes, socks. Is this the only way we humans can make sense of such a monumental discovery? We have to put it into a context we can comprehend. Socks! I'm starting

166

to love this writing.) "Launderers speculate that the telescope could soon pull into view an Argyle galaxy and, quite possibly, with greater focus, some sheer knee-highs."

"Across the nation, formerly flummoxed consumers of hose stopped searching under beds and hampers." (He conjures a great image. An entire nation heaves a sigh a relief. We can now understand the universe and give up our futile search for those socks. We can even throw the odd singles away . . . God forbid!) "Indeed, experts allowed as how the new discovery could revolutionize a field in which they have invested countless hours. Linda Haddock, the manager of Immaculate Hand Laundry & Dry Cleaning, on West Seventy-second Street, declared herself amazed. 'Our theory before was that the socks were stuck inside people's pants and they got lost in the dry-cleaning process,' she said. 'But maybe this is right. This could be the answer.' " (Here, I'm wishing the writer would go back to the galaxies. I want the two tied more closely. Is this really just about socks? What is this about? If someone stopped and asked me right now, I'd say that it is a sardonic piece linking the ordinary to the extraordinary. I guess, but is there more? I read the last paragraph.)

"Surely the discovery of forty billion galaxies will make Alvy Singer (late of *Annie Hall* and Coney Island) the front-runner for next year's Nobel Prize for Physics (or whatever)." (My eyes stop. My heart leaps. "YES!" I yell out loud and leap from my comfortable perch. *Annie Hall* is one of my five all-time favorite movies—I must have seen it forty times. I adore Alvy Singer. He makes my neuroses seem insignificant. He makes David's mother seem psychologically healthy! This is why I love *The New Yorker*. Alvy Singer!) "It was Singer who, decades back, told his mother that the source of his anomie was rooted in his firm knowledge (the profound insight!) that the universe is expanding—rendering homework near to meaningless. Singer's mother was heard to respond, 'What is that your business?!' " ("What is that your business?" I can hear her saying this. I can see her face. I want to say the phrase over and over. Now I believe this whole piece turns on that sentence. This is a piece about the futility of our lives in relation to the immensity of the universe, and that futility is funny!)

Now we know. (Now we do know. I remember the scene from *Annie Hall* so vividly. That recollection makes these five short paragraphs fit together. I have decided what this piece is about. For me, this little puzzle has four pieces. No five, I just thought of a fifth. It's about the indescribable enormity of the universe, now scientifically proven. It's about our need to translate the extraordinary into ordinary terms. It's about the inescapable frustrations of our daily lives—the missing socks and all they represent viewed in a universal (literally) context. It's about the humor and logic of a child who, in understanding the first (extraordinary) piece of the mosaic—that the universe is expanding—concludes that there isn't much point in doing the second (ordinary) piece of the mosaic, homework. Little wonder. Finally, I decide it is about not taking ourselves—and our science—too seriously. (What is that your business?))

Susan tells me she has found a little piece in *The New Yorker* that may work for our chapter on synthesis. I read it and find myself rereading sentences as I go, trying to make sense of its elements. Susan is watching me. It's hard to make sense of a piece when someone is watching you try to make sense of it. I have more questions than answers, until I read the second to last paragraph about Alvy Singer—a character remembered by possibly twelve people in America. Then I get it. It all fits. I explode in laughter. Susan looks at me as if I have been writing this book much too long.

I feel compelled to read it aloud, pressing into service techniques from my eleventh-grade drama class. I pause just into the fourth paragraph, look heavenward and say, with reverence, "Alvy Singer. The joy!" Woody Allen's face and the character's charming neuroses come back to me. I glance at Susan—not a Woody Allen fan—sitting at her kitchen table. She doesn't get it about Alvy. She continues to look at me with some concern. That's okay, I think to myself, David will get it. I finish reading. "This is perfect!" I whoop. "I love this. Do you know what this piece is about?"

"Socks and the universe?" she asks tentatively. "I thought it was very funny."

"Funny? Funny like King Kong is a big monkey!" I'm cranked

now. "Oh, no Susan, it's much more. This piece is about our role in the vastness of time and space. It's about how socks represent the meaninglessness of the everyday experience. It's about hopelessness and despair (Woody Allen's hyperbole isn't lost on me), but it's also about how one writer can, in five paragraphs, illuminate the universe in terms we can understand and bring to mind a character who, though pathetic, had a deep and profound sense of our place in time and space!"

Susan shakes her head, chuckling and says, "I guess we've found the piece for the beginning of the synthesis chapter. And I think you just synthesized it."

Even after years of studying reading comprehension instruction, observing children as they struggle to create meaning for themselves, and talking to hundreds of teachers about what proficient readers do to make sense of text, our definitions for each strategy continue to evolve. This has been especially true as we have come to understand how readers synthesize.

To me synthesis is the mind's mosaic artistry. I remember seeing ancient Byzantine mosaics while traveling in Europe, and being awestruck at the artist's ability to conceptualize a complex and splendid whole while holding only a tiny fragment in his hand. So it is with synthesis.

Synthesis is the process of ordering, recalling, retelling, and recreating into a coherent whole the information with which our minds are bombarded every day. It is the uniquely human trait that permits us to sift through a myriad of details and focus on those pieces we need to know and remember. It is the ability to collect a disparate array of facts and connect them to a central theme or idea. It is the process by which we forsake much of what we learn in order to make sense of that which we determine is most pivotal for us. Synthesis is about organizing the different pieces to create a mosaic, a meaning, a beauty, greater than the sum of each shiny piece. It is a complex process in which children, even the youngest, engage very naturally every day.

When we sit around our dinner tables at night and share the

events of the day, we are synthesizing, sorting out the unimportant, creating our interpretation of the day for our families. When a child recalls an adventure from the playground or grabs her teacher's arm, whispering "Guess what?" she is synthesizing. When we curl up in bed at night to ruminate about the day in our minds or in a journal, when we remember an image from our childhoods, we synthesize. When we read, we have the opportunity to construct and manipulate a road map of our meaning. Synthesis is a way of saying, "I have been there and this is what I remember. Let me see if by retelling it, I can come to understand it better."

When I read "Lost in the Stars," I synthesized during and after I read. My mind kept an ongoing record as I read and I knew, even if it was a subconscious awareness, what I thought the piece was about. From the moment I read the title and first couple of sentences, to my tongue-in-cheek pontification on the vastness of the universe after I read it aloud, I was creating a synthesis—a personal composite of what the piece was about. I created a new way to describe the piece— to myself as I read, to Susan after I read. By synthesizing, even if it is in the form of mental notes as I read, I am more likely to remember and transfer my learning to new situations.

My synthesis didn't occur accidentally. It was the result of the other comprehension strategies I used as I read. Early in my reading, I posed questions. I focused on what I thought was important. I made connections to prior knowledge. I considered images. And I (liberally) inferred. The end result—my articulated synthesis—was an amalgam of the strategies used most frequently by proficient readers.

It was more than a single inference. It included parts of my prior knowledge, mixed in questions and judgments, and created something new, a synthesis that would be at least slightly different from anyone else's. My synthesis was a mosaic composed of a myriad of tiny mental pieces that represented my understanding of the text.

We all recall experiences from our schooling where teachers demanded we summarize a book, usually in writing. They didn't want much—just a succinct report that touched upon (what they believed to be, but wouldn't tell us) all the critical elements and themes in the book. The summary had to be less than a page long with no editorializing or accounts of personal experiences mixed in. "Oh, geeze," we'd groan. It was not a process we relished.

Though our memories of being asked to summarize might not be fond, research (Pearson, Roehler, Dole, and Duffy, 1992) has long indicated that teaching children to summarize is a helpful tool in teaching reading comprehension. The research confirms what we know through experience and common sense: Proficient readers are able to summarize as a way of helping them recall what they read and then communicate it to others.

We also know that as they reach the upper grades, students are expected to summarize more frequently; and upper-grade teachers express frustration about their students' underdeveloped summaries, particularly for nonfiction.

In the PEC's Reading Project work in Denver-area schools, we began by teaching the traditional concept of summarizing, a succinct retelling of the key points in a text. We soon modified the traditional definition of summary, however, to include students' opinions. We knew, especially for young children, that their summaries would have imaginative inclusions and other elements they, rather than just the teacher, believed were important to the overall meaning. We modeled for children, thinking aloud about exactly how we might retell something we had read—how we would choose what elements to include, how we considered what the audience already knew, how we might capture the most engaging pieces without retelling the entire text.

We emphasized that a summary could help someone who had never read a book understand what it is about. A number of teachers experimented with new ways to teach summary, but it was the children, as usual, who surprised us by taking the traditional concept of summary to a whole new level, to the broader, more encompassing notion of synthesis.

We first noticed and began to make a distinction between synthesis and summary when the youngest readers' summaries included (what they believed to be) the highlights of the text, but went much further. Their summaries were spirited, somewhat rambling stories about the stories infused with details from their own lives. They very naturally added new details, images, inferences, and bits of prior knowledge that seemed to extend the meaning of the story for them. Through their retellings, they actually created new narratives, verbal or written syntheses that fixed the meaning of the piece firmly in their memories.

Seven-year-old Alicia's retelling of Cynthia Rylant's *Dog Heaven* drove the distinction between synthesis and summary home for me. I recall the day I pulled up next to Alicia for a conference.

"Alicia, you've been talking about summary in your classroom for a while now. You've just finished reading *Dog Heaven*. Can you summarize it for me?"

"Well it's about dogs who go to heaven, not just one dog, what happens when any dog goes to heaven. Here's how it works. A dog dies and you bury him in the back yard and part of him, like the exact shape of him, but not really his body, goes to heaven and God is waiting with lots of biscuits, only they're not just the kind that we have here, they're better and in shapes like ham sandwiches and stuff. But it's supposed to make you feel better if your dog (pause), or just any pet, has died because heaven is almost better for the dog than earth and they can come back any time and they can be invisible!"

Her description was more than a summary, more than a simple retelling, and, yet, it was true to the themes in the book. Alicia elaborated her retelling, possibly to make it more memorable. She actually added concrete details about a dog's burial, not found in the book, and then extrapolated the story to all pets without compromising the key themes in Cynthia Rylant's text. She used details from the text (ham sandwiches, invisible visits to earth) to help her arrive at a key theme—it may be better for the dogs in heaven. She went beyond summary. She synthesized.

Several years ago, during one of our quick yogurt lunches early in the life of the Reading Project, Debbie Miller, a first/second-grade teacher at Denver's University Park Elementary School, and I discussed synthesis. (Debbie and a group of other teacher researchers led by PEC staff developer Steph Harvey would go on to publish an article on synthesis in *Language Arts*, December 1996.)

"Ellin, what is synthesis, really? I mean how does it differ from summarizing? I know summarizing helps kids identify key points and organize their thoughts, but I have this hunch synthesis takes them much further."

"Debbie, you always ask the easy questions, don't you?" I said, thinking back to the many conversations we'd had over the years when Debbie had probed and pushed for clarification so that she could better take the ideas back to her classroom. "I guess when I think of synthesis, I think in terms of 'beyond summary.' A summary usually comes at the end of something and is meant to hit all the main points."

"Right, it can be fairly mechanical, it seems to me. Sometimes that's all we want from the children, but sometimes we're looking for more," Debbie said.

I agreed. "Yeah. I see synthesis as something different, and really more important. A summary is a listing of the parts and synthesis is somehow the creation of a whole. It requires real creative, critical thought. It should go on throughout the process of reading—not just at the end. In a way it's a matter of bringing together different ideas and facts, from the text and from the reader's experience, and weaving them together into a tapestry, something larger, more complete than all the threads."

Debbie began her class' comprehension strategy study of synthesis by reading and modeling with *The Kissing Hand*, by Audrey Penn, a story of a raccoon's first and somewhat scary day in school, and his mother's touching way of helping him get through it. We reasoned that its straightforward text and message would be simple to comprehend, permitting the children to focus on a new strategy.

Debbie read the book aloud to the class several times over several days. After she read each time, she synthesized, emphasizing what she believed to be the key themes in the book, but showing how her synthesis became slightly different with each rereading.

"You know, you guys," she began after reading *The Kissing Hand* for the third time, "my synthesis for this book is really changing each time I read it. Remember Monday when I said it was a book about Chester raccoon who was afraid to go to school for the first time and how his mother made him feel better? I still think that's true, but now that I've reread the book, now I think it's also a book about anyone trying anything new and how thinking about people you love, even if they haven't kissed the palm of your hand, can help you feel strong inside. I think it's about how we give each other strength to do things that are new and challenging for us. It reminds me of Tony (one of the second-graders) showing Kenny around our room on his first day with us. It was like Tony was showing Kenny how not to be afraid in a new classroom. Do you remember?"

A chorus of related stories from the children followed. Debbie carefully related each to *The Kissing Hand*, emphasizing how proficient readers use their background knowledge and experiences to help them synthesize a book and how individual background knowledge makes each synthesis of a text different.

As the comprehension strategy study progressed, Debbie modeled nearly every day, increasing the sophistication of her syntheses in a wide variety of texts. She used newspaper articles, nonfiction pieces from magazines, and picture books.

The class also kept an ongoing synthesis on chart paper as Debbie read Laura Ingalls Wilder's *Little House in the Big Woods* aloud. When reading *Little House* she paused once or twice a chapter for the children to add to the class synthesis. They discussed how they decided what to include and what to leave out. They learned that the central elements found in fiction—character, setting, conflict, a sequence of events, and resolution—are usually included in a fiction synthesis. They talked about how each element helped readers focus on what was important as they read and how those central elements anchored the readers' synthesis after they read.

Jamal loved the *Jimmy's Boa* books by Trinka Hakes Noble and was reading *Jimmy's Boa Bounces Back* during reader's workshop one morning. He had read it through once and was four pages into rereading it when Debbie and I stopped by for a conference.

"Jamal," I began, "have you thought about how you'll synthesize this book after you read?"

"Nope."

Brief, but direct, I thought. "Why don't you signal us when you've finished, and we'll come back to hear your synthesis?"

"Okay."

As predicted, the signal never came and when we returned to press Jamal for a synthesis, he still wasn't into verbosity. His synthesis consisted of, "The boa scared a bunch of old ladies." Debbie looked to me and I looked to her, hoping a plan would emerge.

She asked, "What else?"

"Not much."

We tried again. "Jamal, what can you tell us about the events in the story?" I asked.

Same response. Then we stumbled onto a tactic that would change the way we taught synthesis.

"Let's go back to the beginning page, Jamal." Debbie looked like she knew what she was doing, but I'm fairly sure it was accidental. She read a couple of pages, paused, and said, "Here's what I think this is about so far, Jamal; you tell me if you think I'm right. It's about how Jimmy's boa ran away from the farm and ended up outside Meggie's house, cold and tired in a tree. Meggie's mom decided to wear the boa as part of her outfit for the garden club meeting and that's how Jimmy's boa ended up in a meeting with all those old ladies. How was that, Jamal?"

"Pretty good, except you forgot about how that lady's wig flew off!"

"Ooops! That's true. That's where all the trouble begins, isn't it, because then we find out that Mrs. Rosebud's wig came off because it got caught on Mrs. Greenleaf's alligator purse."

"Yeah because Mrs. Greenleaf got sneezed on by Mrs. Peachtree's poodle. He was in the punch."

Debbie said, "You know, you're right Jamal, I forgot about the poodle in the punch. Jamal, you've really helped us figure out something important about synthesis. Great readers like you don't wait until the end of a book to figure out what it is all about, they keep track while they read."

Debbie flipped the book open to a page early in the text. "See, Jamal, on this page we're just thinking this whole book is going to be about Meggie serving cookies at her mother's garden club meeting, but by this page," she flipped to a page near the end, "we know that the real story is about how Meggie tells Jimmy this really incredible story about how his boa constrictor causes all kinds of trouble at the garden club meeting and, if you are really looking at the illustrations as you read, you know it's funny to watch all the ladies get scared by the boa. Great readers have to keep track of the words and the pictures and decide what the book is about all the time as they read. Jamal, have you ever heard the saying a chain reaction?"

Through this type of conference, we began to realize that synthesis is as much about what a reader does during reading as it is about a coherent retelling after reading. We found that many of Debbie's students didn't seem to mentally keep track of the meaning as they read.

Debbie was also concerned that, for too many children, when asked what a book was about after they had read, their responses were like Jamal's initial description of *Jimmy's Boa Bounces Back*— vague and incomplete. She suspected that, for many of her students, the detail they recalled after was almost too overwhelming to condense into a synthesis. We decided we had to get into their heads to find out if they were keeping track of the gist of the text as they read.

Prodding children to think aloud about their reading as they read permits us to look through a window into their thinking processes. We can assess their in-progress understanding of a text by asking them to read aloud and stopping them periodically to describe what the piece is about at that point and to add opinion, interpretation, and prediction. By listening to Debbie's children think aloud, we discovered that the more proficient readers maintained an intricate mental synthesis as they read, while the less proficient readers weren't always aware of the evolving plot or information as they read.

Ruben's fascination with whales was legendary. Debbie and I decided to get him to think aloud so we could peer into a developing synthesis in nonfiction. We stopped Ruben during his umpteenth reading of the Eyewitness Book, *Whale*, by Vassili Papastavrou. He was engrossed in the Orca section when we asked him to read aloud and stop when he became aware of his synthesis—his idea about what the section on Orcas was about so far. He read several paragraphs interspersed with beautiful photographs of Orcas before he stopped.

Ruben said, "Okay, Orcas and killers are the same thing and you know them because their dorsal fin—do you know what that is?—is so tall. Just the fin is taller than my dad. You can always tell an Orca because they're black and white which is their camouflage because you can't see their shape under water. These two pages are about how Orcas live, like that they live in every ocean in the world and how they come up to the beach on purpose sometimes to eat seals and how when they eat something, they toss it around in the air first, but they don't eat people. Also they're the fastest swimmers in the water."

Later Debbie and I looked over the two pages Ruben had synthesized and marveled at the bases he had covered. In a very natural way, Ruben had included all the elements many teachers ask children to include in their summaries. He talked about the whale's size, speed, eating habits, appearance, and global distribution. Yet he omitted dozens of facts from his synthesis. He made split-second decisions about what he believed was important and was able to articulate those highlights when asked.

Debbie asked Ruben to co-teach the mini lesson the following day, stopping as he read to tell what the sections in his book were about so far. The class asked him to defend his inclusions and exclusions from the passages he read. Not surprising, he did so with logic and conviction.

Through studying synthesis in primary, intermediate, and middle-grade classrooms, we discovered that children's syntheses are often a composite of the strategies proficient readers use. When asked to think aloud, children speak of what they believe to be important in a text, connections they made to relevant prior knowledge, questions they had as they read, remembered images, and conclusions or inferences they created.

Their syntheses appear to be updated constantly as they read, changing to accommodate new information from the text. Also, their mid-course synthesis may differ significantly from their reflections about the piece after reading it in its entirety. In addition, the synthesis is likely to change each time they reread all or part of the piece.

Teaching synthesis is a challenge. It may require more think-aloud modeling on the teacher's part, and more conferences focused on helping children think aloud than any other comprehension strategy. We have found it is well worth the effort. When children pay attention to the evolving meaning as they read and create new ways to think about and share the information later, there is a significant improvement in students' abilities to remember books and transfer the information they've synthesized to new learning situations.

It was one of those mid-year mornings. I was with Chryse Hutchins, a PEC staff developer, visiting Jody Cohn's fifth-grade classroom at Denver's Samuels Elementary.

"Your touch is so evident, Chryse," I said. "Every classroom is brimming with teachers and kids who read and write with such depth and quality. It's clear that these kids are able to do what they do because of Samuels' focus on literacy learning for all teachers and kids. A lot of work, but look at the payoff!"

Chryse was the PEC staff developer who had worked with Jody for the past two years. "We've created a real sense of community. I really think that's where this started. Look at how these children work together now and then think back to what it was like at the beginning of the year." Chryse looked over at Jody, who shook her head in agreement.

Chryse, Jody, and I stood with clipboards in hand, ready to jot down observations.

I looked across the room. "Ellin," Chryse said, "Jody and I decided to try something different this year. We're having the kids study the Revolutionary War, Civil War, and World War II simultaneously. They've never done anything this comprehensive before, but we thought it would be a great challenge and they'd develop terrific research skills."

My mouth dropped at the magnitude of the undertaking. Right away, I noticed twenty-four fifth-graders digging in. Some took notes. Some sketched. Some mapped key ideas. Some marked key themes in their books, using self-adhesive notes. One child recorded his thoughts into a dictaphone. Another pair compiled a list on a large butcher-paper chart. They largely ignored us.

We began to wander around the room, peering over shoulders.

"What energy, Jody! What have you done?" I asked.

"This starts the moment the school year begins, and builds on everything the other teachers in this building have done," Jody said. "I have the privilege to work in a setting where many of my colleagues share my teaching philosophy."

I remember stopping by Marissa's desk. She had developed a system using self-adhesive notes in six colors to mark her use of comprehension strategies in her book, *My Brother Sam Is Dead*. She had jotted notes, some decipherable only to her, on the adhesive notes. She was busily recording questions, images, conclusions, connections to prior knowledge, and mid-course syntheses—each on a different color note. I was flabbergasted. As I watched she carefully tucked the end of each protruding note around the page where she placed it, creating a rainbow along the pages of the closed book.

On that morning, Jaquil was working on a time line of the Civil War. He read at a long table in the back of the room, alternating between *Across Five Aprils*, two nonfiction books on the Civil War, and notes he had taken from a PBS documentary, *The Civil War*. His time line was taped to the long table with warnings to his classmates not to touch posted above it. His intricate drawings and captions above and below each date on the time line formed a complex synthesis of material about the Civil War.

Jody stopped behind him, "Jaquil, would you be willing to share your time line with some of the kids who are studying the Revolutionary War? They've struggled to find a way to synthesize all of their reading. You might be able to help."

Jaquil was too engaged to do more than nod.

The group reading books from World War II had called an impromptu meeting. They gathered around a table in the corner and we stopped nearby to listen to their conversation—a conversation that sounded more like an argument.

"Don't go over yet," Chryse whispers. "Let's see what happens."

"It belongs!" Maria's eyes grew intense, her hands grasping her knees as she leaned across the table, speaking directly to Khoa. Chryse explains that they are creating a top ten list of issues from World War II. Their plan is to list the issues, present information to define and describe each, and draw conclusions about whether the top ten issues correlated to issues from the Revolutionary or Civil Wars.

"That's good. I've never seen Maria so engaged about anything having to do with school," Jody says.

"Progress," Chryse retorts.

"Definitely progress. But I wonder about Kaylie. She's had a hard time really getting into this and I'm not sure why. I think I'll go talk to her," Jody said, heading in her direction.

Kaylie sat across the room, staring out the window. Jody and I knelt beside her desk.

"Heh, Kaylie, what's up?"

"I'm supposed to be meeting with them," she gestured toward the Revolutionary War group. "But I haven't read the books and so I don't have anything to say." She paused and looked out the window again. "My grandpa died in a war and there are pictures of him all over our house and I have to hear about him all the time at home and we even went to Washington to find his name on the memorial and we did and he wasn't in any of these wars. I could do a top ten list for Vietnam and I have about two thousand books about it at home and I could even bring some of his stuff in and Mrs. Wall in the library has some other books and she told me there is tons of stuff on the Internet about the Vietnam war."

"You don't have much time." Jody glanced at her watch. "About ten minutes till lunch, but why don't you go to the library and see what you can find on Vietnam. I have a feeling you're going to add some very important information to the discussion."

"Do you mean I can do another war?" Kaylie asked.

"If you can find the information and make the connections to the others we're studying."

"Thanks, Mrs. Cohn. I didn't want to do those wars."

"I bet she'll get more done in ten minutes than she's done in the last three days," Jody said. "I guess we've got to be flexible. Right?"

"And she's the reason," I said, thinking how important it is to watch children carefully.

Jody glanced at the wall clock and said, "There's time for one more conference before lunch. Julia-Claire transferred from another school a couple of months ago and the transition hasn't been easy. Let's see how she's doing."

A pile of computer printouts from CD-Rom encyclopedias surrounded Julia-Claire.

I began, "Julia-Claire, you've been so engrossed this morning, I can't wait to see what you're pulling out of all this information." I scan the piles of paper on her desk and see she has used a highlighting marker liberally (excessively?). As I rifle through the piles, the yellow lines thin out. "What happened when you got here?" I asked, pointing to a printout with only a few highlights. "Didn't you find very much that was important?"

"No, I read that stuff the day we had a mini lesson on text structure. Remember Chryse told us there is, like, cause and effect, chronological, problem-solution, comparison-contrast, and all those ways of organizing in nonfiction."

"Whoa!" Jody exclaimed. "I'm so proud of you for remembering all of that." Jody turned to me and whispered, "Where's the principal at the great moments? Who would believe it?"

"Well," Julia-Claire continued, oblivious to our mumbles, "I started to look for words that show it is that kind of pattern, what did you call it?"

"Evidence of text patterns," Jody responded.

"Yeah, I started to look for words that would give me an idea of how the text was organized and it really helped me to pay attention to the parts that I really need to get and now I'm working on my synthesis of all the stuff I read."

"What's your plan now?" Jody asked.

"I was thinking I would do a diary of a kid my age who lived through the Revolutionary War and tell all these facts I've found out by letting her talk. Is that okay?"

"Sounds great to me," Jody said and smiled as we walked away.

During my visit, I observed Jody's students sifting through information on three (now four) major wars, finding common themes and patterns in each, and developing ways to present their research. That's not where they were at the beginning of the school year. Now they managed the information cognitively—discussing, thinking about, organizing—before trying to manage it in a formal presentation. They were more than active, they were hyperaware as they read, tuning into the important issues, themes, and ideas, asking questions, creating images, relating what they read to prior knowledge, drawing conclusions, making judgments, predicting, and keeping track of what it all means—*synthesizing*.

Jody's classroom was not transformed overnight. She is a superb teacher and Chryse Hutchins, a highly skilled staff developer, has worked with her in her classroom for two years. Samuels School has been involved in PEC's professional development projects for six years, so it is a receptive environment for change and innovation. Many of Samuels' teachers have dramatically changed their teaching and the results show in the children. Nonetheless, this is not a privileged group of students. Eighty-five percent of these children are bused in from one of Denver's poorest neighborhoods.

As I left Jody's room that day, my eyes were drawn to the mess of learning materials: papers, charts, double entry diary forms, markers, staplers, and piles and piles of books. I was reminded of my dorm room when I was preparing for a major presentation in college and remember the feelings of efficacy, industry, and ultimately, accomplishment. Those were some of my first real feelings of excitement about learning. I left Samuels heartened to see—and a bit envious of—these children who are experiencing those feelings of intellectual rigor and excitement while still in elementary school.

When David and I were first married, we played a game we called the question of the week. On alternating weeks, we posed questions to each other and took a week to answer them. I would ask something like what are the three greatest gifts to humankind and we would debate for a week. He would ask what character from history I would dine with if given the opportunity. We asked each other what we would say now to the parent—his father, my mother—each of us had lost to early deaths. I think our game must have been our way of getting to know each other. Our rambling week-long conversations were a way of synthesizing what was important in our lives until that point, our way of carving out a future together.

I realize now that synthesis is absolutely basic—in the air and water category—if we are talking about essentials for learning: literacy learning, life learning. The magnitude and complexity of the information we and the children with whom we work must manage every day is staggering. The magnitude and complexity we have to learn about those we love is staggering. In order to construct any kind of meaning in our literacy learning and our life learning, we must find ways to cull and prune the details with which we are bombarded. We must reorganize and create our own explanations for what we are learning, our own definitions of our lives at any particular juncture.

As with readers we cannot wait until the end to figure out what our lives have meant. The work in progress that is our lives must be synthesized along the way. When we pause long enough to reflect—to consider the synthesis of our lives—we are also bestowed with the gift of better knowing and understanding ourselves and what we care about. No small undertaking. No small gift for our children.

Synthesizing: Some Key Ideas

The process of synthesizing occurs during reading:

- Proficient readers maintain a cognitive synthesis as they read. They monitor the overall meaning, important concepts, and themes in the text as they read and are aware of ways text elements fit together to create that overall meaning and theme. A proficient reader's synthesis is likely to extend the literal meaning of a text to the inferential level.
- Proficient readers are aware of text elements and patterns in fiction and nonfiction and understand that being aware of them as they read helps them predict and understand the overall meanings or themes.
- As they read, proficient readers attend more directly to character, setting, conflict, sequence of events, resolution, and theme in fiction and to text patterns such as description, chronological, cause and effect, comparison/contrast, and problem/solution in nonfiction. They use their knowledge of these elements to make decisions about the overall meaning of a passage, chapter, or book.
- Proficient readers actively revise their cognitive syntheses as they read. New information is assimilated into the reader's evolving ideas about the text, rendering some earlier decisions about the text obsolete.

The process of synthesizing occurs after reading:

- Proficient readers are able to express, through a variety of means, a synthesis of what they have read. The synthesis includes ideas and themes relevant to the overall meaning from the text and is cogently presented.

· Proficient readers use synthesis to share, recommend, and critically review books they have read.

· Proficient readers purposefully use synthesis to better understand what they have read. Syntheses are frequently an amalgam of all comprehension strategies used by proficient readers.

TEN

From Problem to Resolution
Empowering Children to Solve Reading Problems Independently

Comrade Past and Mister Present

Can the misfortune of a dog owned by vegetarians
be felt by a woolen creature exuding class privilege?
Looking through windows to glimpse tits I saw this
instead. It wasn't in the manual. But
applying private cures to collective diseases
occupied every page, it was *The Book of
the Transparent Tombstone.* You could see
all the heroes inside, and downtown Chicago,
men like Mr. Wrigley and buildings like the Tribune
Tower, and what they felt being there like that,
men and buildings squashed inside the look
of a drunk poet chased by wind
like a Sunday supplement on Monday morn.
You could read their desires but not their thoughts,
because you can read those like cigarettes in Lebanon
or Madagascar, and they said,
The thing to be is dead. Complete
thought evacuation. The cold wind
said that. The buildings themselves said
other things, having to do with stubbornness,
heart, commerce, stability, the will
of large men who know the world well
enough to sell it, and when.

You cannot throw up a building in Chicago,
my friend Debra says, and what, say I,
do I look big enough to throw up buildings?
Maybe my steak, but not a whole edifice, no.
You cannot, she says, do that unless it says
something, and the buildings in Chicago say
some pretty strange things these days. I look.
They do. . . .

ANDRE CODRESCU,
Comrade Past and Mister Present

On a blistering hot Sunday, I bought *Comrade Past and Mister Present* at the Tattered Cover—the largest independent bookstore in the United States (it's a converted department store) and much-loved Denver institution that is dotted with overstuffed chairs and sofas, helpful salespeople, and a browse-as-long-as-you'd-like attitude.

I bought *Comrade* because the author, Andre Codrescu, is one of my favorite weekly contributors to National Public Radio's *All Things Considered*. The syncopation and cadence of his voice—still thick with the accent he brought to the United States from Sibiu, Romania, in 1966—speaks to me of exotic people and places. His raw wit is laced with piercing insight into America's eccentricities. I listen intently when his voice drifts out from my car radio, aware that if I miss a word in the dense, fast-paced commentary, I have probably missed the whole point. The editor of *Exquisite Corpse, a Journal of Books & Ideas* and a professor of writing and literature at Louisiana State University, Codrescu has written numerous books of poetry, essays, and commentary. Fascinated with the man, I bought the book.

I took it home and stretched out on the couch in the den eager for a good laugh and for the fresh perspective Codrescu brings to the monumental and routine in American life. Neither were forthcoming. I read and reread the first piece, "Dear Masoch," that begins with the stanza:

Dear Masoch doodling with his contracts
pens Venus in Furs on the margin of the document
he is preparing where it says
how many lashes he must receive, and where,
when the door opens & in the gaping doorway
a head framed by Viennese blue says:

It goes on, but to me it took on no semblance of comprehensibility. Some of the language is intriguing, but the vivid voice of the author didn't resonate as I read the words. They were just words . . . when— the—door—opens—&—in—the—gaping—doorway—a—head— framed—by—Viennese—blue—says . . .

I skipped to page forty-one, the title poem "Comrade Past & Mister Present," hoping the poem with the same title as the book would be less opaque. The title itself was understandable enough. Codrescu came from Eastern Europe. This poem would, I imagined, explore his journey from the repressive communism of Romania to his life in the United States.

As I read, my eyes lost focus on the page. I struggled to keep my eyes opened, yawned, and lost the battle.

It was months later—while writing this book—that I went back to "Comrade Past," committed to make something of it, acutely aware of the times I had urged children to do the same: "You have to work hard to read well. You have to solve the problems you encounter as you read," I have told countless children. "It's not like TV or a movie where the action spills over you like water in the shower."

I deliberately chose this piece because I was looking for a challenging piece and remembered all too well that nap and the frustration I felt when I stashed the book in my bedroom bookcase, realizing as I stored it away that I might never pick it up again. This time I was determined to do what I asked children to do, to stay focused and work hard to fix up my comprehension problems.

I waited until Elizabeth was asleep, curled up in my favorite chair, flipped on the reading lamp that arches over it, and began by reading the piece several times, letting its words sink into my mind. My first reaction was the same I had months before when "Comrade" literally put me to sleep. But with each reread, I found myself a little more dazzled by the poem's absurdity and the quirky mind of the poet.

> Can the misfortune of a dog owned by vegetarians
> be felt by a woolen creature exuding class privilege?

Why do I find this line so funny and incongruous? It strikes me as a bizarre example of total noncommunication. The dog, a natural predator and carnivore, cared for by vegetarians!

Any meaning I might have derived from the first line is lost, however, as I read the second. It seems completely dissonant and makes no sense. I connect "exuding class privilege" to communism's attempt to stomp out classes but can't connect it to the dog. I read it a couple of times and think perhaps the dog is the "woolen creature," but I remain puzzled.

"Looking through windows to glimpse tits I saw this instead. It wasn't in the manual. But applying private cures to collective diseases occupied every page, it was *The Book of the Transparent Tombstone*." Now I see the poet walking at night, looking into the windows of the buildings he passes, displaying the voyeurism we all share when walking at night and seeing in, but knowing those inside can't see out. He is looking, perhaps, for a beautiful, undressed woman. Instead of finding what he seeks, his mind moves on. Again I hear a political allusion in Codrescu's words, "applying private cures to collective diseases." Isn't that what capitalism—the free enterprise system—is all about? I ask myself, then reread, "It wasn't in the manual." David walks in. "Would you take a look at this?" I ask. "I need help. I'm having real trouble making sense of it."

David reads the piece. A smile comes to his face and then a few chuckles. "Whoa. This is obscure, but carefully crafted. I have a feeling there's a lot to it. I get this sense of an inebriated poet who feels particularly small as he walks down the streets of Chicago at night, looking up at huge buildings. It's surrealistic and really provocative. It reminds me of Nabokov. You know one of those brilliant Eastern Europeans who ends up a master of the English language with an odd twist. I think the manual must be *Das Capital*, Karl Marx' Bible for intellectual Communists. At least that's a possibility. It bears further study, Ellin."

We talk for a few minutes and I find my appreciation and understanding of the poem growing. I keep going.

What does Codrescu mean "The Book of the Transparent Tombstone"? Are Chicago's buildings themselves that "Book"? Are they—the buildings—the legacy left behind by "all the heroes inside, and downtown Chicago, men like Mr. Wrigley and buildings like the Tribune Tower?"

The poem remains fuzzy and there are many ways to interpret it, but I am starting to get a sense of the gist, at least a gist for me. Before it was gobbledygook. Now I sense a kind of brilliance—what I had expected from Codrescu. "Men and buildings squashed inside the look of a drunk poet chased by wind like a Sunday supplement on Monday morn." This sentence becomes the crux of the poem for me. I see a drunken poet, late at night—no, early in the morning, having never gone to sleep—and somehow through the haze of his alcohol-sodden brain, he has narrow, piercing insights into the fleeting quality of life (of all things) even the "men and buildings" that surround him and are reflected in his pupils ("squashed inside the look").

The woebegone image of the wind blowing the Sunday supplement down a city street on a Monday morning comes next. We have all seen it, an out-of-date newspaper (how quickly news is old) caught in a gust of wind, now trash to be tossed away with no thought given to what was written there. Are the poet and the men and the buildings like that Sunday supplement?

What is Codrescu trying to say? I feel sadness and then more sadness with the lines, "You could read their desires but not their thoughts, because you can read those like cigarettes in Lebanon or Madagascar, and they said, the thing to be is dead." This conjures a dissonant set of images: cigarettes kill; bombing in Beirut; I don't know anything about Madagascar other than it's a large island off the east coast of Africa; the builders of the buildings, all now dead. I can't connect the thoughts, but I'm intrigued and a bit relieved with the sentences that follow, "Complete thought evacuation. The cold wind said that." Do these sentences let me off the hook a bit? Are they saying that it's okay not to understand everything, that some of the words are the random thoughts of a drunk poet out too late? Does the cold wind clear the cobwebs and confusion away? Does it clear the muddle in the poet's—and the reader's—head? Am I on the right track, even a little bit?

I move on. "The buildings themselves said other things, having to do with stubbornness, heart, commerce, stability, the will of large men who know the world well enough to sell it, and when." I sense a grudging respect for the "large men," the captains of capitalism who built those buildings and left something behind, though they are long gone. There is a paradox here: the commercialism and materialism, but also the heart and stability. Codrescu has captured something important about this country, but again I'm not really sure. I don't feel confident about my interpretation.

"You cannot throw up a building in Chicago, my friend Debra says." "Whoa," I say. How does this fit? Is Debra walking beside the drunken poet? Is he remembering a conversation with Debra that comes to his mind because it is early morning in Chicago? Because he's drunk, is he seeing things differently? I think of that vertical city and agree it would be impossible to "throw up" a building there. Does he remember that line from Debra because he stands in awe of those buildings?

"And what, say I, do I look big enough to throw up buildings? Maybe my steak, but not a whole edifice, no." "Phew," I find myself laughing, relieved with this word play and the comic relief it provides, telling me I don't have to take all of this too seriously.

Now I'm thinking about the first line, that dog owned by vegetarians. Is there some connection with the steak? Perhaps Codrescu is reminding us to laugh, to see things differently, to mix the profound with the ludicrous, and, in this free country, to be thankful for all those buildings in Chicago and what they stand for.

"Comrade Past & Mister Present" was hard work for me, so hard that I fell asleep with it on my first try and on my second almost flipped by it, but stopped myself. I wanted to experience the struggle children often face when presented with a piece just beyond their grasp. I wanted to see if the fix-up strategies we teach children to use when they read would work with me as the guinea pig. "Comrade Past & Mister Present" was a good test. I still don't have it. It is the type of piece that will change and expand with each reading. But through reading it numerous times, thinking about it, jotting down my thoughts, and then talking with my husband David about it, I understand much more. It was a rewarding intellectual challenge for me, but more importantly, it helped me understand the process children frequently must embark upon in order to comprehend what they are reading.

In thinking back on my struggle to comprehend "Comrade," I see the faces of dozens of children who experience similar frustration every day as they read. I also recall children who don't experience that frustration but who, like me, might benefit from such a challenge. I realize that if I am to learn from my experiences as a reader, I must extrapolate and purposely relate my insights to their experiences. I must compare my own befuddlement and sense of accomplishment in meeting a challenge to their daily lives as readers. To do less is to forego a prime opportunity to teach more effectively.

In my mind I review the common stumbling blocks children encounter as they read. I analyze how I surmounted the obstacles and what mental gymnastics I used to arrive at my interpretation of "Comrade Past & Mister Present." I wonder, for example, if the comprehension problems I experienced with "Comrade" are connected to what reading theorists call *surface structure*, the visible aspects of the text: the letters, words, or grammatical structures.

Was mine a problem of deciphering difficult words I was unable to sound out? I glance back over the text. No, that certainly wasn't it. I recognized and could pronounce every word.

Did the text fail to make grammatical sense? A phrase like "you cannot throw up a building in Chicago" caused a double take. But it wasn't a grammatical problem. The sentence is syntactically correct.

My comprehension problems must have related more to the *deep structure* (see Table 10.1 on page 199) of the poem: the meanings, concepts, and associations underlying the words and phrases; my relevant prior knowledge; and my purpose and context for reading. When I first read it, nothing seemed to fit. The thoughts seemed randomly thrown together. But why? Where did the meaning break down?

I thought about word meanings and connotations in this piece. Were there any words I didn't understand, any I should have looked up in the dictionary? No, I knew the word meanings, but words I thought I understood meant little to me in the particular combination Codrescu chose for this poem.

Next I reflected on my prior knowledge or schema for the piece. My prior knowledge, at least that which I tried to use to make sense of the poem, did little to help me paint the picture of the overall meaning of the piece. I knew I would have understood this piece better if I knew more about Madagascar, Romania, and Marxism. I even tried to hear Codrescu's voice in my mind, wondering if an auditory image might provide a road map.

It was only after several careful rereadings and a conversation about it with David that the pieces of the puzzle began to come together. David and I talked about the piece at length, combining his prior knowledge with my own to create an interpretation that seemed to make sense. We read sections of it aloud to each other. I'd recently returned from Chicago, so I added my impressions of its vertical architecture to our discussion. We spent time talking about the Sunday supplement on Monday morning image and relating it to our own life experiences—that "has-been" feeling—before connecting it to the poem.

Also, I had a compelling purpose that motivated me. I wanted to write about the poem for this chapter. I wanted an authentically challenging reading experience so that I could experience personally the frustrations and challenges children face.

Cris Tovani is a take-no-hostages, tell-it-like-it-is type of person with an infectious laugh. She is also a superb teacher. Cris has been a member of the Public Education Coalition's staff development team for seven years and recently returned to full-time teaching. Cris has studied the reading research with other staff developers and worked with teachers to deepen their understanding of reading. Last year she decided she was ready to test what she'd learned. She signed on to teach remedial reading courses at Smoky Hill High School in the Cherry Creek School District. She wanted to see for herself how all the research and her work in elementary classrooms played out in one of the toughest settings of all.

Two days before spring break I stopped by her sixth-hour class. The summer-like weather had seduced several students not to return to school after lunch. The rest shuffled in. Some flopped into over-stuffed chairs bordered by bookshelves while others slid onto stiff chairs behind desks. The way their shoulders slumped and heads hung revealed a body language of defeat from years of painful academic experiences.

Cris has forty-two minutes a day for a semester—for some students a year—to reverse years of reading frustration and failure. On this particular day she introduced the concept of *fix-up strategies*, the collection of tools proficient readers use to solve word and comprehension problems when they occur.

Cris and I had talked about whether fix-ups, as they are often called, are really a separate comprehension strategy or simply a set of tools readers can use to solve problems and to resolve conflicts in their reading. We concluded that it didn't matter how we categorized fix-ups, but it mattered very much that all readers have a well-developed arsenal of tools they use flexibly, adaptively, and independently to solve comprehension and word identification problems when they arise.

Cris built on that definition when she introduced fix-ups to her students. "We have been talking all semester about being aware of when you're understanding what you read and when you're not," she began. "We've called that metacognition—knowing when you know, knowing when you don't know, and thinking about your own thinking. Well, there is another really important part of metacognition. You have to know what you need to know when you are reading and how to solve problems you have when meaning breaks down."

"Huh?" a few students queried.

"Okay, when you get stuck, there are a bunch of things you can do to get unstuck. Any idea what some of those things are?"

No response.

It was time to model. Cris had an eclectic collection of pieces ready to share. On this day she chose a particularly dense journal article describing a research study. In subsequent mini lessons, she would use poetry, newspaper editorials, college application instructions, SAT directions, excerpts from Barbara Kingsolver's novel *The Bean Trees*, and a few bureaucratic memos.

"Okay," she began, "I'm going to read this summary of a research study called, 'The processing of lexically stressed syllables in read and spontaneous speech.'"

Loud groans.

"I know, but let's say I have to read it to understand the research behind some of the stuff I'm teaching you guys, okay? Let's say I have to understand it. Now listen, because I'm going to think aloud about how I can fix up or solve some of the problems I have as I read. Ready? 'This research describes four experiments which examined the processing of words with stressed and unstressed initial syllable in both read and spontaneous speech.' Okay, that's a short summary of the article. From those words, I know there are four experiments. I know a lot about how educators set up research experiments, so I'm okay with that part. I start to have trouble with the part about processing words. What does that mean? I know that one way I can fix up meaning is to keep reading and see if it becomes clearer. That's what I'm going to do, because I haven't read very much yet and I'm going to see if this gets clearer in the next few sentences. If it doesn't, I'll have to go back and try something else. I'm going to read on."

Cris continued. " 'In the first experiment, which focused on read materials . . .' Okay, I read that as read with a long *e*, but that didn't make sense with materials, so I have to go back and change the way I pronounce it to read with a short vowel sound. 'Trisyllabic nouns.' Whoa! Trisyllabic isn't a word I come across very often. Let's see, because that word has a prefix, tri, and a root word, syllabic, I can take that word apart to see what it means. The prefix t-r-i, I know means three, like tri-county, three counties, or even triplets, and syllable means a word part that makes one sound, so trisyllabic must mean three syllable words. Why don't they just say that?!"

Laughter comes from the students who are now so engaged in watching Cris think aloud that their whole affect has changed.

Cris goes on. " '. . .were presented in three contextually defined conditions.' What in the world is a 'contextually defined condition'? I don't think I have background knowledge for that one! I'm going to skip it and see if I think it's important to come back to it later. If it is important, I can ask my friend Sheila McAuliffe who is a researcher, and she can tell me what 'contextually defined conditions' means."

Cris then reads, " '. . . to 36 subjects.' Wow, finally something I can understand! My background knowledge tells me that, in research studies, thirty-six subjects or people with whom the experiment was conducted, is a pretty small number. I know that the smaller the number of subjects, the tougher it is to draw conclusions that the findings would be true for all kids. I know now that I won't take the findings of this study real seriously because it was so small. I'll keep reading."

She does. " 'Analysis of the responses made by subjects . . .' Okay, this isn't subject like math or science or English. This subject means the people who were in the experiment. There are at least two definitions for the word subject and if you emphasize the second syllable, like this—sub-ject'—it means to force someone to do something, which is another meaning. I know it means people in the experiment because of the sentence it is found in 'responses made by the subjects.' I'm going to keep reading: 'hearing only the initial syllable of the stimuli revealed that stressed initial syllables were markedly more intelligible than their unstressed counterparts; but when subjects were presented with the full stimulus, there were no reliable intelligibility differences.' "

Cris says to the students, "Wow, now I'm really asking myself what I must know in order to understand this stuff. So much of it is unclear. I have to make myself stop and ask what kind of problems I'm having. Do I really need to know this stuff? If I do, can I solve my comprehension problems alone? I may need to ask Sheila to read this with me and help me figure out what it means. I'll give it one more sentence. 'In Experiment Two, a large number of polysyllabic content words, excised'— somehow that just reminded me of having a tooth pulled! I must have heard the word excised being used to describe a tooth being pulled—'from the speech of six speakers, were presented without supporting contexts.'"

I watched from the sidelines in Cris' classroom, impressed with the scope of what she modeled for them. Cris had, for the umpteenth time, shown the students that all readers struggle in some texts. She gave her students a glimpse into the vast array of fix-ups a proficient reader uses. She demonstrated that different fix-ups are useful in different problematic situations and for different purposes.

Most importantly, Cris showed that proficient readers, though they may struggle, are active in solving comprehension problems. Her lesson that day—and on the days that followed—provided solutions to surface structure and deep structure problems. Throughout it was clear that the purpose for solving the problems was to comprehend.

Cris' work with the high school readers reminded me again that in order to be proficient, readers must be flexible, adaptive, and independent in using fix-ups.

A surgical analogy comes to mind. Proficient readers, like surgeons, have a tray of instruments (fix-ups) they can use to operate on comprehension problems. They can use these tools flexibly and interchangeably. They are not limited to a scalpel; they have scissors, tweezers, spreaders—many tools they can use to operate on each problem. When Cris told her students she was going to try to read on to decide whether she needed to understand the phrase "contextually defined conditions," and if she did need to know, she would ask her colleague for help, she revealed the flexibility a proficient reader uses, choosing from several problem-solving strategies (see Table 10.1).

Like a surgeon, proficient readers are adaptive. They assess a problem and thoughtfully (though quickly) select the instrument or fix-up most likely to work most effectively in that situation. When Cris realized she could use her skills in word analysis to arrive at the meaning of "trisyllabic," she modeled how a proficient reader care-

The term *cueing systems* refers to the channels or sources through which the human mind receives information during reading. Some theorists suggest there are three, others as many as six or seven. Cueing systems have been defined with some variation by different theorists. The configuration we have found most useful in helping students solve reading problems is listed below.

Grapho-Phonic System—provides information about letters, features of letters, combinations of letters, and the sounds associated with them

Lexical or Orthographic System—provides information about words including instantaneous recognition of words, but not including the meaning associated with the word

Syntactic System—provides information about the form and structure of the language, including whether or not the text sounds correct when pronounced

Semantic System—provides information about the generally accepted meaning(s) associated with words and longer pieces of text

Schematic System—provides information from a reader's prior knowledge and/or personal associations with text and the structure of text; also governs the grouping and organization of new information in memory stores

Pragmatic System—provides information about the purposes and needs the reader has while reading; governs what the reader considers important and what the reader needs to understand

Many theorists (e.g., Rumelhart, 1976; Kintch and Van Dijk, 1984) believe that these cueing systems operate in the mind simultaneously, providing the reader with an abundance of information from all six sources at every moment he or she reads. The reader relies on different sources of information more or less heavily depending upon the purpose and context for reading. For example, a reader with little legal background knowledge may rely more heavily on the grapho-phonic system to decipher technical words in a legal text. That same reader may use the grapho-phonic system rarely while reading a novel by a favorite author.

TABLE 10.1 *Defining Cueing Systems*

fully selects or adapts a problem-solving strategy to match the problem at hand.

Similarly, Cris demonstrated throughout that she can and did solve comprehension problems independently. Through this lesson, and many other demonstrations, she revealed explicitly and implicitly that comprehension strategies, including fix-ups, can be used in all reading situations—in class, at home, alone, or with other readers nearby. She talked with the students about the variety of reading tasks they face each day and, specifically, which fix-ups might be used if problems are encountered in each.

Over the three weeks of the fix-up strategy study, Cris' students talked about tackling the density of content in a science book, the technical instructions they had to decipher in computer manuals, and the difficulty of sorting out a lengthy dialogue between several characters in a novel. They spoke openly of the frustration of having a limited repertoire of solutions to the comprehension problems they faced and they began to build and diversify their arsenal of problem-solving strategies.

A list of reading problems and possible solutions took shape on chart paper around the classroom. Together Cris and the students defined problems and discussed ways in which they could actively and purposefully operate on them. For example, they talked about ways in which the comprehension strategies of questioning, inferring, synthesizing, determining importance, and activating background knowledge could be pressed into service as tools for solving problems that had to do with the meaning of words, passages, and whole text. And they continued to discuss how tools like decoding, word analysis, and using clues from the context can be used to help when the problem relates to recognition, pronunciation, and word definition. (See Table 10.2)

Cris found that when she listened carefully to her students as they described their reading problems, she could respond by modeling a variety of techniques to address surface and deep structure problems. She watched as her students gradually grew more flexible, adaptive, and independent in their use of the tools.

Unfortunately, in too many classrooms, it is assumed that there

Cueing System	Sample Problem	Sample Solutions
Grapho-Phonic System—recognizing that letters have associated sounds and knowing how to pronounce and blend those sounds to decipher unknown words	Difficulty pronouncing words	· Teaching children to sound the word out by identifying beginning and ending sounds, attempting a word, then checking to see if the sounds heard as the word was pronounced match the letters in the text · Point and slide—a technique where children use a finger to gradually reveal the letters in a word, saying the sound that is associated with each letter as it is revealed until the word is pronounced · Children become independent by attempting a pronunciation of a word and asking themselves, Do the letters match the sounds?
Lexical or Orthographic System— Instantaneous word recognition	Difficulty recognizing a word when it is seen in a text other than the one in which it was originally learned Difficulty recognizing a different form of a word, e.g., a contraction, root word with an affix, or a compound word	· Demonstrating the various graphic word representations of a single word, showing children how a single word may look quite different in their own writing and in various books · Helping children to look for words in the surrounding text they do recognize—do those words give clues as to what an unknown word might be? · Word analysis: What does the prefix, suffix, root word mean? Is it a compound word? Do you recognize the words that combine to make the longer word?

TABLE 10.2 *Cueing Systems, Sample Problems, and Sample Solutions*

Cueing System	Sample Problem	Sample Solutions
		· Children become independent by recognizing different forms of the same word and dissecting word parts to support recognition of a new form of the word
Syntactic System— Understanding the correct structure or architecture of written or spoken language; the ability to recognize when language is not structured correctly	Substituting a word that disrupts the meaning of the passage, e.g., *horse* for *house* in the sentence, "My family is building a new house"	· The teacher models how she recognizes correct syntactic arrangement of words. She asks herself, Does this sound like language? · Children are encouraged to read aloud and ask themselves, Does this sound like language? · Children are taught how to stop reading when something doesn't sound right, adjust their rate of reading, and reread asking themselves, Does it make better sense if I read faster or slower? · Children are taught to use language conventions like periods, commas, quotation marks, semicolons as markers of meaning. When they read, they are encouraged to exaggerate the pause for a comma or period, for example, to support clearer meaning · Children study different syntactic styles used by authors to achieve different effects, e.g., when does an author use short, syncopated sentences vs. longer sentences? What type of effect is achieved with each?

TABLE 10.2 *Continued*

Cueing System	Sample Problem	Sample Solutions
Semantic System—The recognition that words and longer pieces of text have associated meanings and concepts, and that those meanings vary slightly from reader to reader; the conceptual meanings can vary from concrete to abstract	Reading words fluently, but experiencing difficulty defining what is meant by a word, sentence, or text	· Children are encouraged to stop, consider a word that would make sense in the context, insert that word, and ask themselves, Does it make sense? · Children are encouraged to stop, reread, read ahead, and otherwise use the context to confirm the meaning of passage; stop yourself when it doesn't make sense: try to ask questions of the book, the author, synthesize or retell what is happening so far, what the author's major points are
Schematic System—The reader's prior knowledge used to comprehend text. Schema is built and/or activated from long-term memory stores when relevant in a reading experience. Schema also refers to the ways—the categories and classification—in which information is stored and retrieved from memory	Inadequate background knowledge or difficulty in activating background knowledge	· Children are encouraged to stop, ask themselves what they already know that is like what this author is trying to communicate · They are encouraged to create a visual image in their minds and ask themselves, What is happening here? How can I draw conclusions, make judgments, assume a critical stance to try to understand subtle points? · Children are encouraged to imagine the author and consider what he or she had in mind when writing · Children are encouraged to ask themselves what they know about this author that might help them comprehend

TABLE 10.2 *Continued*

203

Cueing System	Sample Problem	Sample Solutions
		· Children are encouraged to ask themselves what they know about the text format itself, what is often true of social studies or science text formats
Pragmatic System	Lack of purpose for reading, perception that text is not interesting or useful A setting that prohibits interaction with other readers to construct meaning collectively	· Children are asked to consider what they need to know in order to understand the text · Children are encouraged to ask what is most important from the text in relation to their purpose for reading · Children are encouraged to consider working with another person to discuss, write about, sketch, or act out pieces of the text in order to better comprehend it

TABLE 10.2 *Continued*

are only two kinds of reading problems: failure to decode words and failure to understand word meanings. If we can understand the more subtle features of the reading obstacles themselves, the solutions we teach will be more effective and tailored.

"I don't know what to do about Anne, Ellin. Will you think this through with me?" Kristin Venable, a second-grade teacher in Denver, often poses provocative questions that lead into uncharted waters. That simple question began a conversation in which we invented a host of fix-ups to which I've returned many times in other classrooms.

"Anne is a great reader, Ellin. She gobbles up everything in the room and comes to school with loads of library books. My biggest challenge is keeping her challenged! She came in today with a copy of *The Secret Garden* she was given for Christmas, saying she wants to read it during reader's workshop. It's a beautiful edition with those silky pages and color illustrations sprinkled through it. She has seen the movie and is excited about reading a *challenge* book, but I'm concerned: As I looked through the text, the sentences are lengthy and complex; the language is full of British colloquialisms; it's a long book; and I don't want her to feel frustrated and lose confidence as a reader."

I waited, knowing Kristin would have thought through both sides of the dilemma.

"On the other hand, I've been encouraging all the kids to vary their reading diet. You know, I've said, 'Read in a variety of genres. Read books that are easy or well-loved. Read books that are just right for you and books that are a challenge.' Now Anne wants to do what I've suggested. I'm not sure I can confer with her enough to keep her going through the whole book, but I want to capitalize on her enthusiasm. Do you hear me contradicting myself?" Kristin laughed.

What I heard was nothing like a contradiction. It was a well thought out set of questions about a perplexing problem.

"What do you think about asking Anne?" I proposed. "We could tell her exactly what you've told me and ask her to help make a decision about whether she tackles this project."

Kristin agreed. We spent a recess with Anne, discussing the pros and cons.

"Well, remember what you tell us all the time, Kristin? We don't have to finish everything we start reading and I can always finish reading it in third grade if I can't get it done. I really want to try!"

We agreed. During reader's workshop the next day, Kristin conferred with Anne. "Anne, we've been talking a lot lately about how readers prevent comprehension problems and how they solve those problems if they have them. Let's talk about what you might do to prevent problems before you read."

Anne said, "Well, one of the things good readers do is to think about what they know that's like the book and what they need to know to understand the book."

"Great, we've been calling that activating schema, right? What do you think you know about this book, its author, or the way it is put together—its format?"

Anne replied, "Well, I know what happens because I've seen the movie. Colin walks and his father gets nicer to them all. I don't know anything about the author and I know that it will be the longest chapter book I've ever read!"

"Do you know what country this book is set in?" Kristin asked.

"No, but it's not here and it's a long time ago and it isn't in the city and Mary's parents are both dead."

"That's quite a little spurt of schema, Anne." They both laughed. Kristin quickly went on to build on Anne's knowledge by giving her information about the sentence length, the British figures of speech, and about the relationship between Britain and India in 1911 when the book was published.

"Now, Anne, I want you to read the first few pages by yourself while I confer with a couple of other readers. Why don't you use these little yellow sticky notes to mark places in the text where you are confused by words or ideas. Then I'll come back and we'll talk about ways you can solve problems you might have. Okay?"

When Kristin returned, Anne was intensely engaged in reading and had read most of the first chapter—about five pages. She had marked several places where she had problems. They went to work.

Kristin kept the conference short, five or six minutes, but was able to help Anne solve most of the problems, using a variety of different fix-up strategies. In a couple of cases, Kristin made an on-the-spot decision not to deal with the problem. She said later that she chose to ignore the mistakes when correct pronunciation or word identification had little to do with whether Anne would understand the story.

Anne began by pointing to the text. "When Mary Lennox was sent to Misselthwaite Manor to live with her uncle everybody said she was the most disagreeable-looking child ever seen. It was true, too. She had a little thin face and a little thin body, thin light hair and a sour expression. Her hair was yellow and her face was yellow because she was born in India and had always been ill in one way or another."

"I don't know these words," Anne said, her index finger moving from Misselthwaite to disagreeable to sour expression.

"Let's give them a try sounding them out."

"Miss-eel-th-white," Anne said.

Anne didn't get it quite right, but Kristin said, "Go on Anne. That's not really important and you did well with it. Let's move on."

Kristin pointed to the other words that had given Anne trouble: disagreeable and sour expression. "Give them a try."

"Dis-grace-able . . . No that's not right. Dis-agree-able." Anne corrected her initial pronunciation of the word.

"Great, Anne, how did you know that was disagreeable?"

"Well, I took the word apart in my mind. My mind said disagree. Dis-agree helped me get it."

"So you took the end off that word and saw a smaller word inside?" Kristin asked.

"Yep."

"Did you already know the word disagree?"

"Yep."

"Is there an even smaller word that means something in the word disagreeable?"

"Nope."

Kristin didn't push further. "Okay, where's your next sticky note? What kind of a problem did you have here?"

"I don't know what this is." Anne pointed at sour expression.

"How could you try to figure it out?"

Anne said what she thought the words were. "Sore expedition, sore expedition," Anne said, visibly frustrated. "I can't say it."

"What if I told you the first word was sour?" Kristin asked.

"Sour . . ." Anne looked relieved and reread the sentence.

"Let's see ex-pid-ition? No! expression!"

"How do you know?"

"See? Ex-pres-sion." Anne pointed to each syllable.

"Yes, great Anne. How did you figure that out?"

"Well it was talking about the way she looked and expedition didn't fit that, but light hair and a sour (pause) expression did fit!"

"Great Anne. Go on," Kristin said.

"Her father had held a position under the English Government and had always been bossy and ill himself." Anne read bossy instead of busy. Kristin did not stop Anne as she read this sentence. Anne had not labeled it with a sticky note and the word bossy did little to change the overall meaning Anne seemed to be getting. It matched Anne's background knowledge, having seen the movie in which a bossy Mary Lennox changes gradually into a thoughtful child.

Anne kept reading. "She had not wanted a little girl at all, and when Mary was born she handed her over to the care of an Ayah, who was made to understand that if she wanted to please the Mem Sahib she must keep the child out of sight as much as possible."

"I know I didn't read that right." Anne pointed to Ayah. "And I don't know what it is, that's why I marked it."

"Actually, Anne, you pronounced it perfectly. How did you decide how it should be pronounced?" Kristin asked.

"Because it had an a at the beginning and I just tried to make the rest of the sound of the word with my mouth."

"Well that was really a smart way to do it. Any guesses about what it might mean?"

"I guess a nanny," Anne said.

"How did you know that?"

"Because it said 'to the care of an Ayah' and that sounded like a nanny and also I know people who had nannies that lived with them when they were babies. Their nannies were called something weird, too, like a pear.'"

Kristin and I couldn't resist laughing out loud.

"An au pair is the term the French use for a nanny who lives with a family and takes care of their kids. You're right, though, I think an Ayah is like a nanny or an au pair. Anne, you did exactly what great readers do when they have problems in pronouncing a word and knowing what it means. You figured out how to say the word by sounding it out and you figured out what it meant by looking at the sentence it was in, thinking about your background knowledge, and then guessing at the meaning. That's exactly what great readers do to solve problems."

They moved on to "Mem Sahib."

"I just can't say it, this isn't anything," Anne said, shaking her head. "Mim shahab . . . Meem shabib." Anne tried the words twice, stopped, and spent time rereading before turning to Kristin.

"I don't get it."

"Do you need help with pronouncing the words or with understanding what they mean?" asks Kristin.

"Both," Anne said.

Kristin took a quick glance at the text. Later she told me that she concluded the context would reveal little about the words in question and that, at first, even she was a little unsure about the exact meaning of the words Mem Sahib. From a glance at earlier paragraphs, she drew a conclusion.

"Let me help you with that one," Kristin said to Anne. "That's the name they gave to Mary's mother. I think it means mistress of the house or something like that. Let me tell you how I decided that. I read up here that her mother 'had been a great beauty who cared only to go to parties and amuse herself with gay people.' And then I read that nannies called Ayahs took care of Mary, so I decided that Mem Sahib must be the mother when I read that the Ayah has to keep the child out of sight as much as possible."

I took notes as Kristin conferred, amazed at the territory she covered in five or six minutes. Through her responses to problems Anne identified, she armed Anne with problem-solving strategies that addressed phonics, word identification, word and text meaning, background knowledge, and purpose for reading. Kristin helped Anne to identify problem-solving strategies that were immediately relevant in a text Anne desperately wanted to read. Anne's motivation was a key factor in her application of the problem-solving strategies Kristin taught her that day. She needed to know how to solve problems flexibly, adaptively, and independently if she was to finish the book.

In subsequent conferences, Kristin and Anne talked about getting a reading mentor for her as she read *The Secret Garden*. They were able to identify a fifth-grader who had read the book and was willing to meet with Anne twice a week to coach her through the book. This relieved Kristin of the need to confer with Anne daily and led to the development of a strong relationship with a reader whose proficiency exceeded Anne's. The fifth-grader was taught to converse with Anne and pose questions rather than telling her how to interpret the events she read. As with my struggle through Andre Codrescu's poetry and the value of David's insights, Anne benefitted significantly from the relaxed conversation with another reader.

Kristin told me that Anne struggled through the entire book, exactly as she had told us emphatically she would. Did she recognize the subtleties of meaning an older reader might have? Perhaps not. Will she reread the book in fifth or eighth grade or as a parent? I hope so, and if she does, the layers of meaning she uncovers will no doubt surprise her. The monumental effort she expended as a second-grader to make her way through this book will have, I imagine, an equally lasting impact. She learned that she can set her mind to something and do it. She can move through and beyond the hurdles.

Now I'm glad I bought "Comrade Past & Mister Present," glad I returned to the title poem after many months, and pleased I struggled through its thorny obstacles to a point where, at least in part, I drew some conclusions about its meaning. It makes me wonder whether I challenge myself enough as a reader, realizing after this foray into an obscure mind jungle that I revel in making my way through the dense forest to a place of light and understanding. Having observed Anne and seen the faces of the high school students in Cris' class as they tackled tough comprehension problems, I know that they share a similar sense of accomplishment.

For better or worse, we all learn the most from adversity, not just as readers, but in the wider circles of our lives. Ultimately, confronting our personal challenges, confusions, and losses and moving through them strengthens and deepens us. The same is true of readers. If we can learn to see adversity as opportunity in our lives and in our classrooms, perhaps we will come to view challenges, comprehension problems, and other obstacles as fascinating intellectual opportunities to face together. The satisfaction in emerging on the other side of these hurdles is deeply personal, memorable, and satisfying. If we can make our way through our own Codrescu poetry, perhaps we can find a way to lead our children into their own secret gardens.

Epilogue
Mosaic of Meaning

Dark human shapes could be made out in the distance, flitting indistinctly against the gloomy border of the forest, and near the river two bronze figures, leaning on tall spears, stood in the sunlight under fantastic head-dresses of spotted skins, warlike and still in statuesque repose. And from right to left along the lighted shore moved a wild and gorgeous apparition of a woman.

She walked with measured steps, draped in striped and fringed cloths, treading the earth proudly, with a slight jingle and flash of barbarous ornaments. She carried her head high; her hair was done in the shape of a helmet; she had brass leggings to the knee, brass wire gauntlets to the elbow, a crimson spot on her tawny cheek, innumerable necklaces of glass beads on her neck; bizarre things, charms, gifts of witch-men, that hung about her, glittered and trembled at every step. She must have had the value of several elephant tusks upon her. She was savage and superb, wild-eyed and magnificent; there was something ominous and stately in her deliberate progress. And in the hush that had fallen suddenly upon the whole sorrowful land, the immense wilderness, the colossal body of the fecund and mysterious life seemed to look at her, pensive, as though it had been looking at the image of its own tenebrous and passionate soul.

She came abreast of the steamer, stood still, and faced us. Her long shadow fell to the water's edge. Her face had a tragic and fierce aspect of wild sorrow and of dumb pain mingled with the fear of some struggling, half-shaped resolve. She stood looking at us without a stir, and like the wilderness itself, with an air of brooding over an inscrutable purpose. A whole minute passed, and then she made a step forward. There was a low jingle, a glint of yellow metal, a sway of fringed draperies, and she stopped as if her heart had failed her. The young fellow by my side growled. The pilgrims murmured at my back. She looked at us all as if her life had depended upon the unswerving steadiness of her glance. Suddenly she opened her bared arms and threw them up rigid above her head, as though in an uncontrollable desire to touch the sky, and at the same time the swift shadows darted out on the earth, swept around on the river, gathering the steamer into a shadowy embrace. A formidable silence hung over the scene.

She turned away slowly, walked on, following the bank, and passed into the bushes to the left. Once only her eyes gleamed back at us in the dusk of the thickets before she disappeared.

"If she had offered to come aboard, I really think I would have tried to shoot her," said the man of patches nervously . . .

JOSEPH CONRAD,
Heart of Darkness

It was this page that caught my eye as I flipped through *A Conrad Argosy*, a Joseph Conrad collection illustrated with wood cuts by Hans Mueller. It is a large, heavy book that has been carefully mended with adhesive tape to keep the cover from loosening further. In black ink on the first page is the inscription "Mrs. Paul D. Phillips, October 1942." I picture Rita, my husband Paul's mother, carefully writing her name there over fifty years ago. It was, I believe, a difficult autograph for her. At that time she was a young woman of twenty-two, recently married, receiving the book perhaps as a birthday gift from her parents with whom she then lived in Baltimore. Just months before, her husband Paul Sr. had been captured by the Japanese in the Philippines. For over three years—during the period that Paul Sr. was a prisoner of war, experiencing his own heart of darkness—she would not hear from him.

It is fitting that this is the book I pull out, searching for a final piece. Rita is now dead; yet I feel her careful hands where, long ago, she repaired this book with tape. I am grateful the book is now in our library. It has been much loved and cared for, and somehow, I want to capture in this last chapter a sense of the love, care, and thoughtful consideration that must go into the work teachers do.

This passage leaps out at me from the page. It is the woman who captures my imagination. The first time I read it, my heart beats faster and my palms sweat. The questions begin: Why do I feel such fear for this amazing woman? Why do I sense her coming demise and with that the loss of something incalculably precious? Why, as I read, am I overwhelmed with foreboding and fascinated with this being Conrad has described?

"Dark human shapes could be made out in the distance, flitting indistinctly against the gloomy border of the forest . . ." I am taken into a dream, into a dark, murky place, a jungle completely foreign to me, a place of nightmares. My eyes and ears open and are full of images. I hear the rustling of branches and see vague shapes moving ominously on the bank, as the principal character in this scene appears: ". . . from right to left along the lighted shore moved a wild and gorgeous apparition of a woman." She is, I suppose, a tribal leader or priestess of some sort. A vivid picture of her adorned body forms in my mind: "brass leggings to the knee," "innumerable necklaces of glass beads on her neck," "the value of several elephant tusks upon her." She is statuesque, strong, and silent. Nowhere in the passage does she make a sound. Something about Conrad's description makes me think of a leopard, an elegant, ferocious cat that cannot be tamed.

As I read on, the woman grows in my mind. I begin making inferences. She is more than a human; she is a force—that wildness in woman that has been repressed over the centuries. She becomes for me a character of mythic proportion, harkening back to the goddesses of pre-Christian times.

Joseph Conrad wrote *Heart of Darkness* nearly a century ago, yet this passage remains eternal. The heathen woman embodies a female power and beauty before which men stand speechless, utterly unable to respond, "the hush that had fallen suddenly upon the whole sorrowful land."

In turn the woman seems puzzled by and frightened of the

steamer, the men on it, and all it represents. "Her face had a tragic and fierce aspect of wild sorrow and of dumb pain mingled with the fear of some struggling, half-shaped resolve." Is the woman the symbol of Africa, that mysterious land whose wildness continues to frighten the developed world? Is she the darkness in each of us, that wild part of our unconscious which we fear to confront, let alone acknowledge? Is she, in Jungian terms, a female archetype, representing a power that has been passed down through the ages?

What is her half-shaped resolve? As the dying Kurtz—one of literature's truly evil characters—is taken away on the steamer, does she know that the destruction he has caused can never be repaired? Is the wild sorrow and dumb pain a realization of all that has been lost? The questions continue, a critical part of my effort to make sense of this passage—my synthesis.

"And she stopped as if her heart had failed her . . . She looked at us all as if her life had depended upon the unswerving steadiness of her glance. Suddenly she opened her bared arms and threw them up rigid above her head, as though in an uncontrollable desire to touch the sky, and at the same time the swift shadows darted out on the earth, swept around on the river, gathering the steamer into a shadowy embrace." What is she doing here? It is as if she knows her fate and yet there is something in her that goes beyond fate. Is this shadowy embrace a gesture of forgiveness, or is it her way of showing the men on the steamer that she has them in her embrace and will never let them go, though they may think they've escaped?

I read again and see that the woman's gesture is also one of futility and hopelessness. No one can really touch the sky, though we all may want to at times. Is she throwing up her arms in despair? Does she know she has lost and all she can do is make one last powerful, but futile, gesture?

What is it about the woman that the men on the steamer cannot abide? Is it her wildness, her strength, her willingness to forgive, or her inability to let go that brings out their guilt and evil? "If she had offered to come aboard, I really think I would have tried to shoot her . . ." I infer that there is something here about the repression of those things we fear and don't understand. In this brief passage, Conrad creates a creature imbued with mystery and strength and with a few strokes shows how quickly man is prepared to destroy that which threatens or puzzles him.

I find myself reading the passage again and again, each time seeing more. Here are white men coming up the mighty river in a steamer that clangs and whistles, imposing itself on a land where it doesn't belong. The men carry rifles. They act in total disregard for the natives on the shore. They invade and plunder, believing they have every right to do so. I see the tragic clash between native peoples and western civilization's greed. I see that the price of colonization was the destruction of cultures.

I wonder if the modern era will be remembered as that time in our history when thousands of diverse cultures were obliterated forever. I connect my experience to this writing and remember arriving at the Istanbul airport several years ago and being greeted by a huge picture of the Marlboro man. I think of Tina Turner's "What's love got to do, got to do with it . . ." blasting from the loudspeaker at a sacred hot springs turned swimming pool in Pammukkale, a remote Turkish town with an ancient Greek theater and white travertine cliffs. And I think little has changed since Conrad's time. Our means of conquering are just different today.

I go back and reread the whole story. I first read it in college and remember skimming it again years later, before going to see *Apocalypse Now*, a modern-day rendition in which Vietnam was the Heart of Darkness and Marlon Brando the tyrant Kurtz. I get up early and read voraciously, mesmerized by the shadowy evil Conrad portrays. And as I read, I wonder if each of us has within us the potential to become a Kurtz—to be eaten up and embraced by darkness so deep and penetrating that no light can get through.

I go back to the passage of the woman, now able to put it in context and I am, more than ever, struck by the power and poetry of Conrad's language and by the dichotomies that flow through his writing, creating a mood as complex as life itself: wild and gorgeous, savage and superb, wild-eyed and magnificent, ominous and stately, tragic and fierce, wild sorrow and dumb pain, "half-shaped" resolve, and "inscrutable" purpose.

My prediction that the woman would be destroyed comes true, or perhaps it does. Conrad wraps even that in ambiguity: "I pulled the string [of the steam boat whistle] time after time . . . Only the barbarous and superb woman did not so much as flinch, and stretched tragically her bare arms after us over the somber and glittering river . . . And then that imbecile crowd [the men with rifles] down on the deck started their little fun, and I could see nothing more for the smoke."

As I read, I consciously and subconsciously use the strategies we've discussed in this book. I synthesize. I question. I infer. I create vivid sensory images. I relate the piece to my own experience. I tease out what I think is most important. I draw conclusions about what I think the key points of the passage are. Sometimes I use the strategies purposefully, other times they surface randomly. They are tools I use, sometimes effortlessly, sometimes purposefully to construct a meaning. They intertwine and merge and I switch quickly among them, frequently using them simultaneously. They are the instruments which, as I became more familiar with them, gave me the ability to read more critically. They are a means to an end. For proficient readers, they are second nature.

Years ago, Ellin gave me *Where the Bluebird Sings to the Lemonade Springs*, a series of essays by Wallace Stegner. She gave it to me as I left the Public Education Coalition to embark on a writer's life and inscribed it "to call forth that all important sense of place; to surround you with peace and wonder on your journey."

Many essays in that book have guided me, but the last one I come back to year after year. In it Stegner says, "The writers I admired, and still admire, were not carpenters but sculptors. Their art was and is a real probe of troubling human confusions. They spurned replicas, they despised commercialized entertainment. They were after the mystery implicit in the stone."

Repeatedly, I have found myself substituting the word teacher for writer in that passage. The teachers I admire—the teachers whose classrooms we have visited in this book as well as many others—are not carpenters but sculptors. They are after the mystery implicit in the stone. They guide their students on a search for the mystery and ponder with them as "troubling human confusions" are revealed.

These are teachers who create the environment and give students the tools they need to read deeply and thoughtfully, so that they can contemplate ideas alone and with others, and write persuasively about what they read. They are teachers who embrace the wide range of responses their students give to the same text, and challenge the students to read books they believe they cannot.

We have all had those teachers—inside and outside the classroom. People who believed in us, who trusted our uniqueness, who unleashed our dormant talents, and who gave us the skills and confidence to carve away at the stone ourselves. We remember them for their gifts to us. But, perhaps their greatest gift was the standard they set as curious and passionate learners.

We cannot expect to be able to teach these techniques for increasing the scope and depth of a child's comprehension unless we use them ourselves. It is through our own experience in reading—using these strategies very consciously at times—that we internalize and are able to teach them. By teaching the strategies, we give children the tools they need to exercise their critical thinking faculties, to struggle with human confusions, and to embark on their own explorations of the mystery and beauty of life.

John Cheever once said that he wrote "to try to make sense of my life." We read, I think, for the same reason: to make sense of our lives and to connect to those who have come before us and those who now share the planet with us. We read to do our jobs, to learn, to explore, to adventure, to bring order to chaos, to open new vistas, to better understand the world around us, and to develop compassion for the human condition.

Great writing leaves us with more questions than answers. Each of us must look deep within to determine what a great novel, poem, or essay means to us. The comprehension strategies discussed in this book are tools to chisel meaning deep into a reader's long-term memory as he or she discusses with others, writes about the piece, or explores it further through research or additional reading.

Each time we encounter a great piece of writing, we set out on a personal journey of self-discovery with a destination as unknown as that of Columbus. By the mysterious alchemy of the written word, we range over time and space, expanding our experiences, enriching our souls, and ultimately becoming more fully, more consciously human.

Appendix One
The Big Picture in Reading

Where does comprehension instruction fit in to an overall reader's workshop?

The table in this appendix represents a model of reading that includes many of the elements we consider critical to a successful reader's workshop. It begins with a redefinition of the *content* in reading—a model (adapted from Rumelhart) outlining six systems (types of information readers rely upon during reading) and below, the strategies proficient readers use to ensure the successful functioning of all six systems. As we consider other elements in a well-rounded reader's workshop, we have included information about text elements and genre study, both regular and appropriate focuses for instruction, and a brief sampling of elements found in richly literate classrooms. Though we feel all are critical success factors in elementary- and middle-school classrooms, this book focuses primarily on the strategies proficient readers use to comprehend well, a critically important component of the content in reading.

Content		Text Elements	
Surface Structure Systems	**Deep Structure Systems**	**Narrative Text Elements:**	**Expository Text Elements:**
Grapho-Phonic (letter/sound knowledge)	*Semantic* (word meanings/ associations)	Character Setting Conflict Plot Structure	Text Structure: cause/effect chronological problem/solution classification
Lexical (word knowledge)	*Schematic* (prior knowledge)	Table of Contents	Table of Contents
Syntactic (language structure)	*Pragmatic* (knowledge of audience/ purpose)	Dedication Title Illustrations	Index Graphic Elements Appendices

Metacognition
Cognitive Strategies
for Solving Problems

Use of Context	Monitoring for Meaning
Word Recognition	Determining Importance
Word Analysis (prefixes, suffixes, compound)	Creating Mental Images Synthesizing
Rereading	Relating New to Known (Schema)
Reading Ahead	Questioning
Decoding	Inferring

Redefining Reading from Content to Context

Genre Study	*Living in a Literate Classroom*
Poetry	Understanding the processes
Picture Book	and rituals of the readers' workshop
Memoir/Autobiography	
Biography	Selecting books
Realistic Fiction	
Historical Fiction	Contributing to and learning from book clubs;
Narrative Nonfiction	sharing recommendations
Textbooks	
Tests	Understanding options for oral, artistic, and
	written responses to literature
	Creating an environment conducive to in-depth
	study of books and comprehension strategies
	Teachers live literate lives and serve as models
	Selecting their own text

Appendix Two

Is there a schedule for reader's workshop that is more useful than others?

No, though teachers have experimented successfully with a variety of formats. Two are presented below.

Sample One

Silent Reading—5–20 minutes for focused silent reading; often the teacher spends part of this time reading his or her own text

Mini Lesson—5–15 minutes where the teacher works with large or small groups to introduce, model, reinforce, demonstrate, and/or record her own or the children's thinking about a reading comprehension strategy, a reading skill, a classroom procedure such as a book club, or a reading/writing connection

Workshop—20–40 minutes for individual reading, teacher conferring and/or meeting with small, needs-based groups, book club meetings, other responses to reading

Sharing—5–10 minutes in which students share insights from their reading, pose questions for other readers, share responses, or debrief experiences such as book clubs

Note—In this model, writer's workshop, using a similar structure, may occur immediately before or after reader's workshop, or at another time during the school day.

Sample Two

Silent Reading/Writing—5–20 minutes for children to select silent reading or writing—teacher spends part of this time reading or writing

Mini Lesson—10–20 minutes during which the teacher may introduce, model, demonstrate, reinforce and/or record teacher's or children's thinking in relation to a reading and/or writing strategy. In this model, reading and writing instruction is integrated

Reader's/Writer's Workshop—30–60 minutes during which children read, write, or both. Children are encouraged to balance their time between reading and writing, but are permitted to choose which area to focus on any given day or week.

Sharing—15–20 minutes for students to share insights and questions as well as sections of their writing for comment

Workshop may end with another short, focused silent reading/writing time.

Both formats assume long periods of flexibly scheduled time that is structured according to children's needs rather than school schedules, to the degree possible. It is important to note that many highly effective teachers use these large blocks of time to integrate reading, writing, and research from other content areas. Children may use reading and writing, for example, as the tools through which they study social studies, science, mathematics, or art.

Appendix Three

What is the balance between teacher and student involvement during the course of a comprehension strategy study?

Though the subtleties of each class and the knowledge base of each teacher affects the course of a comprehension strategy study, the model below, *The Gradual Release of Responsibility Model* (adapted from Gallagher & Pearson, 1983), represents a gradual transition from teachers' exposition and modeling to student responsibility for demonstrating and articulating his or her use of the strategy. The wavy line represents increased teacher responsibility for modeling when introducing the strategy in a new genre or in very challenging text.

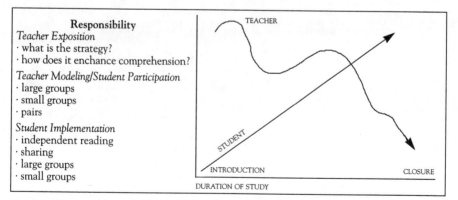

Gradual Release of Responsibility for Comprehension Strategy (Gallagher & Pearson; adapted by Keene)

Appendix Four

Is there a way to assess students' understanding and application of reading comprehension strategies?

There wasn't! We struggled to find a more formal and consistent way to assess children's use of comprehension strategies than relying on records kept during reading conferences. The Major Point Interview for Readers developed by Ellin Keene with input from dozens of teachers and staff developers is an instrument designed to be used in two ways: It was initially designed as a beginning and end of the year (major point) assessment of children's use of all comprehension strategies. Some teachers assessed all students in their classroom as they had extra time in the first and last two months of the school year; others chose a representative sample of ten or twelve students and drew conclusions about the whole class by reviewing the data from those students. Depending on the age of the child, it takes between twenty and forty-five minutes to administer the instrument in its entirety.

The second use for the MPIR involves using only the questions and rubrics that focus on the strategy being studied. For example, a teacher could ask, during individual conferences, the MPIR questions involving synthesis at the beginning and again at the end of a comprehension strategy study of synthesis to assess the student's growth during that study. Each time a new strategy study is undertaken, he or she would use only the questions that relate to that study.

The rubric that follows the MPIR is designed to permit teachers to quantify student growth in use of a given strategy. Each number represents twenty percent of the overall scale. The rubric has been a useful way to quantify and describe a student's growth to parents and administrators.

Public Education & Business Coalition
Reading Project
Major Point Interview for Readers

Text-Based Assessment and Think-Aloud

I want you to read several pages of this book. [Alternative for children who are not voice/print matching: I want you to tell me as much as you can about the first few pages of this book. Be sure to tell me if you recognize any of the words.] I will stop you every once in a while. [Identify logical stopping places roughly every third or fourth page in picture books, and every two to three paragraphs in longer text.] Then tell me exactly what you are thinking about. Tell me what you were thinking about *as you read* the story (or text). The important thing is that you pay attention and remember, so that you can tell me what you were thinking about while you read the piece. You can tell me anything the book makes you think about, any problems you had while reading it, and what you think it is about.

Strategy Use Interview

Now I want to ask you some questions about what you think about while you read.

Uses Schema
1. When you read that story (text) did it remind you of anything you know about? What? Why did it remind you of? [If response is no] Did it remind you of any experiences or things that have happened?

228

2. Are there things you know about or things in your life that help you to understand this book? How does that help?
3. We have just discussed (talked about) what this book reminds you of. [Restate child's response.] What do you understand now that you didn't understand before?

Infers
[Select an event or fact that would call for a conclusion or interpretation. Refer to the event or fact when asking questions under number 2 below.]

1. [For narrative text] Can you predict what is about to happen? Why did you make that prediction? Can you point to (or identify) something in the book that helped you to make that prediction? [Or] What do you already know that helped you to make that prediction?
2. What did the author mean by _____? What in the story (text) helped you to know that? What do you already know that helped you to decide that?
3. We have just discussed (talked about) predicting and inferring. [Restate child's response.] What do you understand now that you didn't understand before?

Asks Questions
1. What did you wonder about (or question) while you were reading this story (text)?
2. What questions do you have about this book now? (or wonder about now?)
3. We have just discussed (talked about) the questions you asked. [Restate child's response.] What do you understand now that you didn't understand before?

Determines What Is Important in Text
1. Are there some parts of this story (text) that are more important than the others? Which ones? Why do you think they were the most important?

2. What do you think the author [name author] thought was most important so far in this story (text)? Why do you think so?

3. We have just discussed (talked about) important parts of the story. [Restate child's response.] What do you understand now that you didn't understand before?

Repeat Think-Aloud with Subsequent Text

Monitors Comprehension/Uses Appropriate Fix-Up Strategies

1. Did you have any problems while you were reading this story (text)? What could you do to solve the problem?

2. When you are reading other stories (texts) what kinds of problems do you have? What are all the ways you solve the problems?

3. We have just discussed (talked about) problems you have. [Restate child's response.] What do you understand now that you didn't understand before?

Visualizes and Creates Mental Images While Reading

1. When you were reading this story (text) did you make any pictures or images in your head? Tell me everything you can about that picture or image you made while you were reading just now. Do the pictures or images that you just told me about help you to understand the story (text) better? How?

2. [If no response] Can you think of a story where you made your own pictures or images in your head? Tell me everything you can about that picture or image. Do those pictures or images help you to understand the story (text) better? How?

3. We have just discussed (talked about) the pictures or images you make in your head. [Restate child's response.] What do you understand now that you didn't understand before?

Synthesizes
1. If you were to tell another person about the story (text) you just read, and you could only use a few sentences, what would you tell them?
2. Think about what you have just said about the story. What do you understand now that you didn't understand before?

Keene, 1995

Public Education & Business Coalition
Reading Project
Major Point Interview for Readers
Scoring Rubric

There is an overall criterion to bear in mind: When the reader can go beyond explaining his or her thinking and begins to articulate how using a strategy helps him or her to comprehend better, the response should be scored at least a 4.

Thinks Aloud
1. No response, random thoughts unconnected to the text
2. Disconnected thoughts relating more to the pictures than text
3. Thinking is tied to text events/text content; beginning inferences, may be inaccurate in relation to text, more tied to personal experience; may identify problems (word level) during reading
4. Generates questions, identifies problems, infers, elaborates text events with own experience, may make predictions about overall book meaning
5. Clearly expresses own thinking, may speculate about theme, discusses how own thinking supports or inhibits comprehension

Uses Schema
1. No response/schematic connection
2. Can talk about what text reminds him or her of, but cannot explain; reference to schema may not be clearly connected to text
3. Relates background knowledge/experience to text
4. Expands interpretation of text using schema; may discuss schema related to author, text structure; may pose questions based on apparent discrepancies between text and background knowledge
5. Explains how schema enriches interpretation of text; talks about use of schema to enhance interpretation and comprehension of other texts; connections extend beyond life experience and immediate text

Infers
1. No response/inference
2. Attempts a prediction or conclusion, inaccurate or unsubstantiated with text information
3. Draws conclusions or makes predictions that are consistent with text or schema
4. Draws conclusions and/or makes predictions and can explain the source of the conclusion or prediction
5. Develops predictions, interpretations, and/or conclusions about the text that include connections between the text and the reader's background knowledge or ideas and beliefs

Questions
1. No questions/irrelevant questions
2. Poses literal question(s)
3. Poses questions to clarify meaning
4. Poses questions to enhance meaning of text (critical response; big idea), may explain how posing questions deepens comprehension

5. Uses questions to challenge the validity of print, author's stance, motive, or point of view

Determines What Is Important in Text

1. No response, random guessing, inaccurate attempt to identify important elements
2. Identifies some elements (primarily pictures) as more important to text meaning
3. Identifies words, characters, and/or events as more important to overall meaning—makes some attempt to explain reasoning
4. Identifies at least one key concept, idea, or theme as important in overall text meaning, and clearly explains why
5. Identifies multiple ideas or themes, may attribute them to different points of view, discusses author's stance or purpose and its relation to key themes and ideas in the text

Following a Second Reading and Think-Aloud

Monitors Comprehension

1. Little or no conscious awareness of reading process
2. Identifies difficulties—problems are often at word level; little or no sense of the need to solve the problem; does not articulate strengths; identifies need to concentrate; says sound it out
3. Identifies problems at word, sentence, or schema level; can articulate and use a strategy to solve problems, usually at the word or sentence level
4. Articulates and uses more than one strategy for solving problems; focuses on problems at the schema (more global) level
5. Identifies problems at all levels; uses a variety of strategies flexibly and appropriately given the context and the problem

Visualizes

1. No response
2. Describes some visual or other sensory images; may be tied directly to text or a description of the picture in the text
3. Describes own mental images, usually visual; images are somewhat elaborated from the literal text or existing picture
4. Creates and describes multisensory images that extend and enrich the text
5. Elaborates multisensory images to enhance comprehension; can articulate how the process enhances comprehension

Synthesizes

1. Random or no response; may give title
2. Identifies some text events; random or nonsensical order
3. Synthesizes with some awareness of event sequence: beginning, middle, end
4. Enhances meaning in text with synthesis; may incorporate own schema; uses story elements to enhance the synthesis, may identify key themes
5. Succinct synthesis using internalized story/genre structure, identifies key themes; may articulate how synthesizing promotes deeper comprehension

Retelling

1. Random response; may be related to story (text); may give title
2. Retelling reveals beginning awareness of event sequence
3. Uses story elements (character, setting, conflict, sequence of events, resolution) and/or genre structure to organize a relatively accurate retelling (beginning, middle, end)
4. Story elements/genre structure clear in an accurate retelling; refers to interactions between story elements

(how problem affects character, how setting changes problem, etc.)

5. Uses all story elements/genre structure and inferences to capture key themes in piece; points out interrelationships between elements; talks about how the overall meaning is influenced

Keene, Goudvis, Schwartz (1995)

Appendix Five

Has the effectiveness of reading comprehension instruction been studied?

The summary that follows is one of several studies the Public Education Coalition has undertaken to measure children's growth in reading comprehension strategies in classrooms where Coalition staff developers focused on comprehension strategies with teachers for at least twenty days. The MPIR and rubric were used to show growth in 119 students in their use of comprehension strategies. That growth was compared to the students' performance on the Flynt/Cooter Informal Reading Inventory. In general, we have found that students' growth in reading comprehension strategies correlates closely with their growth in comprehending at the literal and inferential level, and in their overall comprehension as measured by retelling. This study has been replicated for five years and the results are similar each year.

1994–1995 Reading Project Evaluation Summary

Purpose

The purpose of the 1994–1995 Reading Project Evaluation was to *assess the effect of intensive staff development in reading comprehension strategy instruction in PEBC Reading Project schools.* Schools in the Reading Project are designated *intervention* schools. Teachers receive intensive in-class training over a three year period and commit to teaching reading comprehension strategies as an integral part of their reading instruction. *Nonintervention* schools were PEBC schools currently participating in another PEBC project (such as Literacy League) but which did not receive specific training in reading comprehension instruction.

Sample

A total of 119 children were assessed. Sixty children comprised the intervention sample and fifty-nine comprised the nonintervention sample. Schools were matched for similar socioeconomic and demographic characteristics. The sample included:

Grade Two (whole class case study)
Grade Two, intervention/nonintervention samples
Grades Three, Four, Five, intervention/nonintervention samples
Grade Four (whole class case study)

Evaluation Measures

Measures used to assess children's reading comprehension include the Reading Project's Major Point Interview which measures children's use of the eight proficient reader strategies. A widely used informal reading inventory, the Flynt/Cooter, was used to assess children's responses to comprehension questions and their ability to retell a story.

Assessment of Reading

Results (Major Point Interview)

The Major Point Interview assesses children's ability to use the eight strategies most commonly associated with proficient readers as they read unfamiliar text. Individual interviews were conducted with 119 children in the fall of 1994 and again in the spring of 1995. Children's responses to in-depth interview questions were scored on a five point rubric, measuring their level of sophistication in using each reading comprehension strategy.

Average Percentage Growth on the Major Point Interview from Fall to Spring 1994–1995				
	Intervention Group		*Nonintervention Group*	
Grade 2	n=12	25%	n=12	10%
Grades 3,4,5	n=37	18%	n=36	6%
	Whole Class Case Study Classrooms: *Percentage Gain, Fall to Spring*			
Grade 2	n=19	27% growth		
Grade 4	n=10	21% growth		

Average Percentage Growth on Major Point Interview from Fall to Spring by Ethnic Group				
	Intervention Group		*Nonintervention Group*	
African American	n= 6	27%	n=10	–.25%
Hispanic/Latino	n=24	16%	n=31	6%
Caucasian	n=28	21%	n=18	9%
*Asian American sample is still too small to analyze				

Results (Flynt/Cooter Informal Reading Inventory)

The Flynt/Cooter measures children's ability to answer literal, inferential, and evaluative reading comprehension questions. It is also used to measure children's retelling of a narrative, which is a good indication of how much they understand of what they read.

Average Percentage Growth on Comprehension Questions (Literal vs. Inferential and Evaluative Questions)				
	Intervention Group		Nonintervention Group	
	Literal	Inferential	Literal	Inferential
Grade 3	34%	44%	7%	.4%
Grade 4	19%	47%	−1.8%	21%
Grade 5	14%	50%	−14%	35%

Overall growth for children in grades two through five in the intervention group illustrates that comprehension strategy instruction has an effect on this more global measure of comprehension. The reading intervention is particularly effective in strengthening children's abilities to think inferentially about and evaluate what they read. Again, staff development has a significant impact on students' overall reading comprehension.

Percentage Growth on Retelling Task from Fall to Spring		
	Intervention Group	Nonintervention Group
Grade 3	28%	11%
Grade 4	16%	9%
Grade 5	10%	10%
Grade 2 case study shows a 38% improvement		

Although the increases in children's retelling scores over the course of the year were not as dramatic as in other measures, children's steady improvement in their ability to retell narratives provides additional evidence of the effectiveness of reading comprehension strategy instruction.

Children in intervention classrooms made significantly greater gains than children in the nonintervention classrooms. The gains held across different ethnic groups illustrates that reading comprehension strategy instruction is a powerful intervention with children of all backgrounds and abilities, and that staff development in reading correlates to higher achievement for students.

Appendix Six
Literature Response Options

Are there tools you have used to help children "work with" each compre-
hension strategy during the course of a long strategy study?

We have found that certain tools or strategy applications have been
helpful for children learning to use a strategy for the first time or in particularly challenging text. Many of the applications are used effectively
for all the strategies; others have a more limited and obvious application to only one or two strategies. Children are often asked to show
their thinking through the use of these tools. We have found that the
most authentic, and therefore, successful application of the strategies is
in the context of book clubs—small groups of children talking regularly about books and the strategies they used to understand them.

The sampling of tools provided below is only a small compilation
of the innovative ways teachers have designed and adapted to help
children *see* the mental architecture that underlies successful comprehension. Most of the ideas have been adapted or paraphrased from
the work of teachers and researchers in many sites around the country. Our thanks to all who have contributed to this small collection.

Literature Response Options/Strategy Applications:
Ways to Hold Thinking in Comprehension Strategy Study

The following response options are only a sample of the dozens of
ways teachers have helped young readers to remember or *hold their*

thinking while learning to use comprehension strategies. These techniques have been used in strategy studies of every comprehension strategy.

The goal is for children to understand these response options as tools to help them hold their thinking about a book or about their use of a particular strategy. Ultimately, our hope is that they use them independently when reading a text that is challenging, or when learning to use a strategy that is new to them.

Written or Artistic Response Options/Strategy Applications

· Letters (hypothetical or real) to or from authors, characters, illustrators, or other readers often help children to understand the stance or point of view an author or a character within a book has taken.

· Quick Write—readers pause for a very brief time to write about the gist of the text so far and/or the strategies the reader is using to make sense of the text.

· Double Entry Journals or Diaries—used in a variety of ways to help children simultaneously compare two components of their reading. Teachers often create open-ended tables, such as the one in the sample below, and ask children to determine what will be recorded on either side of the blank chart. Others ask children to use steno notebooks which have a light line dividing the page vertically. I have found that providing children with a double entry journal format and leaving to their discretion a particular use of it is most successful.

· Highlighting markers and self-adhesive notes—Students use markers or self-adhesive notes to mark or code (see below) text where the reader became aware of or used a strategy. The reader may use the code to hold his or her thinking to share with a teacher during a reading conference or with the children during a sharing session.

Story Maps or Webs—Children can build visual representations of key themes, questions, important ideas, images, conclusions, story elements, etc. Story maps help children

Samples	
Facts from the text	Reader's response to the facts
Quote from the text	Reader's response—may include examples of reader's use of a specific strategy
Strategy being studied	Reader's thoughts about how use of that strategy enhanced comprehension of the text
One reader's opinion	Another reader's response to that opinion and his or her own opinion

organize, connect, categorize, and prioritize key concepts in fiction or nonfiction.

· Transparency Text—Teachers copy a page or more of text onto a transparency so the teacher or student can visually demonstrate use of a strategy while other readers watch. The reader marks the transparency using codes or marks the margins with questions and thinks aloud while reading the projected text. The technique provides a way for children to see as well as hear a proficient reader think aloud. Often children have a copy of that text on their desks to mark as the demonstration proceeds.

· Coding Text—Students invent or use a code such as the one below. The code may be laminated onto bookmarks and kept by each child in each book he or she reads.

I = Important
PK = Prior Knowledge
S = Synthesis
MI = Mental Images
! = An inference (conclusion, judgment, belief, opinion based on text)
? = Question
P = Prediction
C = Prediction Confirmed
D/C = Prediction Disconfirmed

· Thinking Records—Chart paper or large artists' notebooks (no lines) are used to record and display strategy definitions, examples generated by the children, questions, and insights about the use of a strategy. The records are best when developed by children and revised throughout a school year so the charts or artist's notebook becomes a living record of the strategies studied and used by the children in a classroom.

· K/W/L—Records of what children *know, what they want to know, and what they learned* are compiled before, during, and after reading a book, article, or before and after a strategy study in which case the K/W/L refers to use of the strategy itself.

· Time lines—Large time lines in the classroom or small ones in a reading log can record information chronologically about what is being learned in a strategy study or what is understood from text.

· Venn Diagrams—Teachers create blank Venn Diagrams with two, three, or four circles. Children can use to show relationships among different strategies or elements of a text.

· Bar and Line Graphs—Teachers create graphs with a horizontal and vertical axis that children can use to represent different use of different strategies, story elements, or changes within a text.

· Photographs of the Mind—Students pause during their reading to sketch an immediate impression, image, or question from the text. They can exchange sketches with another reader and add to that reader's images in order to share impressions of the book with another reader.

Oral Response Options/Strategy Applications

· Book Clubs—Children participate in regularly scheduled meetings of groups (usually with the same group) who meet over time to discuss books they read and strategies they use.

· Pair Shares—Two children, usually sitting knee-to-knee,

share some application of a comprehension strategy or key concepts from a book.

· Think/Pair/Share—Children record their thoughts about a strategy or book and share with a partner. That pair shares with another pair, then with eight children, and eventually with the whole class.

· Notice and Share—Groups of students are assigned a *stance* from which to observe another child or teacher think aloud as they read a text. For example, one group watches a model's use of a comprehension strategy, such as questioning, while another watches for use of determining importance, etc. Students can also assume the stance of a literary critic, a character from the book, a researcher gathering information from the book and/or the author, and share their impressions with others.

· Strategy Study Groups—Students can form ad hoc study groups to reflect on and improve their own use of a comprehension strategy. Occasionally these groups work with the whole class or other small groups to enhance their understanding of the strategy.

· Strategy Instruction Groups—Students work in small groups to develop think-alouds for other groups, including younger children, who are learning to use a particular strategy. They may create posters or other visual aids to share their thinking and help other readers learn to use the strategy.

Appendix Seven
Appropriate Texts for Teachers and Children

Are there certain books you use to teach each strategy?

We have found that most well-written books are usable for all strategies. Teachers have used poorly written or very difficult text to demonstrate the need for very conscious use of strategies in challenging reading situations. We frequently use picture books in mini lessons, as they are short enough to be conducive to modeling during a mini lesson. Many teachers use a novel they are reading aloud as they model use of a comprehension strategy.

Many teachers with whom we work select a group of books from which a group of students can choose. Limiting text selection occurs at different times in the school year *for a specific purpose, such as an author study or a genre study, because a book club wants to read the same book, and/or because a child needs to have a very limited selection of books.*

We have found that *all children need strategy instruction if they are reading sufficiently challenging material.* Hence, highly able readers need strategy instruction as well as children who struggle, if they are reading challenging text. Here are some guidelines we've found helpful in the never-ending task of helping children to choose appropriate text.

Clearly, the most critical book selection is that made by the children (after careful instruction from their teacher) for their independent applications of the strategy. What follows is an outline of key points teachers try to keep in mind when teaching students to make wise, challenging text selections.

We must begin by considering what makes a given text appropriate for a given child. The child's schema is the single most important influence on the readability of a text. This includes

- Schema for text content and author (relevant prior knowledge/experiences), and;
- Schema for text format (print style, layout, density, illustrations and graphs)

We must also consider the needs and interests of each reader. Several additional elements affect the appropriateness of a given text:

- The likelihood that a child will flexibly and independently apply comprehension strategies to make sense of a given text;
- Prereading experiences including the opportunity to hear a read-aloud from the text the child will read and/or discussion about the text content or format;
- The reader's need and desire to comprehend.

We need to consider the long-term diet for each reader: Variety is critical.

- Children need to read and apply comprehension strategies in a variety of genres;
- Children should read text that challenges them in different ways, i.e. a new genre, a new author, increasingly difficult text, choosing text that must be reread in order to be comprehended, etc.;
- Children and their teachers must devise ways keep track of their choices to ensure variety.

Some key points to consider when teaching children to make wise selections and/or when assisting children in their selection of text:

· Quality text is essential—application of comprehension strategies in poorly written text is of limited value;
· Children need to gradually assume responsibility for selecting appropriate text—teachers must continue to interact with students throughout the school year about their selections;
· Modeling is critical—teachers need to model ways in which they select and recommend books;
· Children may need to field test text—they try a page or two or a section and think aloud about the appropriateness of the text with their teacher or book club.

References

Afflerbach, P. P., and P. H. Johnston. 1986. "What Do Expert Readers Do When the Main Idea Is Not Explicit?" In J. F. Baumann, ed., *Teaching Main Idea Comprehension.* Newark, DE: International Reading Association.

Anderson, R. C., and P. D. Pearson. 1984. "A Schema-Theoretic View of Basic Processes in Reading." In P. D. Pearson, ed., *Handbook of Reading Research.* White Plains, NY: Longman.

Andre, M. E., and T. H. Anderson. 1970. "The Development and the Evaluation of a Self-Questioning Study Technique." *Reading Research Quarterly* 161: 605–623.

Baumann, J. F. 1986. "The Direct Instruction of Main Idea Comprehension Ability." In J. F. Baumann, ed., *Teaching Main Idea Comprehension.* Newark, DE: International Reading Association.

Brown, A. L., J. D. Day, and E. S. Jones. 1983. "The Development of Plans for Summarizing Texts." *Child Development* 54: 968–979.

Brown, A. L., and A. S. Palinscar. 1985. *Reciprocal Teaching of Comprehension Strategies: A Natural History of One Program to Enhance Learning.* (Tech. Rep. No. 334). Urbana, IL: University of Illinois Center for the Study of Reading.

Burns, O. A. 1986. *Cold Sassy Tree.* New York: Dell.

Cisneros, S. 1991. *Woman Hollering Creek and Other Stories.* New York: Random House.

Codrescu, A. 1986. *Comrade Past and Mister Present*. Minneapolis, MN: Coffee House.

Collins, B. 1991. *Questions About Angels: Poems*. New York: Morrow.

Conrad, J. 1994. *Heart of Darkness*. New York: Viking Penguin.

Duffy, G. G., et al. 1987. "Effects of Explaining the Reasoning Associated with Using Reading Strategies." *Reading Research Quarterly* 22: 347–368.

Frankl, V. E. 1988. *Man's Search for Meaning*. New York: Pocket Books.

Gallagher, M., and P. D. Pearson. 1983. *The Instruction of Reading Comprehension in Contemporary Educational Psychology*.

Garner, R. 1987. *Metacognition and Reading Comprehension*. J. Orasanu, ed. Norwood, NJ: Ablex.

Gordon, C. J., and P. D. Pearson. 1983. *The Effects of Instruction on Meta-comprehension and Inferencing on Children's Comprehension Abilities*. (Tech Rep. No. 227). Urbana, IL: University of Illinois Center for the Study of Reading.

Griffin, S. 1993. *A Chorus of Stones: A Private Life of War*. New York: Doubleday.

Hansen, J. 1981. "The Effects of Inference Training and Practice on Young Children's Reading Comprehension." *Reading Research Quarterly* 16: 391–417.

———. 1987. *When Writers Read*. Portsmouth, NH: Heinemann.

"If You Can Read This . . . You Learned Phonics. Or So It's Supporters Say." May 13, 1996. *Newsweek*.

Kenyon, J. 1993. *Constance: Poems*. St. Paul, MN: Graywolf.

Kintch, W., and T. A. Van Dijk. 1978. "Toward a Model of Text Comprehension and Production." *Psychological Review* 363–398.

Maria, K. 1990. *Reading Comprehension Instruction: Issues and Strategies*. Timonium, MD: York Press.

Martin, B. Jr., and J. Archambault. 1987. *Knots on a Counting Rope*. New York: Henry Holt.

References

Microsoft Corporation. 1992–1994. *Encarta CD-ROM Multimedia Encyclopedia '94 Edition for Windows*.

Moskowitz, F. 1987. *A Leak in the Heart: Tales from a Woman's Life*. Boston, MA: David R. Godine.

National Commission on Excellence in Education. 1983. *A Nation at Risk: The Imperative for Educational Reform*. Washington, DC: U.S. Government Printing Office.

Paris, S. G., D. R. Cross, and M. Y. Lipson. 1984. "Informed Strategies for Learning: A Program to Improve Children's Reading Awareness and Comprehension." *Journal of Educational Psychology* 76: 1239–1252.

Pearson, P. D., L. R. Roehler, J. A. Dole, and G. G. Duffy. 1992. "Developing Expertise in Reading Comprehension. In J. Samuels and A. Farstrup, eds., *What Research Has to Say About Reading Instruction*. Newark, DE: International Reading Association.

Remnick, D. January 29, 1996. "Lost in the Stars." *The New Yorker*.

Rumelhart, D. 1976. *Toward an Interactive Model of Reading*. (Tech. Rep. No. 56). San Diego, CA: University of California Center for Human Information Processing.

Tierney, R. J., and J. W. Cunningham. 1984. "Research on Teaching Reading Comprehension." In P. D. Pearson, ed., *Handbook of Reading Research*. White Plains, NY: Longman.

Williams, T. T. 1994. *An Unspoken Hunger: Stories from the Field*. New York: Pantheon.

Winograd, P. N., and C. A. Bridge. 1986. "The Comprehension of Important Information in Written Prose." In J. F. Baumann, ed., *Teaching Main Idea Comprehension*. Newark, DE: International Reading Association.

Zimmermann, S. 1993. Personal journal.

———. 1996. *Grief Dancers: A Journey in the Depths of the Soul*. Golden, CO: Nemo Press.